Patterns

of the

Past

by

Judy Hall

Published in 2000 by
The Wessex Astrologer Ltd
PO Box 2751
Bournemouth
BH6 3ZJ
England
Tel/Fax 01202 424695

ISBN 1902405048 2nd revised and enlarged edition

(Previously published by Penguin Arkana as
The Karmic Journey ISBN 0140192204)

Cover art © Paul F. Newman 2000

Printed and bound in the UK by Biddles Ltd., Guildford and
King's Lynn

A catalogue record for this book is available
at the British Library

For Bayer with love

May your life-path be one of love, joy and fulfilment

You can't kill the Spirit
She is like the mountain
Old but strong, going on and on and on ....

Also by Judy Hall

Principles of Past Life Therapy (Thorsons)

Principles of Psychic Protection (Thorsons)

Principles of Reincarnation (Thorsons)

Deja Who: A New Look at Past Lives (Findhorn Press)

Hands Across Time: The Soulmate Enigma (Findhorn Press)

The Zodiac Pack: A Visual Approach to Astrology (Findhorn Press)

The Hades Moon (Samuel Weiser)

The Illustrated Guide to Astrology (Godsfield Press)

Art of Psychic Protection (Findhorn Press and Samuel Weiser)

Holistic Menopause (Findhorn Press)

The Illustrated Guide to Divination (Godsfield Press)

The Illustrated Guide to Crystals (Godsfield Press)

Karmic Astrology: A Beginners Guide (Godsfield Press)

Other books published by The Wessex Astrologer
The Essentials of Vedic Astrology by Komilla Sutton

Astrolocality Astrology - A guide to what it is and how to use it by Martin Davis

You're not a person - just a birthchart by Paul F. Newman

The Consultation Chart - A guide to what it is and how to use it by Wanda Sellar

The No Nonsense Guide to Astrology - available as 4 separate booklets as *Elements and Modes, Progressions, Transits and Aspects.* By various authors.

CONTENTS

ACKNOWLEDGEMENTS

First of all to Robert Jacobs for all his love, support, good food, cups of coffee and giving me the space to write and rewrite this book, go my love and many thanks.

To Margaret Cahill of The Wessex Astrologer, my thanks and gratitude for so caringly restoring the text to my own words, and allowing me the opportunity of revising the work after 15 years.

To Paul Newman for the wonderful cover, for redrawing the charts and for sharing his wisdom and humour with me for many years, my thanks and appreciation.

Jackie May did an amazing job deciphering my updated text, for that and much else besides, go love and thanks.

I must thank my teachers the late Christine Hartley, Robert Tully, and Howard Sasportas for all the wisdom they imparted to me over the years. Also, to all those others whose work I have absorbed over many years of study and used without acknowledgment, my apologies and thanks.

I am most grateful to John Lahr, Jonathan Cott and the estate of the late Christine Hartley for permission to quote at length from their work, and to publishers CRCS, Element Books, Anodyne, The Aquarian Press and The Women's Press for their assistance.

And to that old wise woman Julie Felix for the words to 'Graduation Day' and for her continuing love and friendship, amor y muchas gracias. And finally, to all my clients and workshop participants, who have helped me to learn so much about lives and living, my loving wish for happy lives.

Foreword

by Melanie Reinhart

'Of time you would make a stream upon whose bank you would sit and watch its flowing........ And that which sings and contemplates in you is still dwelling within the bounds of that first moment which scattered the stars into space.'[1]

In this important book, Judy Hall challenges concepts that most of us take for granted, which perhaps we never thought through properly, but which are actually central to our sense of placement in our own lives. What we 'under-stand' literally 'stands under' us, providing the psychological and metaphysical foundation for what we think is real, which in turn conditions our method of dealing with our own experience, or how we move through time.

Understanding the dynamics of time and timing is central to the process of astrology itself. Our worldly life functions according to 'clock time', which is a man-made construct no longer synchronised with seasonal or cosmic time. Astrological time is cyclic, circular, based as it is upon the dynamics of planetary orbits, conjunctions and movements around the Sun. However, the central Sun of our own Solar System is only a symbolic still point around which the Earth and the planets travel. In reality the whole system is moving at breath-taking speed through the cosmos, on a trajectory through time and space, encompassing many additional supra-physical dimensions. We are told too that the Sun's lifetime is finite, and that it will eventually burn itself out, as all the matter which fuels its fire is spent, or transmuted. It is also one among many other suns.

These images from contemporary astronomical science lend themselves to elaborating the metaphor of the Soul, moving through various lifetimes with the patterns of past experience, personal and impersonal, like a gigantic kaleidoscope revolving around it. In this sense, the deep past that lies behind the moment of birth, etched into the various planetary placements on the horoscope, can be symbolised by the prior movements of the solar system up to any given point in time..... the universe unfolding in time. Furthermore, in the predictive techniques within the astrological tradition, time is seen as 'elastic' in that one unit of time can be equated for another, as in progressions, where a day is equal to a year.[2] In *'Patterns of the Past'*, the reader is sure to find a context which addresses many aspects of traditional astrology in a deeper light.

Pluto, Lord of Transformation, is currently moving through Sagittarius, the sign relating to religion, metaphysics and philosophy. During a previous transit in this sign, from 1502 - 1516, the prophet Nostradamus was born, in 1503.

Whatever we make of his famous prophecies, we can be sure he was well acquainted with the ideas of Copernicus, his elder and contemporary, born in 1473. The Copernican Revolution, as it came to be known, was strengthened by the ground-swell of ideas circulating amongst the itinerant intellectuals and philosophers of the day. The notion that the Sun rather than the Earth was the centre of the Solar System was considered such heresy as to be punishable by the Inquisition. Copernicus avoided this, as his ideas were only published in 1534, nine years before his death. Galileo, however, died in 1642, under house arrest, having been interrogated by the Inquisition, and forced to recant his ideas on pain of death. With this revolutionary process in mind it is possible to understand the work of Nostradamus in a different light. Copernicus died in 1543 and Galileo was born 23 years later, in 1564, perhaps returning to complete his mission of breaking the cosmological stranglehold of the ecclesiastical dogma of those times.

'As above, so below' is the alchemical maxim, and we can indeed see that cosmology parallels psychology, or our understanding of human nature and its psychic structure. The Copernican Revolution progressed us from an Earth-bound cosmology to a Sun-centred one, emphasising individual Ego-consciousness[3]. Now a wider or Galactic perspective beckons, made necessary by the astronomical discoveries of the 20th Century which began with a large stellium of planets in Sagittarius. In other words, by the time Pluto leaves Sagittarius in 2008 it will have submitted to the fires of transformation every one of those planets, signalling that the shift of perspective is complete and ready for further anchoring as it enters Capricorn.

Judy's work is part of this larger movement. It is based on a subtle and intensely practical consideration of an expanded framework of human experience and its application through astrology. Her expertise, gained through many years of research, study, consulting and teaching provides a solid basis, a rich terrain through which she expertly guides us in a fascinating journey. She asks us to reconsider the vexing question of Fate and Freewill, adding the certainty of the availability of Grace, notable by its absence from materialistic Western philosophy. She also greatly expands our understanding of causality, choice and consequence, for as we push the primal causality back in time we arrive at 'that first moment which scattered the stars into space'. This can be seen as symbolising the primal union of the Soul with Source, the end and the beginning of the Journey.

This book is full of interesting anecdotes and rich in case material; it is scholarly, readable, challenging, and above all, immensely practical. The beginner and the seasoned astrologer alike will find in its pages many ideas and references which will help awaken new understanding of the individual horoscope, and also a deeper awareness of the matrix within which it is set. The worldview within which our study of astrology is placed will yield perceptions accordingly. We can be divided from ourselves through the fear, blame and judgement engendered by a narrow reductive view, or we can embrace a more fluid healing perspective, which opens the possibility of Grace, choice and participation.

Melanie Reinhart, London, July 2000.

Introduction

The Rebirth of the Karmic Journey

I am a karmic counsellor, specialising in interpreting how 'past lives' affect the present and interact with our purpose in being here. To do this, I use astrology and far memory, a psychic ability to tune into other lives. My experience of the working of karma is based on many years reading astrological charts, of 'seeing' other lives through my psychic vision, and on regressing hundreds of people to different incarnations and the between-life state.

In 1986-7, at the urging of my great friend Howard Sasportas, I wrote the book that would become *The Karmic Journey*. At the end of the nineties, Arkana decided that the life of the book was finished. I felt a great excitement. It was time to add ten more years of experience with karmic astrology – years during which many of my ideas had expanded and some had changed. The process of finding another publisher was closely analogous to choosing a new body for a fresh life. When I spoke to Margaret Cahill of The Wessex Astrologer, she was very enthusiastic at the prospect of updating the book. The right 'parents' had been found. Margaret allowed me the space to correct a few mistakes that had crept in, to revise a few sections, and to massively rewrite the opening. Talking to Margaret was exactly like the process of planning a new life. We discussed what I had learned and identified the gaps that needed to be filled. What neither of us anticipated at that stage was that the book would grow into two! When I came to look at the section on relationships, it was clear that this would be a book in its own right.

What I had rarely encountered in the fifteen years before I wrote *The Karmic Journey*, but did begin to meet regularly in the next ten years, were souls for whom one life was not enough: they 'split' into two, or more, parts. This should not have surprised me. My mentor, Christine Hartley, who taught me the basics of the Western Mystery tradition approach to reincarnation, had given me a model in which a 'piece' broke off from the main 'pool' of spiritual essence. This piece then dropped its vibratory rate and moved deeper into the earth plane. Along the way it split, then split again, creating soul groups. As we are currently entering a new astrological age and a change of vibration, it is natural that some souls will split, whilst others recombine. This, too, has happened to the book. In the intervening period I had written another book looking at how karma affected the astrology of one man. As the publisher went bankrupt almost immediately, few people ever saw the book. Some of its insights have been incorporated into *Patterns of the Past* and *Karmic Connections* – the companion volume on karmic relationships.

As Chapter 1 has grown out of the introduction to *The Karmic Journey*, for clarity I am setting out here how I personally view the natal chart. We will explore this further throughout the book.

We choose our moment of birth so that the chart, which is the picture of the heavens overhead at that time, maps out our karmic inheritance: both our own and that of the family into which we incarnate. The chart describes the patterns from the past which we are carrying with us and also the potential for the future. It maps out all the issues we intend to deal with in the present lifetime, the imbalances we have created, the things we have done and also those that we intended to do but never quite got round to, or deliberately avoided, in the past. Karma is also of course that which we need to do in the present life. It is a continuing stream; we are constantly meeting the results of our past karma, just as our actions in the present generate karma for the future. This often feels like fate or destiny, things 'happen' to us. But, it is our choice, a choice we may have forgotten we made, but chosen by us nonetheless.

Fortunately, however, we are also born with free will and once we begin to understand that we are learning through these experiences, we can choose how we respond. We also then realise that we actually create the situations, although we often make use of the movements of the planets (transits) to trigger situations and thus bring them into closer focus. This is what karmic astrology is all about: it identifies the patterns and the lessons, shows how we are likely to react or respond, links them to events, and gives us a sense of timing and purpose.

However, whilst the broad pattern of a past life and the resulting tendency to behave in a particular way can be seen in the astrological chart, it is not possible to ascertain the precise details of that life from the chart alone. This has to be done by 'far memory', which entails either a psychic, such as myself, reading the 'Akashic Record' (a record of other incarnations), or by taking the person back to read or relive their own past. Such information can come through as an 'actual' event or as a symbolic experience. It may be personal or it may be a living out of collective experiences. We will see throughout this book numerous examples of the difficulties and pitfalls facing the karmic patterns entails and the questions it raises, as well as the rewards it offers.

You may be wondering what all this has to do with you. Well, it is clear to me from the hundreds of clients I have worked with and the letters I have received over the last twenty five years that we all share 'common ground'. There are certain basic patterns and issues that repeat over and over again. We have the same anguish and crises. We are seemingly taken over by destiny and fate. As an illustration of how this common ground is reflected in the astrological chart, I have used case studies, together with example charts of famous people whose lives are familiar to us all. They live out the archetypal themes that can affect anyone. How they experience karmic patterns is a fascinating, complex interweaving of personal karma with the cosmic necessity for evolution to occur. It often appears in our own lives that events are forcing changes - but underneath it all the influence of the planets is at work, reflecting inner energies and slowly drawing out our potential (whatever our own individual perception of the result of that might be).

And so, by studying the effect of karma and the movement of the planets on others, you will be illuminating many areas of your own life. You will also learn to view the people around you from a totally different perspective. You will become familiar with some of the pitfalls of the spiritual path; these are the ubiquitous and universal traps that lie in wait for the unwary. Following a powerful influx of spiritual energies, anyone can fall into the egocentricity of 'I am the son of the godhead' or 'I was Cleopatra'. Similarly the depressive 'Dark Night of the Soul' or the elevated 'Pink Cloud Syndrome' are reactions to a moment outside time. The 'Doomsday Scenario' when it seems that all is lost is also common. Equally pervasive is the longing for a Soulmate or the worshipping at the feet of a Guru. Not all of these traps can be avoided, even if you are aware of them, but you can learn to handle them wisely for your own spiritual evolution out of the patterns of the past.

1

The Presence of the Past

I hold that when a person dies
His soul returns again to earth;
Arrayed in some new flesh-disguise
the old soul takes the road again,
My road shall be the road I made,
All that I gave shall be repaid
John Masefield, 'A Creed'

Karmic astrology sees the birthchart as a map of the credits
and deficits, potentials and weaknesses brought forward into
the present incarnation from other lives. This form of astrology is based on the premise that each person is an eternal,
spiritual being who reincarnates into a physical body, meeting karma generated in other lives, and that the pattern of those
lives can be identified in the chart for the moment of birth, as
can the structure and purpose of the present incarnation. The
motivating basis of life is perceived as one of compensation
and expansion, which take place through successive incarnations into physical and spiritual bodies. This is the evolutionary
journey of human beings towards perfection:

> In the East the life of man is held to be a pilgrimage, not only
> from the cradle to the grave, but also through that vast period
> of time, stretching from the beginning to the end of a period of
> evolution, and as such he is held to be a spiritual being, the con-
> tinuity of his existence is unbroken ... starting from the great
> ALL, radiating like a spark from the central fire, he gathers ex-
> perience in all ages, under all rulers, civilisations and customs,
> ever engaged in a pilgrimage to the shrine from which he came.[1]

This idea presupposes a string of lives with credits and deficits
passing on down the lives. However, as we shall see, the actual working of karma and reincarnation is neither linear nor

chronological. A pattern healed in a 'past' life can improve the 'present'. Equally, a step forward in the 'present' can act retrospectively on the past. I prefer the term 'other lives' to 'past lives'. I don't feel it is necessary to believe in reincarnation to be able to understand and use the knowledge of karmic patterns. Karma is the working of the law of cause and effect, the 'reaping of what has been sown', an activity which has been set in motion at some point in the past – where the past is whatever has gone before in the particular time-frame one is using. It is therefore possible to read a chart from the karmic perspective without necessarily relating it back to former incarnations.

ASTROLOGY AND PAST LIVES

I personally believe in reincarnation even though I do not feel that all recalled 'past lives' are literal, factual truth – the reasons for this are discussed later. I do, however, believe that they are true at some level, and they are in essence our story. Having carried out hundreds of regressions to past lives, I know they can be used to illuminate and inform our present life. Much of my work is concerned with the identification and removal of blocks created in the past. If a past life helps in this process, then that is what matters to me, not whether the person actually lived out that life as a physical, provable incarnation here on earth or wherever. Having said that, I do also believe that the roots of almost all our experiences here on earth are to be found in other lives.

Past lives add another dimension to the birthchart and may well explain the seemingly inexplicable. Astrologers (and critics of astrology) have always been puzzled as to why people born at exactly the same time and place, or within a few minutes of each other, twins for instance, have distinct and separate personalities from birth even though their lives may share a broadly similar pattern. If the theory that the birthchart indicates a specific temperament which comes into being at the moment of birth is correct, then it would be logical to expect people born in the same place and time, astrological twins, to be identical in behaviour. Clearly this is not the case, although there are many parallels. Karmic astrology supplies the missing link by stating that the experience a person has already had in another life will precondition a unique response to this one.

Looking at a chart from a karmic perspective makes it far easier to reach a deeper level of esoteric meaning, and can explain why natal aspects manifest in different ways according to the previous experience of the incarnating soul. If each baby incarnated with a 'clean slate', it would be logical to expect, particularly from the astrological perspective, its temperament, reaction and approach to the environment into which it is born to be exactly the same as that of another born at the same time, allowing of course for cultural and parental differences. This is manifestly not the case, however. Although sharing some basic characteristics astrological twins, born at the same moment in time, will express themselves differently. Identical twins, born in the same place and into the same family, nevertheless have their own distinct temperament from birth which cannot totally be accounted for astrologically by the relatively short time separating entry into the world, or purely by pre-existence as a foetus during the intra-uterine experience.

It can be argued that: 'Personality is the creation of the parental and ancestral biological inheritance, and is conditioned by social environment. It is an incidental experiment for the widening experience of the individual soul'[2]. However, in the here and now, the personality is the incarnating soul's way of presenting itself to the world in this particular lifetime. The concept that each baby is a soul incarnating with the weight of the past experience of many lifetimes behind it more adequately explains individual difference and the inherent personality. The soul is encountering its karma:

> Karma is the principle of universal causality, perpetuated by one's actions. Every thought, word or deed and desire, has a dynamic quality, producing good or bad results. Some simple act of charity may change a life or mould a destiny. Actions give rise to effects, and the sum total of these actions determines the nature, status and circumstances of happiness or misery of a person in his next life, and so on from incarnation to incarnation.[3]

This is the description of karma that I have found most useful, particularly with regard to thought and intention having just as strong an effect as actions, although I would expand it to include non-action as well. I have found that consistently refusing to grow or change has powerful effects on the resulting karma.

FATE, FREE WILL AND KARMA

Belief in karma and reincarnation does not exclude a belief in fate or chance, nor does it imply the fatalistic view that 'what will be, will be', or that the future is fixed and unmoving, with no evolution. 'Fate', however, is capricious and punitive and offers no explanation as to why people suffer, other than perhaps the medieval Christian monastic belief that suffering has merit in its own right.

In *The Astrology of Fate* Liz Greene considers why some people experience particularly difficult lifescripts – 'a catalogue of apparently unmerited human vicissitudes'[4]. She comments that she cannot talk glibly about karma as many astrologers do, and implies that it was something to do with one's previous incarnations so not to worry, just close your eyes 'and think of England ... '[5] For her, the explanation is seemingly a different one:

> As with many people the presence of extreme suffering invokes in me the question of meaning. But for me, the roads of human perversity and catastrophe ... lead to fate ... Fate means: It has been written. For something to be written with such immovability by an unseen hand is terrifying ... and such a vision of fate threatens an experience of real despair, or a chaotic abreaction when the spinal column of the moral and ethical man collapses.[6]

With respect, it would seem that here she is missing the point of reincarnation. Fate may imply, in the traditional, Eastern approach, 'an unseen hand' at work or reaping penalties for past actions. Equally, however, if one includes the concept of free will in reincarnation, the incarnating soul can choose to encounter the result of its own handiwork or to make reparation for the past – no matter how hard a present life that may lead to. It may also be a positive choice, taking on collective karma, helping someone else to learn a lesson, and so on. It is difficult to evaluate the long-term spiritual effects of traumatic or painful karmic experiences upon the eternal Self; the working of karma is in any case, subtle and far from straightforward. However, in over twenty-five years of supplementing karmic astrology with past life therapy (taking people into other lives) I have explored karma in great depth, and my ideas have developed since I wrote *The Karmic Journey*. Having accompanied hundreds of people into the between life state, I now recognise that whilst most people (certainly of those who ask for karmic counselling) have at least a modicum of choice, there are some people who do not progress far enough in the between life state to make an informed choice. They either simply 'bounce back' into incarnation because of a strong desire to be in a body or to be with a particular person, or they are pulled back by ingrained patterns or old promises or vows that have not been rescinded. The major challenge for the present life may be to break the habits of those lifetimes or to release someone – or oneself – from an outdated promise. It is these people who incarnate without plan or preparation who could be said to be 'fated'.

On the other hand, I have confirmed many times that someone who may appear to be 'fated' because of trauma, illness or difficult life situations has actually prepared most carefully for the incarnation and will have a profound reason for making that choice. It may be for personal growth and learning, or to aid other people in their lessons or intentions. In *The Astrologer's Node Book*, Donna van Toen states that: 'Karma is a promise to pay for what you get'. It is helpful to counter this with: 'For every action there is a reaction'. The first is a statement regarding free will and personal responsibility. The second is a credo of fate and predestination. An insight into these two very different views came to me quite late in my work with karma. Initially I too had implicitly believed what Pauline Stone expressed thus: 'Our experiences on earth are predestined by virtue of our own past behaviour. We have free will in respect of how we will meet our karma'[7]. I had also found Theowald Dethlefsen's pronouncement

5

comforting in a strange sort of way: 'The horoscope shows us the individual's karma – it is the study plan that has become necessary for his present incarnation. The horoscope represents what each of us has acquired through his or her deeds. One cannot complain about it'[8].

There were certainly times when I would like to have complained about my own chart, even though I firmly believe I chose it! But as I worked with more and more people, I came to recognise that there are two pathways, and maybe more. The first is that of free will and personal responsibility; the second is a surrender (not submission) to divine will. This book is concerned with the first pathway: it is one of growth and change on all levels and is in direct antithesis to all those people who say: 'I can't help it, it's my karma'. This pathway says: 'You are responsible. Clean up your mess'. But it also says: 'You only have to do enough', and for some people, that 'enough' might include a genuine surrender to the guidance of divine will – which could well reverse the extreme wilfulness of a former life, for instance. The first pathway also allows you to use the skills, abilities and potentials you bring to your current life, and to heal the wounds of the past.

The second pathway may be a genuine commitment to divine purpose. It all depends on how clear the alignment to divine will is, and how clearly the guidance from the Self or the divine is heard. Unfortunately, many people who believe they are following divine will are actually trapped in the patterns of the past, as they attract the same old scenarios over and over again. Regardless of how cunningly it is disguised, abuse, for example, is abuse no matter whether it is perpetrated by a parent, a lover, or a guru under the guise of aligning to higher will and opening spirituality. An enormous amount of self-awareness is called for on the path to enlightenment.

In the fatalistic approach to karma, the rule is 'an eye for an eye, a tooth for a tooth'. If a man murders, he will become a victim; if he injures, he will be injured. However, there are many ways of making reparation or restitution: the murderer may achieve a degree of spiritual enlightenment and choose a life of service. It does not seem necessary to make direct repayment to the person who has been injured, although the choice may be made to do so. Once the incarnating soul has found another to whom a debt is owed, it will be sufficient reparation to perform the appropriate task. Neither does it seem to be necessary to fulfil every last duty or debt. The karma of grace operates and there is a point when enough has been done, understanding has been reached, and the soul is freed from the karmic round.

Karma implies a belief in continuous causality: what is experienced now is seen as the result of personal or collective prior action, but what one experiences in the future will be the result of present action. The exercise of choice and free will is possible. Therefore, the doctrine of karma adds a dimension of personal responsibility to 'destiny' and anyone aligned to Western thought who takes reincarnation seriously is likely to have an attitude of: 'Let's get it right this time', rather than: 'Well, what does it matter I can always get it right next time'.

In this view of reincarnation, contrary to the fatalistic approach, there is conscious choice which arises out of attunement to the needs of the Self – which Jung described, under the name of the soul, as 'the greatest of all cosmic miracles'. The Self is the holistic, eternal, spiritual part of ourselves and it is seeking to evolve back towards perfection and reintegration into the divine force. It is however a spiritual rather than an intellectual concept, which is approached using meditation as opposed to the rational processes of the mind. Knowledge of the soul cannot be derived from reason, observation or science. It would appear that it is the Self Liz Greene refers to when she says:

> From what I have observed ... there is certainly something –
> whether one calls it fate, Providence, natural law, karma or the
> unconscious - that retaliates when its boundaries are transgressed
> or when it receives no respect or effort at relationship, and which
> seems to possess a kind of 'absolute knowledge', not only of what
> the individual needs but of what he is going to need for his un-
> folding in life. It appears to make arrangements, of the most
> particular and astonishing kind, bringing a person together with
> another person or an external situation at precisely the right
> moment, and it appears to be as much a part of the inner man
> as the outer. It also appears to be both psychic and physical,

personal and collective, 'higher' and 'lower', and can wear the mask of Mephistopheles as readily as it can present itself as God. I make no pretence of knowing what it is, but I am unashamedly prepared to call it fate.[9]

Throughout the book this organising principle is referred to as the Self, and the portion which incarnates into the physical body as the soul. A difficulty I have consistently encountered whilst writing is that the eternal Self has no gender, but the incarnating soul takes on the masculine or feminine character through the physical body. I personally have no problem accepting 'Man' as a generic term for mankind encompassing both sexes, but I can understand that some readers will object to this – so I have resorted to referring to the incarnating soul and the zodiacal energy to which it is attuned in the neutral, sexless form of 'it'. My apologies to anyone who is offended by my decision!

Karma and all its manifestations

Since *The Karmic Journey* I have written several books exploring karma, none of them from an astrological perspective apart from the one which never hit the shops because the publisher went bankrupt (and what a karmic tale that was!), and a beginner's guide that I am writing concurrently with updating *The Karmic Journey*. In writing the first book, I found I was looking at 14 types of karma, but since then the list has grown even longer: it is given below with brief astrological indications. Before we look at the types of karma, however, we need to explore levels of karma and the three karmic 'laws' that I have found confirmed time and time again in regressions to other lives.

KARMIC LAWS

• What we desire, we experience

This can also be phrased as 'What we will, happens'. The problem is, the will or desire can be operating at the deepest, strongest level of the subconscious mind, coming straight from another life. The conscious mind can sincerely believe something completely different but, because of the pattern from the past, the subconscious urge is the strongest. What manifests is the old desire. It pulls us back into the patterns of the past.

One of the most graphic descriptions of how desire operates comes from a book[10] written just after the Second World War. Its author, a doctor, died and was taken to the morgue. His soul, however, was very much alive and went adventuring with a guide. He was taken to a bar. He was somewhat taken aback to see people desperate for a drink or a cigarette trying to snatch one from the people around. Gradually, he came to realise that the people doing the snatching were 'dead' – which was why their hands passed through glasses or cigarettes as though they were not there. Few of these poor souls knew they were 'dead'. Frustrated and angry, they could not understand why such a strong craving could not be satisfied. Occasionally, one of the 'living' would pass out and the doctor observed the 'dead', discarnate souls moving into the unconscious body. The guide who was with him explained that such desires kept these souls trapped. The same kind of desire can pull two people back into incarnation together, as can deathbed decisions such as 'next time he'll marry me', or a promise like 'of course I'll always be there for you'. A strong will can hold two people together, manifest a certain situation, or prevent an outcome desired by one person but not another – it is a question of whose desire and whose will is the strongest. Desire is perhaps the strongest factor in 'bouncing back' into incarnation and on to the karmic treadmill.

- **Our spiritual purpose is paramount**
Eventually even the most unconscious of souls has to heed the call of the Self, which wants to evolve. It has incarnated to grow and to expand its understanding and no matter how cut-off and unaware the soul may have become, the Self never gives up. Some of the events that seem like darkest fate are, in fact, a wake up call from the Self. So many of my clients have looked death in the face, lost all they had, or been forced into a totally new way of being, only to say 'Thank god'. They feel they are back on track and able to fulfil their purpose. One woman in particular embodies this story of purpose – her orientation was strongly spiritual. A reflexologist who successfully treated

many people, she became involved in soul retrieval and shamanic work. As her second Saturn return loomed, this previously fit and healthy woman was suddenly diagnosed as suffering from an hereditary heart condition. She could barely move, had to stop her work, and simply 'be'. She was undergoing a classic shamanic test. Saturn may be the Lord of Karma but he also watches over our purpose and pushes us back on track when we stray. She worked though a lot of past-life stuff, changed many of her emotional attitudes, and then realised that the relationship she was in – a strongly karmic one – was killing her because it lacked the warmth and intimacy she needed. Finally she has had to let that go too. When everything had been stripped away, she grieved for all she had lost – and then turned around and saw the potential and purpose of her Self. A purpose which was so powerful she wept again – but this time with joy. She was back on her path.

•   **We only have to do enough**

Karma is not intended to go on forever. The law of Grace overcomes that of karmic patterns. It is possible to step out of karma, either by right action or by Grace, and it means that once we have done all we can, the karma dissolves. It also means that we can, at any moment, step out of a pattern from the past and choose something different. Grace is an offer from our Self that we can't refuse and is about 'higher purpose' entering our lives. When we enter into Grace we may decide to move into alignment with divine will, surrendering personal will. Equally we might go with the calls made by our Self – which is, after all, a part of the divine. We may act out collective purpose, or choose to work on a different part of our karma. All possibilities are open with Grace.

KARMIC LEVELS

There are four main levels of karma:

Personal/Individual
Family/Group/Tribe
Collective
Cosmic

Generally, personal karma can be overridden by group karma, which in turn is subordinate to collective karma. It is from the level of collective karma that much so called 'karmic injustice' arises. People get caught up in something bigger than their own personal karma or individual choice – which may in itself seem unfair from the limited perspective of earth. However, as the staff of the 'Cygnus Review' expressed it in an editorial: 'We collide with the eddies and currents of chaos or evil whose origin lies far outside and beyond ourselves, and whose causes are far too vast and complex for our tiny minds to contemplate.' As they go on to point out:

> There is no need for us to waste any time at all looking around for something or someone to blame. For difficult experiences bring us a marvellous opportunity to invoke ... the Law of Grace [thereby overwriting the law of karma}.*

At the **personal** level we deal with our own 'stuff' – what we have generated in the past, what we are setting in motion now, our purpose and our healing. We may well meet other people with whom we have a karmic connection, or discover our 'soul group' – those we have travelled with throughout time and with whom we have a spiritual connection. Individual karma is what we have personally created and is shown in the natal chart. We reap the rewards of 'positive' karma and we try to balance and overcome, or make reparation for, 'negative' karma.

Group karma relates to anything from the family to a racial group, and usually overrides individual karma. It is indicated in the eleventh house in the natal chart. Family karma can also be seen in the fourth-tenth house axis and in the eighth house as well as aspects to Saturn and Pluto.

Collective karma, especially all the guilt, hatred and anger stirred up by mankind over the millennia, in turn usually overrides the needs of the group and is triggered by the day-to-day movements of the planets (transits). It can be seen in the twelfth

---

* Cygnus Review 2000 Issue 5

house of an individual's chart in particular, but may also show up in the eighth and ninth house if the soul has been battling to bring revolutionary ideas or contact the higher energies through several lifetimes. It passes through all the outer planets and Chiron. Certain individuals incarnate with the task of alleviating this burdensome legacy from the Past. Mahatma Gandhi, for instance, whose Libra Sun was placed in the twelfth house, became a focus for peaceful protests against the injustices of the British-ruled Indian political and caste systems. Gandhi's Scorpio Ascendant focuses on the collective need for change and renewal, and his ninth house Uranus in Cancer indicates the revolutionary ideas that enabled him to lead his people to freedom. Similarly, Martin Luther King, the American Civil Rights leader, was a Capricorn who not had not only vision, but also the authority and personal charisma (Sun on the Midheaven) required to lead his oppressed people out of the prison constructed from the outmoded concepts of society in which they lived. His violent death, which could be seen as a sacrifice on behalf of the collective, is indicated in the square of Uranus to his Saturn, in the eighth house, in opposition to aggressive Mars.

The Sleeping Prophet
Edgar Cayce, who 'read' past lives, spent much of his adult life in trance and was known as 'the sleeping prophet'. His prophetic utternaces foretold great disasters, cataclysmic events and social upheaval. Cayce was told that he had abused his gifts in the past and consequently in the present life he had to work unconsciously, that is, in trance. He discovered his healing gift of reading past lives, which was mainly used to uncover the reasons for people's dis-ease, when a throat condition literally rendered him speechless. He had Moon in Taurus in the ninth house, Taurus being connected to the throat and the Moon to the past. When hypnotised, he relayed the past-life reasons for his condition and the way to alleviate it. The throat condition was to spur him into undertaking his spiritual mission (Pisces North Node). Whenever he tried to give up his spiritual work, the readings, the condition returned. In a reading on himself, quoted by Alan Oken, he reported:

This body [Taurus] is controlled in its work through the psychical [Scorpio], or the mystical and spiritual [ninth house]. It is governed by the life that is led by the person who is guiding the subconscious when in this state [i.e. Cayce himself]. As the ideas given the subconscious to obtain its information are good, the body becomes better. The body should keep in close touch with the spiritual side of life if he is to be successful mentally, physically and financially.[11]

Cayce relayed many of his own past lives when in trance and they are an interesting illustration of the diversity of karmic experience. He believed himself to be Pythagoras and several early spiritual teachers. However, the karmic problem that resulted in the enforced trance work seems to have started in ancient Egypt as a High Priest who had a 'weakness of the flesh' and broke his vow of celibacy when tempted by a priestess into making a 'perfect child'. It culminated in two lives as 'John Bainbridge', one in the 18th and the other in the 19th century. Both men were described as troubled, restless souls, 'wanderers and wastrels', each having a lustful disposition and irresponsible character with the problem of promiscuous relationships featuring strongly. The chain of incarnations was self-seeking in all respects, sexually, financially and morally. Cayce said that the reasons behind these lives was that he had to know the extremes in order to help others. At the end of the second John Bainbridge life, he gave his life in order to save another. Interestingly, in the present life Cayce gave readings to two of the surviving illegitimate children of John Bainbridge, illustrating the close links between such souls from the past. Having explored the extremes, he was able to concentrate on working to raise the collective level of consciousness through the work he did with individuals.

A whole generation has been born with Pluto in Scorpio and the potential to penetrate the darkness of disease, death and destruction and bring healing to the earth. In the first draft of this book a typing error converted 'destruction' to 'instruction'; this is passed on for what it says about how we educate our young. Many of these souls will also have the conjunction of Saturn to Uranus in either Sagittarius or Capricorn indicating a need to change the existing structure of beliefs or society.

The opportunity is being offered to these souls to reverse the collective karma of past generations and to give birth to the New Man of the Aquarian Age who will care for and conserve the planet Earth and all who live on her. The parents and grandparents of this new generation may well have Pluto in Leo, signifying the need to explore the meaning and utilisation of power; many of them were born during and immediately following the major confrontation of the Second World War. They will hopefully pass on to their children and grandchildren the knowledge of the consequences of abuse and misuse, of power in any form, together with an awareness of man's capacity for self- destruction.

Collective karma, concerned with the nature and utilisation of power and control, is also indicated in Uranus- Saturn and Pluto-Mars-Saturn contacts. As Liz Greene has pointed out[12], and has been verified by past life regressions, many people with Pluto-Mars-Saturn aspects, particularly the conjunction, remember on one level or another having been part of persecutory events such as the Holocaust or the Inquisition, either as victim or perpetrator. Many of them seem to have incarnated again within an apparently short time, although it must be remembered that spiritual time is relative. A twelfth house Node, explored in Chapter 4, is also indicative of collective karma.

Although 'positive' collective karma is generated, this is greatly outweighed by the 'negative' karma. It is this 'negative' aspect which has to be cleared at the end of an astrological age because **Cosmic** karma, the need for the cosmos itself to evolve, is paramount. Cosmic karma is beyond the horoscope.

LEVELS OF EVOLUTION

Many people ask what level their soul has reached, but this is not apparent from the natal chart, unless you have experience of tuning into both the soul and the chart at an intuitive level - which is the way I usually work. The chart for a 'New-Age child' is shown here (Fig.1) with her mother's planets in the outer ring. In a past-life reading a year before the child was

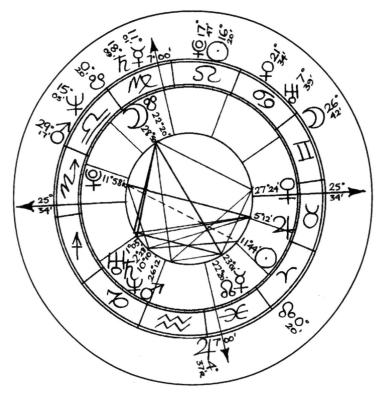

Fig. 1

born, her powerful, creative, Sun/Pluto in Leo mother was told of an Indian incarnation where she had voluntarily given up her child to the temple to keep a vow made when she was childless. She was told that this child was waiting to return to her. She was also shown a South Sea island incarnation where she was a willing sacrificial 'victim' to the sea. On the night she painted her 'memory' of that scene she conceived, and the child was born under water. The mother's South Node is on the child's Moon/South Node conjunction in Virgo opposing Mercury/North Node in Pisces: this was an old connection. The child's chart has a Kite formation and includes the Uranus/Saturn conjunction in Capricorn widely squaring the Nodes, and twelfth house Pluto inconjunct the Sun. She will be brought up both in a village in the interior of Bali (Saturn) – where reincarnation and the interpenetration of spiritual

15

ity into matter is accepted as a fact of life and crime is non-existent – and in California, a centre for New-Age awareness (Uranus) - by parents who are attuned to a spiritual and artistic way of life. When I finally met her, one look into her five-month-old wise and ancient eyes was enough to see that she is a highly evolved soul here to assist mankind with the birth into a new way of Being.

I was obviously tuning into this chart when I did the reading, as I had not met her, but such supposition can at best only be tentative and at worst hampering to correct interpretation if the level is wrongly assessed. The working of karma is subtle and things are not always as they seem. I was later to meet a brain damaged child born on the same day who appeared to have no level of evolution as she was totally unaware of the people around her. But she brought a tremendous spiritual lesson to her parents, and eventually learnt to communicate telepathically with them. It is impossible to judge from extreme signs what is going on karmically. This brings to mind the true story of a disc-jockey who went out to India. He was told by a spiritual teacher that he would meet only one Master during his stay and that it was part of his test to recognise that master. On his return he reported that he had sat at the feet of many gurus and heard much teaching but could not determine which was the true Master. He was asked if he had met anyone else who had made an impression on him. 'Well,' he said, 'I did meet a beggar on a beach. He was different. He didn't ask for money and when I offered him some he told me that he had been blessed with all he needed in life. At the time I didn't understand but I guess now I have my answer. He was the true Master.'

The Soul Group
Today's men and women are used to seeing themselves as individuals and yet esoteric astrology teaches us that we are all reflections of the whole, 'As above, so below' being an ancient maxim that expresses this concept. Karmic astrology says that we are part of soul groups, loosely knit bands of souls who travel the karmic road together, and that these soul groups are in turn a part of the larger whole. Nothing happens in isola-

tion. If we learn a lesson, the soul group evolves and the cosmos benefits. If we raise our level of consciousness, the soul group to which we belong will also raise its level of consciousness and the overall evolution of the whole moves upwards. We can liken this to being part of a tree, say the pip in an orange. The pip is an individual, but at the same time it is enclosed in a segment. That segment is in turn part of a whole, the orange. But the orange is a fruit on a branch, and the branch is part of the tree. The tree is rooted in the earth and reaches up towards the sun that is part of a larger whole. We can extend this to say that the earth is part of the solar system, the universe, etc. We all incarnate with 'our' orange, those with whom we are in close contact (our 'soul group', which is not necessarily our family of origin) and we gradually explore our connection with the tree and move towards encompassing the cosmos with our inner being. Many of us will become aware that there are other levels of existence and yet, at the same time, that everything is part of the divine whole. The microcosm and the macrocosm are one.

The Family and Karma

The birth chart also describes the picture that we carry of 'mother' (the Moon and its aspects) and 'father' (the Sun and its aspects), the karma we have about being parented (fourth/tenth houses – Pluto, Neptune, Uranus, Saturn and Chiron aspects to the Sun and Moon) and sibling karma (third house) and indicates particular attributes that may be carried over from generation to generation (ancestral karma). I believe that we choose our parents and the environment into which we are born with great care because it is part of our long-term soul growth. It may not be apparent from just one lifetime why we are interacting with a particular family; this may only be understandable when seen over a series of lifetimes.

We not only have our own karmic patterns (carried over from previous lives) to work out, but we also have both karmic potential and free will to work with, so we select a family who will create the environment we need to foster these; and who will allow, and hopefully encourage us to develop in a different way if we choose to do so. Our reasons for selecting the particular parents for the present lifetime can be based either on our past relationship with them (we have specific karma and old connections with one or both of them) or we can select parents who will give us the genetic inheritance or upbringing we need for our own personal karma. The second choice is particularly relevant where there is a pattern of family karma which fits the type of experience we have had in the past or need in the present – illnesses which are passed on through the family, for instance, or emotional attitudes, social position, specialised knowledge, etc. This is especially so where we want to develop a special talent or skill – music for example. There need not be prior contact between the individuals who will comprise the new family, although there is almost always at least one member of the wider family with whom we have a special 'soul contact'.

We may also be born in a particular location in order to have the imprint of its unique energies on our developing physical body, or there may be ancestral or collective karma to deal with through the family or racial group into which we incarnate. The most usual family interaction is a combination of these factors. We re-create in our childhood some of the characteristics of past lives which we are struggling to overcome, so we choose parents we have known in the past and with whom we have some personal karma. Parents frequently have planetary combinations in their charts which are reflected in children's charts. It is as though they 'seed' the energies represented by the planets into us, often showing us one way of dealing with them so we can then choose a another. When there are personal issues between parent and child, it will show as inner and outer planet aspects across the charts (interaspects) which repeat both ways. For instance, the powerful, symbiotic bond between a man and his mother – and the strong possibility that she was his mother in a previous life – was shown by her Pluto conjunct his Moon and his Pluto opposing her Moon. If the parent and child share similar issues or are working something out together which is not personal, this will show in one-way interaspects.*

---

* *See* Karmic Connections *for an in-depth examination of family interaction.*

TYPES OF KARMA

There are various types and levels of karma and their work-ings can be both subtle and complex. Certain 'themes' tend to stand out in a chart as karmic patterns are reflected both in planetary aspects and placements by house and sign, with a further indication from the South Node or the Moon. The as-pects associated with karma are personal planet (Sun through to Mars) to outer planet (Saturn through to Pluto) contacts. So far, in my work with clients, I haven't found that Jupiter has specific karmic implications – its function seems to be more one of exaggerating whatever is going on rather than directly influencing it.

Retributive karma is a boomerang effect of something per-petrated coming back. The old idea of 'an eye for an eye, a tooth for a tooth', or someone being born blind who has put out another man's eyes, is an extreme example, but I rarely find this type of retribution in operation unless someone has become totally entrenched in the old pattern of retribution and suffering and refuses to learn any other way. However, retribu-tive karma is at work in most situations where for example, a husband spends all his wife's money, and, when looking back at a past life, the situation was reversed with the wife squan-dering all the husband's money. Of course, retributive karma can also operate within the space of one lifetime. Most of us who are aware of karma notice how quickly the results of our actions come back! Karma is definitely speeding up, and what used to take several lifetimes to work through now happens in a small portion of one lifetime.

Astrologically speaking, retributive karma could be in-dicated in extremely challenging and fixed twelfth-sixth house planets, as the twelfth house is in the area of the natal chart concerned with karma, and the sixth house is connected to health or work. It can also appear in fixed squares, in difficult Saturn aspects, or possibly by Saturn in the first house in a fixed sign. As Saturn is the Lord of Karma it can relate to some pre-vious act, or with clearing collective karma which may well include acting as a scapegoat or making a sacrificial act. Many of my clients suffering from Aids or cancer felt that part of their task was to 'take some of the darkness out of the world' with them. Several of them made the positive choice not to be treated.

Redemptive karma is concerned with willingly making reparation for some previous act, or with deliberately taking on the clearing of collective karma. It may well include what appears to be a scapegoat or sacrificial act. Many of my clients with Aids and cancer, for example, have felt that their task – or part of that task – is to 'take some of the darkness out of the world with them when they left. Redemptive karma can be indicated by Sun, North Node or Neptune in the twelfth: a strong emphasis on Pisces in the chart; and the placement of, and aspects to, Chiron.

There may also be **recompense** karma, something which is 'owed' to us either by another person as a karmic debt (indicated by Saturn or Neptune interaspects with personal planets between the charts), or to compensate for difficult experiences that were not purely of our making (twelfth house planets and 'easy' aspects). For instance, if someone has been severely handicapped or chronically ill in a past life in order to allow someone else to learn a lesson, then in the present life they may well enjoy very good health. On the other hand, a client whose past-life experience was of killing herself because she felt guilty for surviving in a concentration camp, said that in the present life she felt exceedingly fortunate as 'things went so smoothly for her' - this was reflected by several sextiles in her chart.

We also have **merit** karma, which is all the things that we have learned and the karmic resources we have built up; this shows as planets placed in the second house, harmonious aspects between inner and outer planets, and productive Jupiter aspects (together with the potential shown in our chart, particularly in trine and sextile aspects and conjunctions or prominent placing of harmonious planets).

Organic karma relates to previous abuse of the body or old injuries, which create a repeating pattern of disease. One example would be that gluttony in a previous life could produce digestive problems in this, or too much blood letting or shedding could create anaemia. Such karma shows up most strongly in the sixth house of a chart, or aspects to the ruler of the sixth house or to the planet governing that part of the body. Mars placed in the sixth house, for instance, can signify a repeating injury, a karmically 'weak' spot. In Capricorn, the injury could be to the bones or knees, in Sagittarius to the hip or thigh, in Aquarius to the ankles. In Taurus, the throat would be the weak spot, in Scorpio the reproductive organs. An imbalance of planets in earth signs may also be implicated in bodily karma particularly related to abuse of, or disregard for, the body. Chiron's placement and aspects may also delineate organic karma, as can Saturn.

Attitudinal karma, which is the result of long-held, ingrained attitudes or emotions, may have a physical result as the body is where karma finally comes to rest. Arthritis, for example, may be the manifestation of an infexible attitude in the past, arteriosclerosis of being too hard-hearted or too soft-hearted. Opposite attitudes can sometimes induce an opposite physical reaction as the body tries to compensate. Dr Motoyama, a Japanese doctor and Shinto priest, has pointed out that karma results from mental attachment to an emotion no matter how ideal. In other words, fervently pursuing the goal of enlightenment will still create karma.

Here again, it is the planets placed in the sixth-twelfth housesand difficult aspects to them, or challenging placements in signs, associated with the relevant attitudes and the organs affected which indicate the source.

Symbolic karma refers to a situation which is symbolic of the original act – for instance, the American seer Edgar Cayce cites the example of a bed-wetter in the present life having been a witch ducker in a previous life. This karma would show up in the chart in aspects to an appropriate planet.

The rather more specific 'karma of **mockery**' is somewhat similar and arises from having mocked, and thereby judged, a situation for which one knew nothing of the karmic necessity. A Cayce example is that of a polio victim who had been in the audience at Rome when the Christians were thrown to the lions. As Gina Cerminara points out in *Many Mansions*:

> 'He who laughs at the affliction of another is condemning a set of circumstances for which he does not understand the inner necessity; he is despising the right of every man to evolve through even the meanest form of folly; he is deprecating the dignity and worth and divinity which in-here in every soul, no matter how low or ridiculous the estate to which it may have fallen. He is, moreover, asserting his selfhood as being superior to the selfhood of those he laughed at. The act of mockery is an act of self-assertion in the most ignoble sense of the term.'[13]

A twelfth house Mercury; Mercury in Gemini, Virgo or Scorpio, difficult aspects to Mercury, plus the South Node in Gemini or Scorpio, could be indications.

Vocational karma, the continuance of previous work or service, usually shows up in the sixth, tenth or twelfth house. For instance, doctors and healers who are carrying on an old vocation frequently have Pluto near to the Ascendant, most often in the twelfth house. Many musicians or artists carry over their talent from previous lives, which would show up in a strong Neptune placement and productive aspects between Neptune and the personal planets. American General George Patton, a leading soldier in the Second World War, who – to the best of my recollection – believed he was the reincarnation of both Hannibal and Alexander the Great, could be seen to be carrying on a vocation: war. He has both power-hungry Pluto (the 'higher octave' of the aggressive martial planet, Mars) and idealistic Neptune in the twelfth house, with the dark and devious, and equally power-mad, Scorpio Sun in the sixth house, and the South Node of the Moon in Pisces in the tenth house. Clearly there is a powerful connection in his horoscope with death and rebirth, and with the sacrificial Neptunian and Piscean energies.

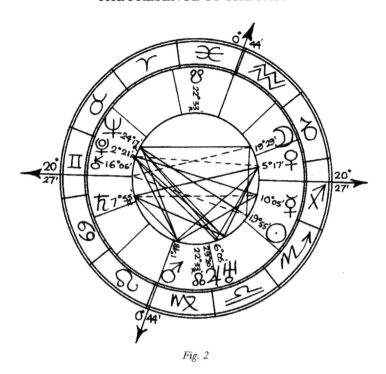

Fig. 2

The Psychic General

This is the first chart I ever saw (Fig. 2). It was put up as an example in my astrology class. Typically for me, I attended an intermediate class before the beginners. I hardly knew what the glyphs (signs) meant, but I found I could read a chart. When asked what struck me about this chart I said: 'He's a General with the soul of a poet'. 'Quite so' said my tutor. Second World War General George S. Patton felt fated almost from birth to be a fighter and a leader of men. As a small boy, he would march about wielding his toy sword on which he had emblazoned: Lt. Gen. G.S. Patton. He believed he had begun his training for this great destiny on the plains of ancient Troy and continued with Caesar's Tenth Roman Legion and then on through recent history. He was also a poet. In 1944 he wrote:

> So as through a glass and darkly
> The age long strife I see

Where I fought in many guises
Many names – but always me.

And I see not in my blindness
What the objects were I wrought
But as God rules o'er our bickerings
It was through His will I fought.
So forever in the future,
Shall I battle as of yore
Dying to be born a fighter
But to die again once more.

His Moon is in authoritarian Capricorn, and powerful Pluto sits in his karmic twelfth house. As a commander he was feared and respected – almost court-martialled for brutality to his men, they would nevertheless do anything for him. He has 'aggressive' karma through his Pluto to Mars aspect which has seen the use, abuse and misuse of power in all its manifestations, and has been in authority many times in the past. His Sun is in masterful Scorpio, co-ruled by the warrior planet Mars and by Pluto the Lord of Fate. His North Node of the Moon is in Virgo, indicating he was here to be of service to mankind. The General's South Node in Pisces gave him the psychic ability to be aware of his past lives, and may also in part explain his poetic soul. What struck me was his twelfth house Neptune which tends to evade human suffering if at all possible. The past lives he was not quite so forthcoming about would undoubtedly have been much more artistic and spiritual in character, and he may well have escaped from the world into a religious order. He has the past-life dilemma of having handed his will over to God (Saturn-Mars and Neptune-Mars) and needing to take it back. Certainly those lines in his poem: 'But as God rules o'er our bickerings, It was through His will I fought' take little responsibility for the results of his actions and is typical of both Neptune and Pisces as well as having made a vow of obedience to God in a past life which is still being lived out in the present life.

The karma of work arises from acts in a previous occupation, or difficult experiences such as confronting the lack of integrity. Positive work karma indicates skills to be drawn on in the present life – look at the sixth and tenth houses and 'easy' aspects such as trines.

Technological karma may well include the placement of Uranus in the Sixth or Twelfth House. This is karma based on having had to make ethical decisions about the use, or stemming from the misuse, of technology, frequently going back to Atlantis or the Industrial Revolution. For instance, a Health and Safety Inspector discovered he had been a mill owner at the start of the Industrial Revolution when many people, particularly children, were killed or injured due to dangerous working conditions.

There may be a repeating pattern of karma – the **Karmic Treadmill**. What has, or has not, been done shows up in planets that form a square aspect between fixed signs (Taurus, Leo, Scorpio, Aquarius). So often our karma is concerned with what we have repeatedly failed to do, or to learn, rather than what we have actually done. The 'sins of omission and commission' can be included here and linked to the appropriate planets and houses, or there may be phobias and fears arising from the past – usually indicated by Pluto or Saturn on one of the angles of the chart.

As we cannot deal with everything at once, there is karma **in suspension** which we will not have to deal with this time round or may come to when we've finished with other karma. This can be shown in wide aspects where the personal planet will move into close orb by progression during the current life. And as we are also creating karma, there is karma **in the making**, shown by cardinal and mutable squares and our present life actions.

Communication karma: some people communicate clearly with no misunderstandings or deviousness, while other people seem unable to communicate at all – especially in the area of emotions or self-expression. Yet others seem fated to be talked about, or slandered. It all comes down to communication karma. How and what you have communicated in the past has repercussions, and this karma is indicated by Mercury, its aspects and placement. Look out especially for Mercury in Gemini or Scorpio, or in the ninth, third or twelfth house – and sextiles to it.

Ideological karma. This involves being attached to certain beliefs or ideas, and coercing or enforcing them on others. It can be indicated by the ninth house placement of Chiron, Saturn, Uranus and Pluto.

The karma of **grace** allows us to move beyond karma when we have done sufficient work, or all we can, in a situation.

REINCARNATION, NEAR DEATH EXPERIENCE (NDE) AND OOBE'S

Reincarnation

From my experience with running seminars on reincarnation and karmic astrology, for over twenty-five years, I know that several questions arise regarding the concept of reincarnation, and that there are other possible explanations for the type of experiences which lead people to accept the reality of an independent, continuous state of Being. We need to explore these questions prior to penetrating the depths of astrological karmic significators and manifestations.

The doctrine of reincarnation is a very ancient one, prevalent world wide, particularly in the so-called 'primitive' societies which have survived with their beliefs intact, and of course throughout Hindu and Buddhist countries. Stated simply, it is the belief that a soul, which formerly inhabited a body on earth and died, is reborn again into a different body. For example, in Bali children are expected to be the reincarnation of deceased family members and are praised for having the 'good' qualities of those ancestors. Many of the Greek philosophers, including Plato, refer matter-of-factly to reincarnation, and the concept was widely accepted in the Western world prior to the Roman version of Christianity. The Jews are expecting a Messiah who will be the reincarnation of one of the prophets and Jesus implies (Matthew 11:14) that John the Baptist was Elias. There are still traces of the doctrine within the four Gospels and in the other books that make up the New Testament. These particular books were finally selected from over two hundred gospels and other writings in existence in the first few centuries after Christ's birth - and there are many more references in the rejected books. Similarly, in his Gallic Wars Julius Caesar mentions the belief in reincarnation in connection with the Celts, a belief which passed into the early Celtic Christian Church.

Many of the early Christian saints expressed the belief that the soul had inhabited other bodies prior to its present life. According to Origen (AD 185-254), every soul comes into this world strengthened by the victories or weakened by the defeats of its previous life. Its place in this world as a vessel appointed to honour or dishonour is determined by its previous merits or demerits. Its work in this world determines its place in the world which is to follow.[14] St Gregory (AD 257-332), whilst not here specifically mentioning the pre-existence of the soul, insists: 'It is an absolute necessity that the soul should be healed and purified, and if this does not take place during its life on earth it must be accomplished in future lives.'[15] St Augustine (AD 354-430), in his Confessions, addressed a question to God concerning his prior existence: 'Say, Lord to me... did my infancy succeed another age of mine that died before it? Was it that which I spent within my mother's womb?... and what before that life again, O God my joy, was I anywhere or in any body?'[16]

However, in AD 553 a Church Council ratified the anathema of the Emperor Justinian against the doctrine of Origen concerning the pre-existence of the human soul, and by implication reincarnation. From this time onwards the belief in reincarnation officially ceased in the Christian Church, although several Gnostic 'heretical' sects, such as the Cathari, strove to reinstate it so it never completely died out in Western thought.

In the West belief in reincarnation was taken up by the

Theosophists and other esoteric and occult organisations at a time of resurgence of interest in the survival and purpose of the human soul, the two concepts being very closely linked. As Dr Ian Stevenson pointed out in his Twenty Cases Suggestive of Reincarnation:

> Survival could occur without reincarnation. On the other hand, reincarnation by definition cannot occur without some preceding survival of a physical death. Thus evidence for reincarnation is ipso facto evidence for survival while the reverse is certainly not true … In mediumistic communication we have the problem of proving that someone clearly dead still lives. In evaluating apparent memories of former incarnations, the problem consists in judging whether someone clearly living once died.[17]

A considerable number of books have been published on the subject of reincarnation, some scholarly and scientific, others experiential, and the reader wishing to pursue the matter further is referred to the Bibliography. So far, despite the considerable efforts of researchers like Dr Ian Stevenson, there is no objective proof of the fact of reincarnation, although stronger cases are arising every day. As Benjamin Walker points out: 'The testimony of tradition is in its favour, while scientific opinion is against it.'[18] There are several other possible explanations for so-called reincarnation memories. However, according to the psychologist and philosopher William James, 'There is a verge of the mind which these things haunt; and whispers therefrom mingle with the operations of our understanding, even as the waters of the infinite ocean send their waves to break among the pebbles that lie upon our shore.'[19]

Many people do not need scientific proof in order to accept the validity of the reincarnation experience. There are subjective states of consciousness which can lead to an acceptance of the survival of the human soul, and thereby to the 'a priori' knowledge of reincarnation. One of these altered states of consciousness is hypnosis*, during which the person is di-

---

* *See* Principles of Past Life Therapy, Principles of Reincarnation *and* Deja Who? *for further details*

rected back to the past, an experience which convinces many people of the veracity of former lives.

Out of Body Experience

Another subjective state, but one which often appears to have objective consciousness as well, is the Out of the Body Experience (OOBE). During an OOBE the etheric or astral body, which houses the soul, becomes temporarily separated from the physical body and serves as a vehicle for consciousness. Such separations take place for a short time in sleep or trance states, OOBE etc., and permanently at death. In a classic book, *The Projection of the Astral Body*, written in 1929, Sylvan Muldoon expressed his certainty of the immortality of man: 'For my part, had a book on immortality never been written, had a lecture on survival never been uttered ... in fact had no-one else in the whole world ever suspected "life after death" I should still believe implicitly that I am immortal – for I have experienced the projection of the astral body.'[20]

Once someone has had that experience, they 'know' and no amount of psychological explanation or rationalisation can remove the knowledge that there is a vehicle for consciousness which can function independently of the physical body. Once in possession of that inner knowing, which is a matter of intuitive apprehension rather than intellectual comprehension, one is truly aware of one's immortality and of the totality of one's being.

Some fifty years after Sylvan Muldoon's experience of OOBEs, Robert Monroe in his book *Journeys Out of the Body*, which is also a classic, sought to differentiate, from his own experience, between the dream state and the OOBE. He cites continuity of conscious awareness and the ability to make and implement decisions in a sequential time-frame as typical of the OOBE. The experience is subtly different from lucid dreaming in which the dreamer knows he or she is dreaming but chooses to go along with the dream, or from dream or imaging work in which the dreamer chooses to explore further or create new scenarios. In the dream state there is very rarely any sense of separation from the physical body, whereas in the OOBE experience there is always a feeling of freedom, of having been released from the necessity for physical sentience – although sense and other perceptions continue. Robert Monroe points out that the astral body, which is the vehicle for the OOBE, responds directly to thought which is the 'vital creative energy' and can, for example, translocate instantaneously if required.

Near Death Experience

Another subjective area which leads many people to believe that they will survive physical death is the Near-Death Experience (NDE) which has been widely documented (see Bibliography). Such an experience occurs when a person is clinically 'dead' or is dying, but consciousness on another level continues and the soul ultimately returns to earthly existence. One of the earliest references to such an experience is found in Plato's Republic and, in the seventh century, the Venerable Bede records a wonderful story of one among the Northumbrians who rose from the dead and related the things he had seen, some exciting terror and others delight' which has all the classic components of an NDE.

Fig.3 is the chart of a somewhat unusual National Health Service psychiatrist: he utilises fairy-tales, myths and Liz Greene's tarot pack in his clinical work with disturbed adolescents. He had an NDE whilst still a medical student. Scorpio intercepted in the sixth house points to a karmic health or career need to penetrate the depths and darkness of the psyche and Chiron in the eighth house indicates a significant life change following an encounter with 'death'. He is the son of a high-ranking army officer and his chart indicates considerable karma involved with power and aggression issues linked to the Pluto-Mars opposition across the MC/IC, and Mars being the ruler of the karmic twelfth house. He has a fascination for military history which may perhaps be an expression of his own past or his family/genetic inheritance.

In addition to Chiron in the eighth house, which points to a significant encounter with death and to the need for an antidote to the 'suffering' he has created, however unconsciously, and endured in the past, the chart also has two

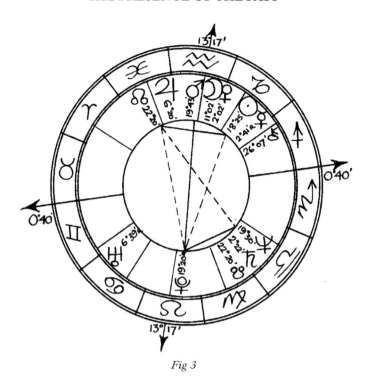

Fig 3

Fingers of Fate (utilising wide karmic orbs for quincunx aspects) involving Pluto, the Nodes, the Sun, Mars and Neptune. Karmically, one would expect him to have been involved in a traumatic event which resulted in the need to integrate these powerful energies that are linked to an understanding of the birth-death-rebirth cycle, and the transformation of his spiritual awareness:

> My near-death experience was the most important event in my life so far. I was told by my physician afterwards that I very nearly died. During the days I was most ill I was entirely unaware of my surroundings, and yet the experience itself had a timeless clarity. In the preceding weeks I had been in continual physical agony, but this was a time of complete tranquillity and absence of pain. The recollection of the actual events is hazy, but the inner certainty of their ultimate validity, over and above ordinary experience is as overwhelmingly real as ever.

During the weeks leading up to the manifestation of his disease, transiting Mars was opposing natal Saturn and bringing out his underlying pain. As the NDE approached, transiting Mars had moved on after opposing natal Neptune, which induces euphoria and expanded states of consciousness, and transiting Saturn was squaring natal Saturn and opposing Mercury, paving the way for a classic NDE 'life review':

My soul came to be in the presence of a completely benign person who was male, was somehow all around and was entirely good. This person was totally uncritical, calm and loving in an unsentimental way. I felt completely safe and at ease. In his presence I appraised my life so far and found that it had been good and worthwhile. I was satisfied and grateful for what had been given and had no desire for it to carry on, or to finish. He let me know that this wasn't meant to be the end of my life but that I would carry on as I had work to do [a need to express the Fingers of Fate and the eleventh house Pisces North Node out to the world]. I accepted this without question. Interestingly, many years later, my mother consulted a clairvoyant who incidentally told her that sometime before I had almost died, but did not because I had important work to do. After recovery, I identified the person as being most like Jesus Christ. After this my life fundamentally changed. I lost all worldly ambition, which seemed to me to be a ridiculous delusion.

Here he was moving out of the earth-orientated Virgo South Node and into the mystical Pisces North Node and the Finger of Fate focused on it, which embodies the karmic need to integrate the transforming, regenerating energy of Pluto and the spiritual consciousness of Neptune. He was also moving beyond the personal power games and egotistical level of the other Finger of Fate, which includes the Sun, Pluto and Mars as well as the Pisces Node, which produces difficulty in assimilating and eliminating the past, and resulted in his bowel disease and consequent NDE. He began to own his own creative and healing power (the constructive manifestation of the Pluto energy) and to develop his spiritual understanding: 'I was endowed with a strong curiosity in spiritual matters which has remained with me. The progressive uncovering of what life signifies has seemed to me ever since to be the only worthwhile quest.' Uranus in opposition to Mercury, fifth house Neptune and Saturn, the Gemini Ascendant, and Chiron in Sagittarius in his chart indicate attunement to the 'higher mind' energies and a need to understand how the spiritual-mind link functions – he also works with Neuro-Linguistic Programming:

> Since then, deep within me, I have the certainty of acquaintance with the transcended reality [the effect of the Sun square Neptune], despite the overlay of my fair share of life's hardships. I regard myself as fortunate in having had this realisation. Having come face to face with my own mortality [exemplified by his earthy Sun in Capricorn and the eighth house Chiron], I have had to come to terms with it, and the vulnerability of my body. Death holds no fear for me.

In an article in the British Journal of Psychiatry, Drs Glenn Roberts and John Owen critically reviewed the NDE literature and experience from both the historical and clinical perspective. They based their criticism of the NDE on the fact that death is notoriously difficult to diagnose and also irreversible and therefore, according to them, no one claiming to have 'died' and returned can have been 'dead'. However, as they point out:

> The process of dying takes a finite time, and if the arrested heart is restarted, the dying process is reversed.[21]

They found that: 'A frequent, consistent and apparently enduring pattern of changes in attitudes, values, beliefs and conduct have been observed in people who have had an NDE.'[22] They also examined the effects of both cultural expectations, psychopathology, epilepsy and drug experiences and concluded that 'all the separate elements can occur in non-life-threatening situations and that typical NDEs can be chemically induced ... it may be that NDEs are common end points of a number of aetiological pathways.'[23] However, the question of the varying impact of the NDE is left unanswered: 'It remains to be explained why some return from a close brush with death with a vivid, extensive and profound experience, and others report nothing. This review has attempted to describe the work done so far; a great deal remains to be explored, described, quantified, tested, understood and applied.'[24] As Roberts and Owen point out, there is a considerable difference between objective and subjective reality but an acceptance of subjective states is a cultural difficulty stemming from the West's insistence on intellectual comprehension rather than intuitive recognition and inner knowing. The East would have no difficulty in accepting the 'evidence' of mystical experience. Healer Matthew Manning's comment on a similar paradox would seem to be appropriate here: 'To those who know, no explanation is required. To those who do not know, no explanation is possible.' And, as Robert Hand pointed out in the Astrological Journal, mystical consciousness encompasses astrological cognisance:

> True mysticism is not merely something that is mystifying as scientists would have us believe. It is the belief that all of the apparent diversity of nature and Man is one whole, an interacting oneness. In this sense astrology is applied mysticism because it is a day-to-day manifestation of the Oneness. Humanity and the movement of the planets are parallel manifestations of the One. In the mystical world view astrology does not require an explanation. In fact astrology's not working would have to be explained.[25]

Deja Vu and 'Ghosts'

As part of the concept of 'Oneness', it has been hypothesised that places can hold 'imprints' of past events or of past lives which have taken place there. Although auto-suggestion can of course be an explanation for this, many people have found, on visiting the sites of old battlefields for example, that they are suddenly able to tune in to what has passed there – and some believe that they actually took part in the events: the déjà vu experience. This 'imprint' theory is one of the explanations for ghosts who haunt a particular spot, endlessly repeating an action, as opposed to a 'spirit' who may appear and interact with the observer.

A print sales representative I knew, normally the most cynical and sceptical of men, arrived at my office much shaken by an experience he had had. He lived in a new house on the site of an old orchard. In the middle of the night he was awakened by an old man bending over the bed. His immediate re-action was to hit out. His fist went straight through the man, who looked quite amused. The next morning the same old man was standing next to the rep's wife in the kitchen and he blurted out: 'What's that ghost doing here?'. 'Don't worry dear,' his wife soothingly replied, 'it's only Fred. He used to work here and likes to pop in for a visit.' She had been com-municating with Fred ever since they moved into the house but had not liked to mention it in case her husband thought she had 'gone screwy'. I suggested that Fred might be an earth-bound spirit and that perhaps they could persuade him to move on to other realms. When this was relayed to Fred, he said he would consider it in his own good time!

Spontaneous Recall

The deja vu experience is a subjective state which produces a sense of re-entering the past, and in which the subject appar-ently 'knows' the place without necessarily having ever been there. This is often explained away as a perception difficulty in that the eye perceives some time before the brain acknowl-edges, or as knowledge acquired as a result of, for example, having seen a picture of the place many years earlier. When my mother had an NDE she suddenly found herself wander-ing on a high moor-like road on which a signpost said 'Winchcomb'. Having since been to that part of the road my-self, I know that it is featureless apart from the sign-posted side-road, and is not particularly memorable. Nevertheless she is convinced that she, in some non-physical form, not only travelled to the place – to which she has never been in the present life – but recognised it as somewhere she had been be-fore.

A friend's elderly father had exactly the same experience on visiting Dunster for the first time. He could describe exactly what was around the next corner and what the buildings had been in the last century. When a friend and I visited Wells Ca-thedral and asked the Chancellor about a particular feature we wanted to see, his reply was that it hadn't been like that since the fourteenth century or thereabouts.

A similar, but usually much more detailed, experience is that of spontaneous past-life recall in which the subject appears to relive a prior experience. I have had many of these experiences. Once, when watching Karnak temple on television, I suddenly found myself 'seeing', superimposed on the ruins, a picture of how the temple was when it was first built and drifted into a long 'reliving' of a life there. One of my first actions on visiting the temple in this life was to seek out a particular 'secret' temple which was still exactly as I had seen it all those years ago. As psychologist Dr Frederick Lenz points out: 'Spontaneous past-life memory tends to occur in dreams, during meditation, via déjà vu experiences and as waking visions. These waking vision cases are the most characteristic. The experiencer usually feels as though he has been literally transported in time back to his or her past life.'

A client was referred to me by the College of Psychic, Studies. A psychotherapist, she had had the unsettling experience of suddenly finding herself trying to commit suicide, but knowing that it was a few centuries ago. She was full of a despair that she could not shake off. During a regression she returned to a life in which she had killed herself. In her present life she had met a person with whom she had been involved in that lifetime, and the meeting had triggered off the memory. Once she recognised it as part of the past and no longer relevant to the present relationship, she was able to let it go.

My own sense of 'knowing' in connection with reincarnation is almost totally subjective and based on NDE, OOBEs, and on many spontaneous regressions to other lives. Prior to these experiences I thought that reincarnation was an interesting theory. After them, reincarnation became an acknowledged causal factor in my life which made sense of the previously inexplicable and which totally changed my notions of both time and the reason for existence. However, this book is not intended to convince the 'unbeliever'. It puts forward one potential answer to the question: 'Why are we here and what can we learn from our experience?' It shows how karma originating in past experiences, which is mapped in the birthchart, may block the progress of the deeper Self, and how an awareness of the pattern laid down may unlock creative energies and potential which the soul can utilise in order to grow.

ANCESTRAL MEMORY AND OTHER EXPLANATIONS

In *The Visions Seminars* Jung speaks of 'The Ghosts' who are the ancestors:

> The ghosts are remnants of former lives, what one calls ancestral spirits, and the ancestral spirits psychologically are the units which constitute our psyche. If one splits up the psyche into its original components ... one part of your psyche comes from the grandfather, another from the great grandmother, and so on: one is a sort of conglomeration of ancestral lives. This of course leads to the idea of reincarnation, that one existed in former ages ... All those ideas come from the vivid recollection of former lives when one is in a certain condition, namely, when an ancestral life is regenerated in one ... It is possible that one sets out to live the ancestral life right in the beginning, as most people do who develop in a reasonable and positive way; they grow out of several ancestral lives into all-round individuals ... But also there are people who have their blossom first ... an ancestral life breaks through, and they become sort of withered mummies ... In living the inherited nature, one is thoroughly alive because one lives for the ancestors, one makes a new attempt to pay off the debts left by the ancestor generations.[26]

This may be an explanation for some 'past-life' experiences, and certainl some of my own past-life regressions may conceivably have been a reliving of my ancestral experience. Within a few short generations I can trace English, Scots, French Huguenot and Romany. But, contemplating the dilution and complexity of the route through which ancestral spirits could have inspired my own vivid 'memories' of three or four thousand years ago, I personally find the reincarnation theory much simpler. And it does appear to explain better the experience of an English participant in a past-life workshop who regressed to about seven or eight, 'fairly recent' Far Eastern incarnations although, as far as he could ascertain, he had no ancestral link. However, it may well be that ancestral memory is a contributory, causal factor in the soul choosing to incarnate into a particular family. (Since writing *The Karmic Journey*, I have also come to realise how many people do carry powerful ancestral memories and incarnate to be a 'lineage breaker' for the family, but this is part of a much deeper and complex question as to just what constitutes the soul and the Self and will have to wait for another book.)

In *Masks of the Soul* Benjamin Walker explores the concept of the psychogene, which would appear to be intimately linked into Jung's concept of the ancestral 'Ghosts' as the carrier of memory:

> It has been suggested that just as the biophysical traits are carried by the genes, there may be an inherited mind-and-memory factor, the psychogene, carrying a mental legacy from one generation to the next... Some psychologists are of the view that a series of such psychogenes, passed on over the centuries, forge a kind of continuing memory chain, a mental continuum built up into instincts, racial and tribal rnemories, and all the mind-stuff of the antecedent line. It is obvious that there can be no possible break in the chain of succession that leads back to our remotest progenitors.[27]

I would postulate an 'etheric' rather than 'physical' gene: a memory cell — a personal Akashic Record — located in the spiritual entity that survives physical death and forms the blueprint for the next body. This entity incarnates again only in the sense that it is assimilated into, and can be accessed through, the Self where it is stored. Such an 'etheric memory cell' could be the 'missing link' in Rupert Sheldrake's theory of 'Morphic Resonance':

> The central idea of morphogenic fields is that these are invisible fields shaping and moulding developing organisms, giving them their form and structure ... If living organisms are shaped or moulded by this new kind of field, the fields themselves must have a structure or organisation ... the structure of these fields is derived from the actual physical structure of similar organisms in the past. It is derived by connection across time and space. Thus the fields represent a kind of cumulative memory of the species - the process of morphic resonance.[28]

In an article in *The Astrological Journal,* Alan Jewsbury describes morphic resonance as:

> ... an exciting concept that, if true, makes astrology seem much more understandable; and the apparent weirdness of a natal imprint that remains active for life whilst it interacts with currently transiting planets is no longer so strange ...
>
> The basic personal and unique field at birth remains in force throughout life; if the planets are significators of the original pattern, then the transiting planets will also resonate with the natal field. It is not unreasonable also to assume that the parents' fields mirroring their emotions, concerns and fears have a strong formative effect on the young child's developing field: which will also be affected by the prevailing cultural field. But this is not a fatalistic doctrine because fields can be modified by learning; although a major influence will always be the presence of the past.[29]

When exploring the need for an astrological discipline, Robert Hand makes the supposition that 'planetary arrangements might cause some kind of pulsing or modulation in the magnetic field of the earth such that certain kinds of thoughts or behaviour are induced in the brain.'[30] This would seem to be consistent with the morphic fields theory, as Sheldrake believes that via morphic resonance it is possible to tune in to not only our own memories, but also those of other people, which would in effect be a communication from the past: 'If we tune in to the large number of memories from large numbers of people in the past, what we would get would not be specific memories of their particular lives, but rather a sort of composite or pooled memory of the species ... The idea of course corresponds very well to Jung's idea of the archetypes in the collective unconscious.'[31]

Jungian theory does, of course, offer another interpretation of past-life recall: the collective unconscious, a Neptunian level of (un)consciousness which links all souls together in the depths of their being:

> During Jung's research into the psyche, he 'uncovered' a bottom layer beneath the personal unconscious where the psychic history of man had been written, as though carved with a knife

into a tree ... It is as if we have part of us that connects to the Infinite ... The planets Uranus, Neptune and Pluto connect us to energies that are beyond everyday experiences, a sort of divine reservoir.[32]

Attunement to this level of unilateral awareness could well bring to the surface buried memories and karma from 'the past' which is both personal and universal. It may be one explanation for why several people can 'share' the memory of having been a person from history.*

Other explanations for reincarnation experiences include 'possession' by 'dead spirits' – which presupposes that some form of survival after death is possible. When I first began psychic development classes, every meditation would bring vivid scenes of Egypt, ancient Greece and Renaissance Venice. 'How nice, dear,' the circle leader would say, 'the Guides are showing you where they used to live.' I always wondered why, then, I had such a sense of recognition and intimate knowing of these places. Christine Hartley's book, which fell off the library shelf into my hands, suggested another explanation: reincarnation. That is not to say that as someone who utilises psychic 'far vision', I am not at times aware of discarnate entities who wish to communicate clairvoyantly, but this has a 'different feel', subjectively, to it from a reading of the record of another incarnate being's past.

Benjamin Walker and others also suggest as explanations of past-life recall the influence of mental states induced by hysteria, epilepsy, or drugs. He also cites the power of suggestion at work. Yet if suggestion, or wishful thinking, were that powerful then all past-life workshop participants would easily and quickly find their previous incarnations, and this unfortunately is not the case. It can however account for the number of Cleopatras, for example, one meets. In the course of working in the NHS I did meet several people who were undergoing treatment in psychiatric hospitals for experiences not unlike my own – the difference being that in their case these interfered with their functioning in the everyday world, and subjective and objective experiences were not differentiated.

---

* *see* Deja Who?

Paramnesia (false memory) and cryptomnesia (hidden memory) in which, for example, a book or film read or seen many years ago will suddenly float into consciousness, might also be explanations for past-life recall. It is true that in past-life workshops participants have expressed recall as being in the form of a film set, and that some past-life readings can be rather like novels. In fact several books, by Joan Grant for example, presented as historical novels were based on her past-life experiences. The inspiration for novels has to come from somewhere and the present-life experiences of many people could be passed off as a 'soap-opera' script! However, with over twenty-five years of experience in evaluating the usefulness of past-life recall and regressions, I have reached the conclusion that whatever is seen during a past-life regression or creative visualisation session is of value in a symbolic form. Symbols are the language of the psyche through which the Self, or the unconscious, communicates – in exactly the same way, but rather more lucidly, as it would in a dream. It is the meaning and effect of the experience which have value and validity, rather than the fact that it can be proved true or false in empirical terms, and this same reasoning is applied to the karmic interpretation of charts. If a past life helps a client to understand, and be released from, or utilise, a part of his or her life hitherto inexplicable or blocked, then it has value and meaning.

Where and When?

Once I had come to accept reincarnation as an explanation for my own experiences and patterns, two questions became crucial: that of space – the 'where' of inter-incarnation states – and time.

I began with the source of the 'new' soul which had never incarnated before. The most convincing answer that I could find was based on the concept of a 'pool' of spiritual essence, the Oneness to which the soul yearns to return, from which an individual Self separates in order to gain experience. As an Indian saying goes, 'God breathed out and Man was created. God breathed in and Man began his journey back to the source.' I then asked where the so-called 'dead' souls who are awaiting reincarnation are. In a channelled communication, a discarnate soul answered: 'All around you. We haven't gone anywhere. Only our vibrations and perceptions are different. Our world interpenetrates yours but because we function at a different level of vibration and consciousness, you are not normally aware of us.' 'A change of world is not brought about by spatial travel but by a change in what we are aware of.'[33]

The Nature of Time

From all my experience and research, I have come to the conclusion that time is far from linear and chronological. We need a sense of past, present and future to order and make sense of our earthly experience. But, once we are removed from the constraints of earth, time is another dimension entirely. Words fail when it comes to describing the real nature of time; it has to be experienced. At best I can describe it as fluid, circular or spiral – we can stand in the middle and access any part, but at some very deep level, everything is happening now. Which is why, when an intervention takes place in a past life, healing occurs in the present life. And why, there can be no such thing as fixed and immutable fate. Our actions have consequences, and our consequences change the future and the past.

I see time as symbolic: chronological, linear time sequences being the means by which the incarnated soul makes sense of the physical world. As Joan Grant points out: 'The concept of successive personalities being threaded by Time like beads on a string is intellectually expedient but misleading.'[34] Once one moves out of physical perception of time into spiritual or mystical apprehension, then time loses its meaning. Jane Roberts expresses this notion of flexible time in a poem:

> Between each ticking of the clock
> Long centuries pass
> In universes hidden from our own.

In order to explain how it is possible to 'tune in' to different lives, it can be postulated that time is circular and that if one stands at its central point, then one can access any point on the circle. However, at a very deep level I have come to believe that there is no such thing as time: no past, present or future: it is all happening Now. And, consequently, there are an infinite number of different realities encompassed within that eternal Now being experienced by the Self.

Astrology is a spatial time-frame reference which allows us to make sense of our experience in the present reality. Karmic astrology adds another dimension to our understanding of the inner processes of life, deepening our spiritual perception and linking us into the greater reality of the expanded, holistic, totally aware Self who is our real Being, and who simply Is.

> I have circled awhile with the Nine Fathers in each Heaven
> For years I have revolved with the stars in their signs.
> I was invisible awhile, I was dwelling with Him.'[35]
>
> Rumi

PATTERNS OF THE PAST

Patterns Past, Present, Future

The soul chooses a time to be born because the astrological pattern fits the experiences needed for the present stage of growth.

Howard Sasportas, The Twelve Houses

CHARTING THE JOURNEY

Viewed from the perspective of the karmic astrologer, the natal chart delineates both the instinctual behaviour and expectations carried forward from the past and possibilities for the future, as represented by the interaction of the energies of the planets and the signs. It reiterates and reinforces major patterns and assumptions, blocks and potential, wisdom and weakness built up over many lifetimes. Areas of imbalance and conflict are mapped, and those for growth and new learning outlined. The pattern of cause and effect laid down in previous incarnations is reflected in the heavens at the moment of birth and the incarnating soul chooses a time of entry which will offer the conditions most conducive to growth and development.

Carl Jung postulated that what happens to a person is characteristic of him or her. He presents a pattern, and all the pieces fit, and one by one, as life proceeds, they fall into place according to some pre-ordained design (the birthchart). In my experience, for most people that is self-selected plan, a matter of choice and intention, and it has freewill built into it. The natal chart, after all, is not static – progressions and transits usher in change and the soul always has the choice of responding constructively or destructively, positively or negatively, to planetary energies.

What we encounter in our lives now can be seen as the direct result of what we have enacted, or omitted, over many lifetimes. In regressions to past lives the 'sins of omission' appear over and over as a soul incarnates time and again into the same conditions until it finally confronts what it has come to learn. Similarly many people 'suffer' the same problems until they recognise that only they are able to change the pattern and that they do in fact create their own reality and can move beyond karma. 'Karmic justice' is not simply a matter of having had a difficult time in one's last life, and therefore now being eligible to have an easy time. The question which must be addressed is: 'Did the incarnating soul learn the lesson for that life or not?' If it did not, then the soul repeats the lesson as many times as it takes to resolve it – or to recognise that it does not have to go on endlessly repeating a pattern. It has the option of changing the way it interacts, of reorganising its own reality and moving beyond the constraints of karma. A knowledge of pre-existing patterns and the plan for the present lifetime, as seen through the chart, is thus a potent tool in understanding, adjusting to, overcoming, and growing through current life circumstances.

It should, however, be borne in mind that if everything is attributed to past causes, in effect living in the past, then the soul misses out on its immediate experience of the life it is currently living. The Self, that eternal part of us which is cosmic and eternal, strives to live in the ever-present Now and to fully experience each moment as it occurs. When it is able to do this, it has reached enlightenment. Enlightenment is not a matter of perpetual bliss, it is entering a state of simple Being; interacting with one's whole experience on the physical, emotional, mental and spiritual levels; recognising that one is a spiritual Self, and finally getting on with the business of fully living each moment.

KARMIC PATTERNS

Every human being is a mass of contradictions and conflicts. When these are recognised as stemming from different personas and from experiences throughout many lives the possibility of integrating the dissonant energies unfolds, offering wholeness. Repression is lifted, blockages freed, and the energies which have been subjugated are released for creative use.

Each incarnation, and natal chart, can therefore be seen as a learning experience set up prior to birth so that the strengths and wisdom acquired in previous lives can be used to overcome inherent weaknesses and areas of imbalance. These areas can be identified through the placement and interaction of the planets within the birthchart. Karmic patterns are carried over from former incarnations and the appropriate environment is created within the family, and early life experience, for them to be recapitulated and intensified. The patterns from childhood will then be carried into adult life and relationships, and in due time they will be brought into conscious awareness. This process offers the possibility of choice and change, with the consequent release from the karmic pattern and growth into a new way of Being. As we have seen, a philosophical dilemma inherent in the concept of reincarnation is the question of whether an incarnating soul is the victim of its immutable fate, or whether it has the free will to control its own destiny. Once it is recognised that the incarnating soul created the circumstances in which it finds itself and that it has a choice in how to meet those circumstances, a resolution of the fate versus freewill dilemma becomes possible. As Pauline Stone points out, 'Our experiences on earth are ... predestined by virtue of our own past behaviour ... We have freewill in respect of how we meet our karma.'[1]

The karmic patterns stemming from vastly different lifetimes are mapped as difficult aspects between inner and outer planets (Chiron acting here as an outer planet), aspects between unsympathetic planets, planets in incompatible signs, or the Sun and Moon in conflicting elements and signs. These aspects and conflicts indicate areas for synthesis or a shift to a new mode of behaviour. 'Difficult' aspects are the square (90^0), opposition (180^0), inconjunct/quincunx (150^0) and semi-sextile (30^0) and at times the conjunction (0^0). We should bear in mind that supposedly 'easy' aspects such as the trine (120^0) or sextile (60^0) can prove to be difficult if the energies are not yet integrated or manifesting positively and, therefore, when an aspect is not specified the comments apply to any major combination of planets. In order to obtain a clear outline of the basic karmic pattern of the incarnating soul, I use only the major planetary aspects and the inconjunct. The quintile aspect (72^0), however, is one of 'fate' or 'destiny' and can indicate an area which the incarnating soul has decided it simply must face up to in this life - there is no choice. I believe it is Alan Oken who refers to this aspect as 'evolutionary potential'. This 'minor' aspect can then become a crucial aspect in attuning to the soul's purpose.

Orbs

For karmic work I have found that the more usual orbs of aspect can be extended. Orbs of up to 8^0 for a square, opposition, conjunction or trine and 6^0 for the sextile will reveal themselves in obvious ways, which then become more subtle in manifestation as the orb moves through 10^0-12^0 and onwards, especially where the personal planet is applying to, that is, moving towards, the outer planet. Planets which are in the same sign but technically not within orb represent energies which are difficult to grasp and bring together, although there is an inherent awareness of the need for integration. For the quincunx it has been found that up to an 8^0 orb may apply despite the fact that this can technically include the bi-quintile (144^0) aspect. Other 'minor' aspects use 2^0/3^0 orbs.

Time of Birth

A difficulty frequently encountered when interpreting charts is that clients do not know their time of birth. For some souls the moment of physical birth may not in any case necessarily coincide with the soul incarnating into the body and beginning its interaction with the earth environment. Under hypnosis and regression many people report being 'loosely attached' for periods ranging from a few minutes to days, weeks and even, in exceptional cases, years before making the final decision to fully incarnate. This is particularly noticeable in autistic children, for example, but there are also seemingly aware adults who nevertheless display all the signs of 'only visiting this planet' and do not appear to have fully incarnated in the physical body. When a time of birth is not available, the symbolism of the sunrise chart with the Sun on the cusp of the first house has been found to work well and to be preferable to a noon chart. It must be borne in mind, however, that the planetary energies may express themselves in a slightly different sphere of life to that of the symbolic house in which the planet falls in the sunrise chart.

How to Use This Book

This book is not intended as an astrological 'cook-book'. It contains insights into the working of karma distilled from a quarter of a century of experience with both astrological charts and individuals. Although certain themes and associated planetary aspects and placements have recurred continuously over the years, others have never arisen. Some planetary aspects or house placements have therefore not been included simply because I do not have the experience or examples to illustrate the possible underlying karma (if there is any). To any reader who feels 'cheated' because his or her particular placement or aspect has not been covered, may I suggest that you apply your own astrological knowledge and speculate on possibilities. Also, at times, planets and aspects are dealt with in other than the conventional, accepted, planetary order because this has allowed exploration of dichotomies or contrasting experiences. Some readers may possibly find this confusing or difficult to follow and for this reason a detailed index has been included. Similarly, a glossary is incorporated at the end of the book to aid those who are unfamiliar with astrological or karmic terminology and concepts. I think we need to remember that the planets do not 'cause' anything to happen, they represent energies and patterns within the psyche which are manifested outwardly as events, and inwardly as personality traits.

ELEMENTAL LESSONS

The balance of planets placed in elements signify karmic imbalance. No planets in an element or more than three planets constitutes an imbalance. Such imbalances can relate to opposite ends of the spectrum of experience and it is not so much the lack of, or emphasis on, an element that is significant as the fact that the imbalance exists. Any or all of the possible scenarios listed can apply.

Earth

Earth is the element of incarnation into matter. This is where the soul takes on a body and uses the physical senses to interact with the world around it. Past life experiences range from abuse, misuse and over-indulgence of the body to being totally ungrounded and hardly aware of having a body at all. Toxic conditions can occur which need to be released on the physical, mental, emotional and spiritual levels. Diet can help in compensating for, and healing, organic karma from past.

Water

Water is the element of intuition, emotions and feelings. Imbalances here relate to suppression and repression of the feelings, unacceptable emotions, and over-indulgence in emotionality or irrationality. Being an out-of-control psychic channel may well form part of this imbalance as can some psychiatric disorders. Control of these emotions or irrational fears may be part of the life lesson.

Air

As the element of the mind and the rational processes, an imbalance of air can indicate too much emphasis on the intellectual processes, or having to balance out a life lived totally irrationally without thought or discrimination. Past lives may include the 'air head' or the intellectual theorist.

Fire

Fire is the element of the spirit and the intuition. Too much fire can burn itself out very quickly, too little has a weak life force. Learning to handle energy is a major lesson for this imbalance.

THE PLANETS

Each planet carries specific karmic vibrations and implications, but it is the outer planets that most strongly hold the karmic patterns because they are 'transpersonal', that is, beyond the purely personal, individual level of consciousness. The **Sun** relates to personal identity, the Self and to the father; the **Moon** to the emotions and to the mother or eternal feminine.

Mercury indicates karma connected with the mind, ideas, communication and siblings. **Venus** is expressed through relationships and aspects to Venus indicate how well love, creativity and relationship will flow. It also indicates the type of woman to whom a man may be karmically attracted and the values held. **Mars**, the god of war, relates to aggression and assertion, to previous experience of war and violence, and specifically to the use of Will. It also indicates the type of man to whom a woman may be karmically attracted.

Jupiter is the planet connected to travel and to philosophy, so the karma here may be 'religious' or secular. It is the point where the soul can expand, where we grow beyond what we have been in the past. It is also the planet of over-expansion and may indicate where someone has gone off the rails in the past and has to compensate for previous excess. Jupiter symbolises the power to bring things into manifestation. It is the 'old tapes' that we run based on our past experience, which may need to be re-programmed before we can grow, but it can also be our greatest gifts.

Saturn on the other hand is the planet of constriction, discipline, boundaries. It is the Lord of Karma in the chart, so obviously the position of Saturn in a house indicates karma to be worked on which will be expressed through the area of life related to that house. However, Saturn is also the wisdom that has been acquired in previous lives and the inner strength that develops from overcoming adversity and lessons learned.

Chiron is the wounded healer, the modern shaman, and indicates our karmic wound and where healing and integration are needed. Both Chiron and Neptune have an intimate connection with suffering and scapegoating. **Neptune** is also vision, or escapism. It is the planet of enlightenment and mystic consciousness, or delusion, illusion and deception. **Uranus**, the awakener, is the rebel and a catalyst for change, it brings in new ideas. Uranian karma has to do with revolution and the use or misuse of technology, but it can also have been subversive or unstable, bringing in chaos rather than constructive change. It is the intuitive planet and the one with a deep understanding of vibrations and how they manifest.

Pluto is the planet of birth, death and rebirth, and of

elimination and transformation. The karma connected with Pluto almost always has to do with the use and abuse of power, fanaticism, obsession and with transmutation. We can look at Pluto as representing our karma, and also having to do with fate working itself out. It was Pluto who, in mythology, broke out from his abode below the ground, i.e. unconsciousness, and abducted the maiden Persephone: innocent, untouched and undifferentiated awareness. As a result her grieving mother, Demeter, the creative principle, laid barren the earth until her daughter was returned to her. The Eleusinian Mysteries were born out of this myth, with initiates being sworn to secrecy: so potent was the oath that no-one betrayed it. But we do know that initiation consisted of several stages, part of which was a re-enactment of the Persephone myth, a recreation of the death and rebirth cycle. Initiates renounced their old self, let go of the world, and were reborn to their deeper Self. The mysteries taught that death was not to be feared, but rather welcomed as an opportunity to grow.

Greek mythology also offers us the three sisters who are known as the Fates. The threads they spin (fate) encircle the world but rarely interfere with everyday life. Occasionally, however, one of the threads will reach out and touch a human, who would then act out fate. It was his destiny to act out this role – he could not escape it. This is very similar to the idea of the archetypes or the planets being activated, or of collective or cosmic karma taking over. So wherever Pluto is in the chart, here is where a part of us must die in order to be reborn; old attitudes must be released so that something new can be created. Transforming Pluto is a fundamental challenge. It is part of the karmic issue of finding and owning power, and using Will wisely.

The Luminaries

The Sun and Moon are signposts on the karmic journey, indicating characteristics which have been brought forward from the past and attributes to be built into the present. Unlike conventional astrology, karmic astrology sees the Sun's energies as potential to be developed during the present incarnation. The negative qualities of the sign in which the Moon is located indicates karma and deeply ingrained patterns built up over many lifetimes that need to be overcome. The positive qualities of the Moon and Sun sign energies are to be incorporated into the incarnating soul's new way of being.

The Moon reflects instinctual feelings and reactions carried over from other lives and is passive and receptive. It relates to the incarnating soul's deepest security needs and to how it will seek to satisfy them; it has a deep-rooted connection to the Mother, which is primal and immediate. It is the expectation of, and response to, nurturing. It is unconscious, rhythmic and cyclical. Impregnated by the character of its sign, subtly motivated and incited by past experience, the Moon is a causal factor in emotional life. It is what the soul has been.

It contrasts sharply with the Sun: the conscious Self into which the soul is endeavouring to grow, the qualities it is trying to develop here and now, the autonomy it is seeking to manifest, and the ego strength it must gain before it can be merged into the greater whole. The Sun is active and outgoing, it initiates and forges new experience into a tool for its own growth. It is what the soul must be.

THE MOON THROUGH THE SIGNS

In some schools of esoteric astrology the placement of the Moon is seen as an indication of the Sun's sign in the last incarnation. However, Mary Devlin[2], who has researched past-life charts (obtained from birth data given under regression), found no connection between the last-life Sun and the present life Moon, nor did she find evidence to support the related concept of the Ascendant as the past Sun or Moon sign. My own researches show that such birth data is, in any case, somewhat suspect, but the concept is a useful one to bear in mind when exploring the Moon's role in bringing forward powerful influences from the past. The instinctual pattern of the Moon is a deeply ingrained one and must have arisen through considerable experience of the sign in which it is now placed.

A Moon which is out of sympathy with the rest of the chart –

for example a Water Moon in an Earthy chart, or a Moon in an inharmonious sign such as Capricorn, which is uncomfortable with feelings – is an incompatible Moon. It will drastically affect how the rest of the chart functions and will continually fall back into the old pattern delineated by its sign, which is detrimental to the expression of the Sun energy. This type of imbalance is a major cause of difficulty in the present life until the positive, life-enhancing qualities of the Moon are allowed to rise into consciousness, overcoming the destructive, life-failing negative tendencies.

I have investigated lunar expectations and the karma attached to Moon placements in *The Hades Moon*, which summed up some twenty years' work on this ancient light. Time and again I have seen the ingrained patterns that follow surfacing in both regression and my clients' life stories. American astrologer Tracy Marks has explored patterns of parenting and expectations of nurturing relating to the Moon sign and identifies twenty-two positive versus negative expressions of the Moon's energies, including sensitivity/oversensitivity, nurturing/overprotectiveness or smothering, healthy/unhealthy eating patterns. Our books offer suggestions for improving emotional well-being through moving into the positive expression of Moon energies. Tracy Marks also explores the neglected healing power of lunar darkness and points out: 'One of the lessons of the Moon … concerns the healing capacity of consciously chosen unconsciousness … we need to relinquish our solar attempts at order and control, to open to darkness not in order to remain in darkness but to awaken our lunar consciousness and its healing energies.'[3]

This descent into the darkness allows the incarnating soul access to forgotten wisdom that can be used to aid the flowering of the Sun-self. Within this darkness the detritus of outgrown consciousness can make fertile compost for the growth of new awareness; provided that the cyclical light of the Moon is allowed to shine when appropriate. Compost without light and air soon deteriorates into a grim morass of decay, but regularly aerated it becomes a rich and nourishing source of goodness. Tracy Marks also makes the point that 'we must not interrupt the incubation period within us'. It is important to recognise when light is required in the darkness, and when it is inappropriate. We all know that a seed needs time in the darkness to develop roots and to sprout; pulling it up to see how well it is doing will kill it. The Moon has natural cycles of darkness and light; attunement to these inner cycles will indicate the time for inward reflection, the moment when the old has to die, the period of dormancy, and the springing into new life.

The unconscious, unaware Moon energies manifest as a compulsive pull back into the past; the consciously expressed lunar energies nurture the growth of self and others, rectifying the karmic imbalance. The Moon's eclipse cycle, which we will explore later, brings many of the deeper lunar issues up into the light of consciousness.

Moon in Aries

The negative manifestation of the Aries Moon is selfish, self centred and isolated; it pretends to be emotionally self-sufficient, fearing the 'weakness' of dependency, unable to make contact with others. It demands nurturing for itself, seeks ego-boosting dominant relationships, and lacks commitment to anything outside itself. It can be a highly demanding Moon, needing constant reassurance of self-worth.

The positive expression of the lunar energies centres around the Self, recognising its deep needs and being able to self-nurture by meeting those needs. It indicates an individual who has strength and validity because the totality of the Self, including its connection to others, has been rediscovered and is known intimately. Aries is the archetypal knight in shining armour on a white charger, defending the weak and helpless, righting wrongs and battling for good. It is caring, concerned, and able to initiate positive change, handing over its creation when it is appropriate for others to carry it on.

Moon in Taurus

The negative side of the Taurus Moon is manifested as tenacity in holding on to emotions. It harbours a grudge for almost as long as Scorpio and exudes the same kind of brooding resentment. It is a past master at repression, particularly of anger

– like the elephant, it never forgets. As with the Taurus South Node, it seeks sensual gratification and security through the body from people and objects, particularly food. It is fixed, immobile, resistant to change even when obviously hurt by its circumstances. Changing itself is never seen as an option: 'they' are at fault, 'they' must make amends/forgive/alter their behaviour. As a mothering energy it is dominant, overpowering, symbiotic; there is no separation, it is the instinctual Earth. A negative Taurus Moon is stuck in a rut that will ultimately become a grave.

The positive lunar aspects are the ability to nurture through the physical environment and to provide for the needs of others. It finds security within itself. It is loyal, enduring, and perseveres long after everyone else has given up. The Moon in Taurus is often seen in the charts of psychics and healers as it can channel the intuitive levels of awareness down to the earth. It is grounded in the body, a totality of mind/body/spirit/ emotions, using all the senses to interact with the world. It is the earth mother who nourishes and sustains her children, but is then able to let them go at a time appropriate to their growth.

Moon in Gemini

The unconscious Gemini Moon is superficial, fickle, restless, uncommitted, and cerebral. It is cut off from the nourishing source of its emotional energy, and inclined to verbalise out of existence any feeling which does surface.

The consciously expressed lunar energy is able to communicate its feelings freely, without being overly emotional. It holds a balance between the body and the emotions, mediating through the intellect in order to recognise and acknowledge its emotional roots.

Moon in Cancer

The destructive side of the Cancer Moon energy is overly sensitive, possessive, clinging and dependent – those crab claws do not let go easily. It has a hard shell of seeming indifference covering an inner feeling of extreme vulnerability. It suffers from corrosive self-pity which eats away any joy in life. It obliquely demands emotional nourishment for the needy child who is protected by that shell. As a mothering energy it smothers, allowing no autonomy or separation. Its own needs can be totally subjugated to the concept of 'The Family'.

The positive expression of the lunar energy is an unsurpassed capacity for nurturing. It is caring, protective and sympathetic, providing emotional nourishment for all. It mothers in a growth-inducing way, not only its children but anyone who is needy. It is attuned to the life-giving energies of the feminine, the Goddess. It has learned to nurture the Self.

Moon in Leo

The deeply instinctual Moon in Leo is autocratic and overbearing. It demands the admiration which is essential to its emotional sustenance. Its great sin is 'hubris', too much pride. It cannot cope with feeling neglected or helpless, and will unashamedly exert its considerable authority in order to be rewarded by feeling needed and powerful.

When the Leo Moon becomes conscious it is capable of deep loving and generosity of spirit. It becomes centred in its heart, showering benevolent warmth and affection on all people. It knows that 'genuine love is a self-replenishing activity (which is) volitional rather than emotional'.[4]

Moon in Virgo

The unconscious Moon in Virgo is cold, critical and overly analytical. It is not comfortable with emotion and will attempt to rationalise feelings. It seeks order as a means of exerting control – everything in its conscious mind is pigeon-holed, clean, neat and acceptable. Anything else is firmly excluded, relegated to the hold labelled 'Not Wanted on Voyage'. It is sterile and puritanical, trapped in old vows of celibacy.

When the Moon in Virgo is manifested consciously, it taps a wellspring of fertile, creative energy. This sign above all else indicates truly altruistic service springing from an inner state of love and relatedness. It is virgin within the old meaning: 'intact', integrated and whole. Virgo is the sign of the harvest, fruitful and abundant.

Moon in Libra

The old pattern for the Moon in Libra is one of over-compromising; adjusting too much to the needs of others, the soul with this placement is a 'people-pleaser'. It avoids confrontation and assertion and thereby stifles its own emotional needs. Its very 'niceness' is untrustworthy because it can explode unexpectedly when its deeper needs demand to be heard.

The positive lunar pattern opens up to true relationship, interaction with an equal. It is capable of harmonising and balancing its own emotional needs with those of another effecting a creative compromise. It has reached inner emotional equilibrium and is centred on itself and therefore not afraid to be honest and truthful in expressing feelings.

Moon in Scorpio

The deeply mistrustful Scorpio Moon harbours old jealousies, anger, pain and passion. It is resentful, suffers from inner feelings of inadequacy and guilt, and elicits rejection as a defence against the risk of opening up to another person. The biggest fear of the Scorpio Moon is that someone else will have power over it, so feelings are never expressed directly, not even to itself. It is 'paranoid', seeing persecution around every corner: 'they are out to get me/won't let me be happy/are waiting to punish me' are just a few of its inner messages that arise out of past experiences. Emotions are deeply repressed and erupt from time to time in a monumental outburst that bears no relation to the size of the trigger as it has the full weight of the past behind it. That past is a traumatic, unsafe place to venture.

The positive Scorpio Moon can penetrate the depths, the taboo areas where others fear to tread. It is able to go through the pain and trauma and emerge with insights about its own and others' healing and progress. It is intensely passionate and can harness its creative energy to accompany others on the journey into their own darkness, acting as a guide and catalyst for their growth. It is deeply intuitive and is attuned to the cycle of birth, death and regeneration.

Moon in Sagittarius

The negatively manifesting Sagittarian Moon is 'out to lunch' whenever any emotional demands are made. Its response to emotional pressure is to travel, preferably physically, but if this is not possible, mentally. Although it will enjoy exploring the rhetorical question: 'Why do we need feelings?', it will not enjoy exploring those feelings other than in a purely philosophical manner. It is a dual Moon, and when it does allow itself to feel anything there can be oscillation between two emotions or two people; this is an unfaithful Moon. It is the old courtesan, a cultured, entertaining companion but one who is not emotionally engaged in the relationship.

The positively expressed Sagittarius Moon is open, honest and trusting in its relationships and sharing of feelings, allowing joy to manifest in its life. Its philosophy embraces feelings, intuition, and an old knowing into its sense of Being.

Moon in Capricorn

The unconscious Capricorn Moon is cold, judgmental, unresponsive and afraid to express emotion. It gives out a message of isolation and self-sufficiency 'approach with caution', and retreats into 'safe' material expressions of its feelings. It cares financially for the family, often at the cost of emotional closeness and carries an almost paralysing burden of responsibility. As a mothering energy the negative Capricorn Moon is severe, controlling and may be incapable of physically expressing its maternal feelings.

The conscious Capricorn Moon is steadfast, responsible and authoritative, offering dependable support. As a mothering energy it offers consistent discipline leading towards maturity and self-control.

Capricorn has to move from an 'external locus of control' (a voice comprised of all the authority figures, teachers, parents, gurus from its past) into an 'inner locus' that is the voice of the Self. When it achieves this, Capricorn has inner authority and power that act as a guide to life – both for the individual and for society.

Moon in Aquarius

The negatively expressed Aquarian Moon is self-contained, out of touch with its feelings and its past and yet profoundly motivated by both. The soul with this placement finds one-to-one relationships difficult, preferring to relate 'to the whole' in a very detached way, or to retreat into an unreal fantasy relationship in which it perceives little about its partner's feelings and responses. The Aquarian Moon has a distant and formal pattern of relating and takes refuge in a cold, lonely place whenever it is threatened emotionally. It may choose celibacy in preference to the intimacy it finds so challenging.

The positive Aquarian Moon is an expression of universal love. It is connected to the whole, interacting from an objective perspective, unattached to the outcome, and yet capable of expressing its very real feelings of love for the microcosm, a human being, and macrocosm, humankind. It is the true humanitarian. It is detached from the emotions, unaffected by emotional arguments and can therefore evaluate what is most beneficial to the whole. The Aquarian Moon is intuitive and perceptive, attuned through old contacts to the philanthropic ideals behind the new Aquarian Age.

Moon in Pisces

The unconscious Pisces Moon slips into the same old scenarios as the Pisces South Node, falling back into a martyr/victim, rescuer/persecutor or saviour pattern. It is self-sacrificing and self-immolating and induces guilt with facile ease. This too is a dual, unfaithful Moon, although it deceives itself into believing it is not capable of hurting anyone and that, in any case, if no one knows, no one is hurt by the emotional games it plays with two lovers, for example. It cannot bear pain, wallows in self-pity and sympathy, makes promises it will never keep, and then goes its own sweet way.

The conscious Pisces Moon is the natural mystic and medium of the zodiac, bringing unconditional love and inspiration to the world. It is empathetic but discriminating; connected and yet independent. It recognises that 'love involves a change in the self, but this is an extension of the self rather than a sacrifice of the self'[5]. When called upon, it can make great personal sacrifice for the good of the greater whole, but this is not an involuntary reaction, it is the final step in self-integration with the cosmos.

THE SUN THROUGH THE SIGNS

The pathway to true integration and release from the karmic round requires that the question 'Who am I?' be addressed. The instinctual Moon offers one answer, but a conscious shift into the Sun sign energies allows for an expansion of the incarnating soul into the Self – the totality embracing the whole being – where an altogether different answer emerges. Although the following is portrayed as a journey around the zodiac, the intention is not to imply that an incarnating soul progresses inexorably from the preceding sign to the next. The signs are areas of experience which will be used when required and as appropriate in order to balance out previous incarnations. Several experiences may be needed in one particular sign or element before its lessons are properly assimilated; other lessons come easily and a short experience may be all that is required. The zodiac is a spectrum through which the soul progresses in accordance with its own pattern, evolving towards its highest potential.

Sun in Aries

Aries is a sign of birth and isolation. There is an intense awareness of separateness, of being an individual consciousness, surrounded by a vast otherness.[6]

Born into Aries, the incarnating soul becomes conscious of moving into a separate identity after experiencing the interconnectedness and wholeness of the between-life state. It moves from the attunement of sharing space with those in the spiritual realm to a sense of 'otherness'; an alienation from the sense of being at one. A young Norwegian client (eighth house Sun in Aries, five planets in Earth) asked: 'I would like to know from where in the universe I come, and when did I come here. Finally I am interested if there is someone in the family or nearby who has been in connection with me during past lives.' He had a third house Neptune and felt separate, not a part of his family of origin. He was physically aware of this difference, an alien being incarcerated in the body of a stranger with the task of discovering himself.

Aries is concerned with the development of the ego: 'the conscious, thinking subject'[7], the Will: 'desire of sufficient intensity that it is translated into action'[8], and the Self: 'own individuality or essence'[9]. The incarnating soul may evolve through the pathway of identification with itself on the level of individuality; a selfish, self-centred pathway concerned only with 'Me' which generates karma, or through merging with the essence: an unselfish pathway concerned with expression of the eternal 'I' which is beyond karma.

Aries is also concerned with issues of assertion and Will. The Will may be developed in the service of the ego or of the Self. When associated with the ego, it is wilful: 'compulsion or ignorance or accident cannot be pleaded as excuse, intentional, deliberate, due to perversity or self-will, obstinate, headstrong, refractory'[10], and concerned only with self-interest. In the service of the Self it is concerned with self-growth and self-determination. Aries must master the lesson of transmutation of the base impulses of self-will and aggression which are linked to its ruler, Mars. Assertion is the higher octave of the aggressive, violent urge towards destruction. It is concerned with affirmation of the Self, with growth and construction. Courage is an Aries quality, defined by M. Scott Peck as 'not the absence of fear, it is the making of action in spite of fear, the moving out against the resistance engendered by fear into the unknown and into the future'.[11]

It is this experience of travelling into the unknown which will develop the innate Arian leadership potential and pioneering spirit. However, wisdom is required to circumvent disaster brought about by those other Arian qualities – foolhardiness and over-impulsiveness. Aries must learn to think before acting, but not fall into the trap of procrastination. A middle course must be steered, guided by the compass of the Self.

Sun in Taurus

Incarnating in Taurus, the soul becomes aware of the world through sensory perception. Discarnate beings describe inhabiting worlds where the spirit is lightly clothed and each thought or emotion is clearly visible to all. American Episcopalian Bishop Pyke's son, in his communications through the medium

Ena Twigg, described a place where all desires could be satisfied. By the act of desiring something, it was there. Sexual intercourse was a fusion of two beings, not just bodies. Small wonder then that Taurus is so involved with the physical, sensual and sexual level of being; the soul needs physical experience, and there must be no separation between the Self and its vehicle. If it gets stuck on the purely sensual level however, karma will accumulate which will have to be balanced out later. If it learns to move into that fusion of being on all levels which Jeff Mayo describes as 'organic relatedness'[12], then its karmic task is completed.

Taurus is one of the fixed signs; it is obstinate and unmoving, and this soul needs to learn perseverance and endurance. Where Aries would move on, Taurus stays through to the end. However, it must learn when to hang on in there, and when it is merely digging a deeper and deeper rut which will eventually become its grave; Taurus must evolve, slowly and steadily but relentlessly, or expire from inertia.

One of the main lessons that Taurus must learn is to achieve inner security rather than identify with what it owns or possesses. I have repeatedly asked Taurean clients what kept her, or him – it makes no difference – in a marriage which was clearly over years before. The answer was always the same: 'Well, there's the house ...', and of course the marriage, no matter how dead, which was something known and familiar. Fear of change and the unfamiliar can keep many Taureans in their rut. When Taurus feels secure within itself, it has a stable base from which to venture on its journey into the unknown.

Sun in Gemini

Moving into Gemini the incarnating soul finds itself inhabiting a 'mental' realm of intellect and communication. It is concerned with gathering information about the world around it and the people it meets, and with processing these facts to make order and sense out of a jumble of perceptions. We are bombarded with sensory input on a daily basis, and Gemini learns to select only the relevant information for the task at hand. It filters out the unnecessary data. Its essential function is communication: what has been processed must be passed on. It is ruled by Mercury, mediator and messenger for the gods. Singer Julie Felix (Gemini with Scorpio rising, first house Scorpio North Node, and ninth house Venus-Pluto in Cancer) experienced jealousy consciously for the first time at age fifty. She promptly wrote a song 'Graduation Day' to express her pain and new understanding out to the world:

> I guess that you could say
> That this is graduation day
> Cos I just stand here and hear you say
> Like the lines from a play
> That you slept with her
> That was a promise that you kept with her
> You slept with her.
>
> I know we both agreed
> That if we ever felt the need
> To explore some karmic debt
> With a person that we met
> That we could sleep with them
> If there were dreams that we could reap with them
> Then we could sleep with them.
>
> It's funny how the human heart gets broken
> No matter what precautions we might take
> It's not until those painful words are spoken
> That reality defeats philosophy.
>
> How did it feel inside
> Was it guilt or was it pride
> What was it that you said
> To make her crawl into your bed
> And sleep with you
> And were your feelings really deep and true
> To have her sleep with you?
>
> And now you're by my side
> And you held me while I cried
> Until somewhere deep inside
> I felt the turning of the tide
> And you slept with me.

Other songs have communicated her evolving spiritual awareness, and her protests at the exploitation of the earth and its
people.

Gemini is flexible and adaptive, able to adjust easily to changing circumstances. The danger is that it can be too mercurial,
constantly and restlessly seeking new experiences and not allowing time for consolidation. It can be the 'butterfly mind'
alighting here and there as the whim takes it but never completing a task and dissipating its energies in a fruitless search
for satiation. The lesson for the soul attuned to the Gemini Sun
is to discipline its restless mind and focus on communicating
all that has been learnt – then it will be free to move on.

Sun in Cancer

In Cancer the soul enters the world of the emotions and the
eternally nurturing energy of the Great Mother. Here it meets
and consciously integrates the archetypal feminine and matriarchal energies into its being. Just as Taurus faced the lesson
of endurance, Cancer has to learn when to nurture, and when
to let go. This is a very specific lesson for Cancer mothers as
they can fall into the role of the eternal mother, inhibiting both
their own growth and that of their dependant – whether physically related or not – by blotting out separation and difference.
They need to differentiate between mothering and smothering, love and possessiveness.

A client (with twelfth house Sun in Cancer square the
Moon in Libra) was brought up by a mother (Moon in Cancer) who smothered him with love. 'Have you got your hanky,
dear?' she would ask as she waved him off to school, age six-
teen and six feet tall. He was a sensitive, withdrawn child,
absorbing the repressed emotional ambience of a dysfunc-
tional family, and his only outlet was music. His father was a
womaniser and the family moved continually to escape from
the latest affair, but the problem was never acknowledged; both
parents were Pisces. At the age of eleven, apparently in response to pressure to pass his eleven-plus examination, he
developed night-time epilepsy. His twelfth house Venus in
Gemini conjunct Uranus-Mercury in Cancer square to Mars

indicated an old disruption in the brain-wave pattern, but no brain malfunction or injury could be found to explain it. Many years later it was discovered that, when sleeping, he would literally stop breathing and convulsions would ensue. Breath is one of the ways we nourish ourselves and he was manifesting his symbolic suffocation. This always occurred during a period of emotional distress within the family: failing to breathe was his way of withdrawing from the unacknowledged stress. He has a split chart with Pluto sextile Neptune but neither planet aspecting any other, so the withdrawal was an unconscious and dissociative reflex action. The episodes were always preceded by the same terrifying dream (twelfth house Uranus-Mercury communicating an old terror).

Apart from visits to a psychiatric hospital for tests, his problem was never validated within the family by being discussed – a typically Piscean and twelfth house response to a difficult situation. His doting mother was terrified of the convulsions and never went to him during an attack. He married a Taurus 'earth mother' type (Sun conjunct his North Node) who tried to give him the nurturing and grounding he previously lacked. Although the epilepsy subsided, it recurred whenever the family could no longer be ignored. It was only at the age of forty, on his Uranus opposition, that he was able to reassess the problem and begin to live – a life which was free from the unconscious parental pressures and his own desperate, little-boy need for nourishment and protection. So far, however, he has not explored the karmic implications of his twelfth house, which could possibly release him from these difficulties.

When the Cancer Sun energy functions positively, it works through vocations and activities which nurture and nourish those it meets on its journey, especially when undertaken by people who know how to ensure that their own needs are met. It is the cosmic social worker in constructive action.

Sun in Leo

In Leo the soul enters the arena of power and empowerment and develops the urge towards expression of personal authority. Leo is the king of the zodiac and its rule may be despotic, autocratic or benign depending on how that urge is acted out. Leo's lesson is to own the power deep within its Self. As Liz Greene'[13] points, out Leo's initial challenge is to find out why it is 'uniquely itself', and its life-long task is to discover some much-needed self-esteem. She sees Leo's main purpose as making the journey within.

This journey into the centre of its being is linked to the Leo need to be heart-centred. Traditionally Leo rules the heart and a stressed, frustrated Leo is prone to cardiac problems. When Leo becomes centred in its heart, the love energy becomes the source of power, both for the inward and the outward journey. It is empowered. However: 'When power is clearly moving through us, energy pours through and we become 'larger than life'. If it is not let go of afterwards then we begin to misuse it and we become puffed up, 'on a high horse'.[14]

As Debbie Boater (now Shapiro) pointed out many years ago, it is through the attachment to power, trying to hold on to it instead of letting it flow, that problems arise. When Leo is conscious of owning its power, it knows that, paradoxically, the power is not its own: 'owning power is an acknowledgement that there is nothing to own'. A Leo who is grasping at power demands admiration and praise, a Leo who owns power commands it naturally. Watch Leo enter a room: if it is secure its presence illuminates the whole area. It has centre stage. A Pisces woman grumbled, about a good friend: 'When Bren walks into a room it's just like a magnet, every man in it gravitates to her.' Bren was middle-aged and overweight, but she was also Leo. Secure in her own power, she radiated love and warmth and everyone responded, including the Piscean who 'couldn't help herself'. She knew herself to be special, the quality that every Leo yearns for, and yet, paradoxically, she saw everyone else as special too and shone her light upon the world.

When uncomfortable with power, Leo snarls like a bad-tempered old lion protecting his pride from a young challenger. If at ease with power, Leo basks in its warmth like a contented pussycat stretched out in the sun. The aware Leo naturally radiates its Self out to the waiting world. It has become conscious of its creative power. It has authority. It is empowered. The process of becoming aware as an individual is complete.

Sun in Virgo

In Virgo the incarnating soul begins the process of reintegration with the whole, and enters into service as an expression of interconnectedness. Having been acknowledged for its own power in Leo, the soul now submits to the authority of divine love and offers itself in unselfish service as an outpouring of that love. The service that is given is disinterested, there is no ego involvement, neither is the service given so that others, or Virgo itself, will say: What a good person'. It is given without thought of reward or recognition. A smiling greeting to a lonely stranger is an act of service just as much as nursing someone through their final hours. One of the ways Virgo can give service is by entering the world of medicine and healing. Virgo is the intellectual Earth sign and it has a need to understand the body/mind link and the psychosomatic causes of disease – why and how the soul being ill at ease will manifest within the physical body as pain and discomfort.

Virgo is also the craftsperson, the creator on the physical level. Its symbol is the Virgin holding an ear of corn, and it is linked to the old earth goddess and the rituals to ensure an abundant and fruitful harvest. It is part of the fertility cycle and deeply attuned to creative energy. It has an inherent urge towards perfection. Jeff Mayo sees Virgo as having a primal impulse towards the skilful use of energy which avoids wastage or dissipation, and which incorporates self-sufficiency and independence. A purity of Being which is the true meaning of virgin – whole and, intact. He sees Virgo's task as to analyse everything until the pure essence is perceived and assimilated. This purity of essence is essential for Virgo as from it springs a detached service, concerned only with what is required, not with reward or recognition. In true humility Virgo honours the creative love force underlying life and carries it out to the world in loving service.

Sun in Libra

In Libra the soul seeks to expand through relationship with others. It is ready to move on to a path that requires its own boundaries be expanded enough to include, or be penetrated by, A. N. Other; to enlarge its consciousness beyond individual separation into loving interrelation with another.

There is no alternative … to bringing into being a truly conscious relationship with another person. Inevitably it hurts; any birth does. One must dare to suffer the death of illusions, and the dissolution of projections. One must dare to be mistaken. One must dare to be vulnerable, to be inferior, to be magnanimous enough to allow for the failings of others because one is prone to them oneself; and one must dare to incur (and inflict) pain and wounded pride … And one must be willing to accept the element of unconscious collusion in all situations, however much they may seem to be the fault of the other. Nothing comes into a man's life that is not a reflection of something within himself.[15]

This is the karmic task of Libra; to enter into an aware relationship with another human being with all the failings and foibles, the needs and aspirations on both sides taken into account and allowed expression. Where there is a conflict of interest the Libra soul must learn the art of creative compromise, ensuring that its own needs do not become submerged under pressure from the other and that a way is found to encompass both. This can only be achieved when the Libran soul has entered into relationship with its Self first.

Libra attains emotional equilibrium through its relationships, in the widest sense. It learns to accommodate both its own feelings and those of another, and to recognise that while both have validity and value, neither are of overwhelming importance. Conscious awareness of motivation and of where those feelings are coming from will allow a choice to be made – decisions being something Libra is notoriously bad at – whether to incorporate the new point of view which is being represented by the other. In this way Libra is able to grow through its interaction and develops an inner harmony and balance which is reflected in relationships outside of itself.

Sun in Scorpio

In Scorpio the soul makes its descent into darkness. It must regain its understanding of the shadow side of life and integrate this into its awareness; it must then rise to the heights of consciousness. The soul must recognise its own immortality.

As with the Scorpio Moon and Node, the Scorpio Sun can venture into the depths where others fear to tread, the taboo areas wherein lurk death and annihilation, to bring back insights that will help others on their individual journeys. It has an intuitive understanding that here, in the darkness, is where the deepest roots of creativity lie; here is the energy for renewal and new growth. It also has an intuitive knowledge of the fertility cycle, the seasons of conception, birth, death and rebirth and it knows that death comes many times, physically and psychically, only to rise again to new life. And from those depths it brings back an awareness of the purpose of its Being. Scorpio knows the soul can never be extinguished, it will always survive.

Scorpio experiences the sexual act as a transforming and regenerative process intimately linked to the energies of creation, an act of mystical union with another soul which incorporates 'death' through temporary self-forgetfulness and, immolation. Through that union with an other (which is an act of integration), the Scorpio soul fuses with the cosmos and the source of life itself. It is thus uniquely attuned to the on-going, ever-present process of death and rebirth intrinsic in existence. The depth of emotional power which Scorpio generates is also unique and must be harnessed to the evolution of the Self or there is a danger it will become self destructive. In gaining mastery over this power and losing the fear of death, Scorpio fulfils its innermost purpose.

Scorpio has many levels of being. There is the instinctive reaction of the scorpion who lashes out indiscriminately, destroying everything in its path including itself, 'because it is its nature to do so'[16]. There is the level of the eagle who can soar high above the earth, gaining an overview through its penetrating eye and homing in on its target, often with lethal intent. And then there is that of the phoenix, the legendary being who goes through the purifying fire so that all the dross is burnt away and the golden essence is revealed. This is Scorpio at its most evolved: no longer into emotional games or needing revenge for the past, lethal no more. It has entered into relationship with the darkness, mastered it, and brought it into light. Scorpio is then empowered to bring forth the healing and insight necessary for the regeneration of humankind.

Sun in Sagittarius

Sagittarius is the eternal traveller engaged in unceasing exploration of the physical and philosophical worlds. The Sun in Sagittarius soul is a free spirit that ranges far and wide in its search for meaning. It is the ancient philosopher and the Renaissance man for whom there was no division of knowledge; the arts, sciences and humanities were one. Religion came into being in answer to Sagittarius' urgent questions: 'Who am I?', 'Why am I here?'.

These are questions to which Sagittarius must still apply itself today and having found its answers, must then share them in a way that will encourage those less philosophically inclined to move forward into their own understanding of eternal truths. Sagittarius's resources are intuition and old knowledge. Its symbol is the centaur, half man, half beast, a synthesis of instinct and rational thought, capable of making a spontaneous, intuitive leap into the unknown which pulls ever onwards. However, like its polarity sign of Gemini, Sagittarius needs time to ponder, space to assimilate and formulate a belief system which offers a way to Be; and it must follow these beliefs. A centaur paying lip service to ethics is a hollow shell, purposeless and untrustworthy. A Sagittarian true to its path is a sage who leads humankind onwards into knowledge of itself, its world and other dimensions of being.

Sun in Capricorn

In Capricorn the soul meets the archetypal patriarchal energies of 'God the Father' and must assimilate these into its being. It is offered the opportunity of exploring inner discipline in relation to leadership and authority. Capricorn can draw on internal strength, resilience and a disciplined Will in order to establish its own inner authority, which is then translated into and expressed externally as leadership. In the unevolved Capricorn, such leadership can often lack spiritual vision and adheres too closely to an inflexible set of principles:

> Here the unconscious intuitive search for meaning in life is structured and crystallised by the senses into dogma, which attempts to define God and put spiritual reality into concrete form, and translate the numinous into sacrosanct objects – and adherence

to the letter of the law, in other words, an obliviousness to its spirit.[17]

As with the Capricorn Moon, this Sun is striving to develop attunement to, and alignment with, the voice of the Self. When Capricorn is sufficiently confident of its own worth and authority, it can venture away from fixed dogma and into the realms of experiential spirituality and vision. Martin Luther King, Baptist preacher, winner of the Nobel Peace Prize and Civil Rights leader, was a Capricorn who had not only vision, but also the authority and personal charisma (Sun conjunct Midheaven) required to lead his oppressed people out of the prison constructed from the outmoded concepts of the society (Uranus square Saturn) in which they lived:

> Now is the time to make real the promises of democracy. I have a dream that one day this nation will rise up and live out the true meaning of its creed: 'We hold these truths to be self evident, that all men are created equal'. I have a dream that one day ... the sons of former slaves and the sons of former slave-owners will be able to sit down together at the table of brotherhood.[18]

Dr King was a pacifist who believed in non-violent action. He had a wide Sun-Pluto opposition, Sun inconjunct Mars, and Saturn opposing Mars. His karma was concerned with the nature and proper use of power and assertion. He believed in the transforming power of spiritual love (Venus in Pisces) : 'Only through an inner spiritual transformation do we gain the strength to fight vigorously the evils of the world in a humble, loving spirit.'[19] His trine of Ascendant conjunct Jupiter in Taurus to Neptune in Virgo combined idealism with practical action, which took him, through his vision, beyond the limits of the environment in which he was operating.

> Violence brings only temporary victories; violence, by creating many more social problems then it solves, never brings permanent peace. I am convinced that if we succumb to the temptation to use violence in our struggle for freedom, unborn generations will be the recipients of a long and desolate night of bitterness, and our chief legacy to them will be a never ending reign of chaos.[20]

That twelfth house Uranus has old knowledge of revolution, but his vision of spiritual community and love freed from oppression, is one which every Capricorn can share.

Sun in Aquarius

The soul incarnating into Aquarius marches to a different drum from the rest of humanity. It is one step ahead; the social visionary who is able to conceive of new ways of being in which the needs of all of humanity will be met. However, in spite of this it is acutely aware of its connection to its 'brother man'. This is the sign that is most concerned with the ultimate fate of humanity and planet earth.

The unevolved Aquarian is, in the words of Martin Luther King: 'A reformer ... whose rebellion against the evils of society has left him annoyingly rigid and unreasonably impatient.'[21] All too often the detachment of Aquarius actually conceals an 'out-of-touchness' with emotional forces that rage within, pushing Aquarius this way and that until, at last, these feelings rise into consciousness. The evolved Aquarian has become truly centred in Being, no longer attached to the emotions, the mind the servant of the Self: the intuition has blended with rational intelligence to attain true wisdom. The Aquarian Self is attuned to the vibration of universal love and brotherhood which permeates and underlies the functioning of the cosmos. This universal love is expressed by the Aquarian soul through humanitarian ideals and an originality of thought which ushers in Progress. Humankind is entering the Age of Aquarius, the time to move into conscious, caring brotherhood not only with each other, but also with the rest of creation. It is no accident that politics have turned 'green' and are aligned to ecological and conservation issues: the Aquarian Age ordains that this be so, together with a shift into husbanding the resources of the planet and its people.

According to Genesis, Man was given dominion over the earth and appointed to be its steward, a position of responsibility, not despoiler. Brotherhood extends to both creator and creation, including the furthermost stars and levels of existence. The Age of Aquarius demands a return to the state of harmonious inter–connectedness of the organic whole, and the

Aquarian energy will be there, leading the way to universal Being.

Sun in Pisces

In Pisces the soul completes its journey back to the source. It transcends the material world, reaches out to the spiritual realm, and attains union with the divine.

The evolved Piscean develops its powers of unconditional love and compassion as it ministers impartially to those around it. It is moving towards a state of grace, the point where karma is balanced out, obligations sufficiently repaid, potential adequately fulfilled. Release from the wheel of rebirth is a distinct possibility. M. Scott Peck describes this state: 'The call to grace is a call to life of effortful caring; to a life of service and whatever sacrifice seems required. It is a call out of spiritual childhood into adulthood, a call to be a parent unto mankind.'[22]

The Pisces Sun is striving to merge into its greater Self, and the journey appears to have an unbreakable connection with the testing process known as 'The Dark Night of the Soul'. When one is seemingly at last reaching a point of enlightenment; one is plunged into a period of spiritual blackness. For Pisces in particular this may well be linked to the need to avoid 'spiritual pride' (especially when the Sun is in the twelfth house) as this can negate any progress made towards achieving the state of grace. It is a humbling experience to suddenly find that, just as one feels one is getting somewhere, one falls into deepest despair, apparently without cause or reason. In her book *A Case for Reincarnation*, Christine Hartley points out:

> Just because in one sense we know so much, so are they (these states of despair) the more bitter for us than for the unaware because we know that we should be able to conquer the despair and the gloom. But we cannot. To each man must come his Gethsemane, the saints and saviours all experience it and the greater the saint, in all probability the greater the despair. Unless a man has cried 'My God, my God, why hast thou forsaken me?' he cannot understand the despair of others ... only by our own suffering can we truly learn how to help suffering humanity, and only by our acceptance of it and our transmutation of it can we show the world our belief that it is only a moment in the eternal passage of time.[23]

It is the karmic task of Pisces to achieve this transmutation of suffering into a state of grace, and in so doing surrender to the divine, merge and become One.

[Note: see also the Nodes of the Moon for further insight into past/present patterns.]

PROGRESSIONS

I rarely use progressions in karmic work but occasionally will notice that it is time for a new energy to emerge, a new karmic lesson to begin or circumstances to change. This almost invariably corresponds with a progressed planet either changing sign, house or moving up to aspect a natal planet. The method I use for progression is the 'day-for-a-year' which involves counting days in the Ephemeris of planetary positions as though they were years of life – so to see what is happening at age 25, for instance, you would count forward 25 days (including the day of birth). Most planets move slowly by progression, except for the Moon which changes signs frequently. The progressed Moon has a rhythmic unfoldment, identifiable as it passes round the zodiac bringing experience of the different signs and houses – see Chapter 5.

TRANSITS

Transits (the day to day movement of the planets) act as a trigger for the karmic energy patterns. Some triggers occur at a fixed, predetermined time according to the orbit of that planet: the squares, returns and opposition of a planet to its natal place. Others occur according to the distribution of the planets around the natal chart. I work with orbs that are at least 4^0-5^0 each side of exact for outer planet transits (Jupiter onwards) as the effect of these will be felt long before, and long after, the comparatively short time when they will be exact: that is, when they reach the same degree as the planet they are activating in the chart. This is particularly relevant when a planet appears to retrograde (move backwards) as it approaches a major transit aspect to the natal chart. It is especially noticeable when the retrograde motion apparently causes the transiting planet to pass over the degree of the natal planet three times. The effect will be weak at first, then be felt strongly, will then recede, gain strength, recede and gain strength again before moving on.

A personal planet transit, which is much faster, may be needed to 'kickstart' a slower transit into action. The effect of 'personal' planet transits usually lasts for a few days or weeks at the most, rather than the months and even years that an outer planet transit will be felt, but they can be very significant in bringing a karmic issue to the surface for resolution. The transits of the outer planets may be more dramatic and traumatic, their pressure unavoidable. Certain transits bring up both issues of karma and karmic purpose.

Transiting Pluto

Pluto transits inevitably bring up issues of karmic power and compulsion according to the nature of the planet involved in the transit. When Pluto transits Venus, for instance, karmic relationship issues and old emotional patterns come to the fore to be transformed. This is a time of karmic meetings and reconnections.

Transiting Pluto square Pluto is an astrological 'biggy'. This is a critical time as Pluto tears down what is old and outworn so that something new may emerge. Charles Carter said Pluto transits are 'a resurrection of things past and half-forgotten', but it can feel rather like dismemberment (or crucifixion) in someone who is not aware of the positive energies below the surface. This can be a time of regeneration, going through 'the fires of transformation', and a recognition of the creative processes at work in the universe. It is an appropriate time for spiritual pregnancy to end and its fruit be born (Pluto is, of course, the planet of birth as well as death). On the other hand, it is also a time when the conscious mind may appear to be in control, but, as time goes on, the unconscious takes over with disastrous consequences. In other words, karma goes on working itself out. By the time Pluto comes into trine with itself the issues have become clear but may call for further work to integrate the new insights.

In an article on 'The Pluto in Leo Generation', Robert Blaschke wrote about this generation 'coming into their power during the transiting Pluto in Scorpio square'. As he pointed out, this square is occurring at a younger age than it has done in previous generations. He pinpoints one of the lessons as needing to face, and heal inner emotional turmoil in order to be of compassionate service to others. He sees Pluto as provoking the questions: Do I go on controlling others because I fear my vulnerability? Am I driven by compulsions and obsessive thoughts and feeling patterns that cause me to do destructive things in my life, even when I would choose otherwise if I could? He commented that 'The Pluto force is not complete until the individual interacts with others in a transformed way'. This was a 'wake up call for a self-centred generation that is at the threshold of its greatest creative experience – the giving of self for the needs of humanity'. He saw the Aquarian polarity as 'asking for the catharsis of the individual into the collective'. The final paragraph of his article asks: 'How much suffering do we need to witness before we mobilize our generational forces and take action (fire element – Leo) to heal (Pluto) the ills in society that we see all around us (air element – Aquarian polarity)'. A question that is still unfortunately relevant to the Pluto in Sagittarius trine to the Leonine Pluto. We can only hope, and work on resolving the issue before Pluto moves into Capricorn and forces society as a whole to confront this problem.

Blaschke also points out that whatever is buried from the past will surface during a Pluto transit, and that symbolic death and regeneration are an integral part of the Pluto experience. He makes the comment that this placement has great 'strength of self and this is precisely why this generation has manifested the intense karma in its lifetime that it has'.

The Uranus Opposition

One of the major astrological events in anyone's life is the Uranus Opposition, otherwise known as the mid-life crisis. With all major transits, there is a sense of something pending – be it doom, gloom or excited anticipation – for anything up to a year before the transit becomes exact, and the effects can last for two years after the transit. Despite this, the suddeness of Uranian aspects still cause surprise. We are never quite prepared for Uranus events no matter how hard we try to be.

The Uranus Opposition is one of the main periods when people consult an astrologer. It is a major transition phase when we have to ask many questions. We have to reassess what we have accomplished, identify what we have not yet achieved, let go of our inappropriate aims and ambitions, and check out whether we are happy and fulfilled in all areas of our lives. If we are not, then the 'crisis' aspect of the Uranian vibration tends to hit us hard as one by one the drastic changes begin to manifest and we experience the disruptive phase of the energy. Even where we have been going along with the changes we need to make, this transit tends to uncover still more and the advice I usually give people at this time is 'expect the unexpected'. What is happening on the deeper levels is that experience is shifting from 'outer world' orientated events to inner exploration. The higher mind is being activated and the energies flowing through the chakras are able to start transforming the raw energy of creation into a refined, purposeful, flow.

We can take as an example the Uranus in Cancer generation who had the opposition at a comparatively young age at the start of the 1990s. Jeff Green, an American astrologer who has worked extensively with both Uranus and Pluto, says that the Uranus in Cancer generation need to 'liberate from all external forms of emotional security and dependency'. He points out that the inability of most of their parents to support the child's gut level knowledge that he (or she) is unique in himself means that the child will be thrown in on himself for nurturing, leaving unresolved emotional needs behind which are dragged into adulthood. Cyclically, in rhythm with the transits, the child will be brought face to face with the need to learn true independence and emotional security. It is part of the 'cosmic plan' as this experience then changes the ability to parent and to say to his own children 'Be who you are'.

As Jeff Green explains: 'When Uranus is in Cancer it helps break up the crystalized structures of the consensus reality defined by any society. It facilitates and quickens the evolutionary growth rate of the human organism. These people operate planetarily as "seed" people.' He then specifically takes the example of Uranus in Cancer in the ninth house, and says that these people have to break out the biological womb and into the womb of the inner Self. They can become insecure in the process so need to 'define his/her personal sense of identity in cosmological or metaphysical terms'. Then will come the need to communicate their new understanding. He reckons that only about a third of the Uranus-in-Cancer generation will respond in this way. And, he warns: 'He or she will set him – or herself up to be judged as an eclectic thinker, a person who, by the nature of his or her thoughts or philosophies, threatens the philosophical security of mainstream society'. And 'The lesson is also to learn how to deliver, present or teach these things in such a way as to not alienate (ninth house) others to the point of rebellion.'

Transiting Neptune

Neptune is a slippery planet and under its influence it is possible to drift into karmic situations. One of my clients, for instance, somehow found herself married to a violent man with whom she had considerable negative karmic connections. Six months later: 'It was as though I had been hypnotised and someone had snapped their fingers. I realised I had been drawn back into an old, self-destructive pattern and got out as quickly as I could'. Neptune was transiting her fifth house Moon. The day 'the fingers snapped' was the day Neptune moved on.

The problem with Neptune transits is that they can be linked to spiritual enlightenment, mystical experiences and the working out of karmic purpose. They can also bring out the greatest illusions of all time and it is not apparent until the transit is over which is which. This is what I call 'Pink Cloud Syndrome'.

Under Neptune's influence many people believe they have a mission. They believe aliens, God, angels or discarnate beings give them their instructions and it is all too easy to lose touch with everyday reality, as a New Age guru found to his cost. He had been told by a medium that he had a karmic task to carry out for the good of mankind. He began to channel energies to heal the earth, and received a series of channelled teachings which became a best selling book. However, the launch of this book coincided with him undergoing successive transits of Jupiter and Neptune that triggered his Grand Cross of Saturn conjunct Neptune in Libra in the twelfth house opposing Mercury in the sixth, squared by Moon-Uranus in ninth house Cancer opposing Chiron in the third. He rapidly lost contact with 'the brakes' as he calls it and has graphically described the Neptunian 'fog' that descended on him. He had a mystical experience in Peru and on his return immediately called a press conference to announce his ideas to the world: "The 'take-over' of the rational me was at its peak and it needed to be, I can tell you, to stand up in a room of tabloid journalists and announce not only that you were a Son of the Godhead, whatever that meant, but also a long list of fantastic geological events .... standing there was a weird, unreal experience."

It wasn't until October that year that the Neptune transit passed and the rational man returned. 'Almost as though someone had flicked a switch.' In December transiting Uranus contacted his natal Chiron, offering its gift of healing and transformation. He went back on to the media to try and explain what had happened. With their usual flair, the media then said that he had confessed to madness and recanted all that he had previously said (echoes of Neptune). As he says, "It was time to use the interest generated by the 'Son of God period to get over what I am really saying. If I had simply written a book, interest would have long disappeared". As it was, the subjects of karma and the state of the earth were given peak time on both radio and television, an appropriate use of Neptune's energy!

All transits are an opportunity to work more closely with the energies of the planetary combination involved and to develop its qualities within us. If we are strongly attuned to a planet and, therefore, to our own inner energy, we will resonate strongly with its transits and will try to co-operate with the inner adjustments it brings. If we are not, we will be buffeted by the process and believe that 'something out there' is forcing these changes upon us. Expanding inner awareness is reflected in how we handle transits and external events. Things no longer 'happen' to us, we begin to recognise their purpose in the overall scheme of things.

Transits and the Chakras

Astrologically, life can be divided into age-spans which relate to different levels of awareness. This is linked to the flow of the universal creative energy, the life force, through ourselves. Throughout our lives we are balancing the different 'bodies': the physical, emotional, mental and spiritual. The linkage points for these different bodies are the energy centres known as the chakras and there is a powerful interaction between the planets and the chakras via the endocrine system which mediates the changes in the physical body.

Up to age 29, we are dealing with the 'physical' level. This is the period when the lower chakras, governing the sexual organs, are activated and we attune to the life force at the physical creative level. We have to get our career and finances worked out and learn how to interact with the world through a physical body. When transiting Saturn returns to its natal position on the chart (the Saturn Return), around age 29, we shift into the 'emotional body' and the solar plexus and heart chakras are activated. In our thirties we examine the feelings we have about ourselves and others, and our ability to express who we are. We have to work on mastering the emotions rather than being ruled by them. The ideal is to remain centred and calm, and unaffected by extremes of pain and joy. At this stage the life force is expressed through emotional and bodily creativity.

Following the Saturn Return we have the Uranus Opposition, when the planet is opposite its place on the natal chart. At this stage we have to move into the 'mental body' and let go of youth. Detaching from emotional issues in order to understand the world and our place in it. It is also the time when we move the energies up to the throat chakra, activating the higher mind. We can then direct the life force (or kundalini energy) from its 'home' in the base chakra so that it meets the 'mind force' and is expressed through communication and mental creation. Between 48 and 51 we have the Chiron Return, which usually provokes a crisis of meaning when we move into the 'spiritual body' and the soul finds its new form. If we successfully make this transition to the spiritual level, the brow and crown chakras are activated and we have a connection to a wider consciousness than was possible by remaining in our limited individual awareness. We live creatively, uniting heart, mind and spirit.

If we haven't made this transition, the second Saturn Return at around 58 can be quite a painful process as we have to learn to let go of the past or to go back over our lessons about the physical level: re-vision being needed. If we have successfully made the transition, then this is when we reap the rewards of Saturn, the Lord of Karma. We come into our wisdom.

KARMIC ASPECTS

The energies of the planets are symbolic of energies within ourselves that have developed over many lifetimes. The relationship between the planets shows our ease, or dis-ease, with those energies. Karma is shown in outer planet to personal planet contacts. Personal to personal contacts have to do with the present life – and may indicate a pattern that could become karmic and need to be dealt with in the next life.

Aspect patterns indicate how constructively or otherwise the planetary energies will be used by the incarnating soul when dealing with the karma attached to the planetary configuration. On the whole, flowing aspects manifest more easily and hard aspects indicate a struggle to regain and value the planetary principle. Nevertheless, that struggle may be of value if it is required in order to overcome the problem. Without the impetus of the discomfort a hard aspect brings, the delaying tactic of procrastination can recur.

Fixed Squares

Squares which are in fixed signs or houses point to long-term, deeply entrenched, karma which has built up over many lifetimes. The fixed square between Pluto in Leo and the Moon in Taurus or Scorpio, for example, indicates mothering difficulties experienced throughout many incarnations, and associated traumatic emotional experiences such as rejection, abandonment, guilt and resentment. Similarly a fixed square of Uranus to Mars will indicate issues of wilfulness throughout many lifetimes.

Cardinal and Mutable Squares

As a general rule, mutable squares indicate karma that arose in the 'last' incarnation and which can either be dealt with in this incarnation, being close to resolution, or become an ongoing difficulty in future incarnations. Cardinal squares represent karma in the making, patterns arising in the present life and which can be used positively or negatively. However, experience shows that any square can be a deeply ingrained difficulty. For example, a soul with a Neptune-Mars square may choose to face the challenge of spiritualising the Will, moving beyond the personal ego into alignment with the eternal Self; conversely it may fall into the trap of self-destruction, drink or drugs as a way of disintegration.

The Grand Cross

Squares can come together to form a Grand Cross, an aspect with powerful karmic connotations and a deep need to integrate the warring factions of the psyche which are represented by the planetary energies involved. Kenneth Halliwell (Fig. 4), who murdered playwright Joe Orton (see *Karmic Connections*), had a fixed Grand Cross (Venus in Taurus square Neptune in Leo square Moon-Saturn in Scorpio square Jupiter in Aquarius). Jacqueline Clare, the sensitive Piscean who drew the charts for *The Karmic Journey*, described him, through her attunement to his energies, as a 'frustrated soul in torment'. The Orton diaries portray a man wrestling with out-of-control, unconscious, conflicting emotions; depression and elation; self-aggrandisement and deep inadequacy. The emotional separation from his parents was epitomised when his mother, whom he loved obsessively, choked to death when he was a young teenager. Sometime later his father committed suicide. Halliwell appears to have been a man who found it impossible to be happy. His answer to his increasing disintegration and separation from Orton was to kill him, and then himself.

Many charts with a Grand Cross convey a sense of destiny, the incarnating soul choosing to face several old patterns which lock in together. The example shown here (Fig. 5) belongs to an alternative medicine practitioner and past-life therapist who had problems with her endocrine system and

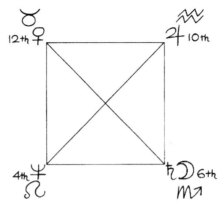

Fig 4

intractable, recurrent back pain. Despite years. of chiropractic, osteopathic, healing and regression sessions, she had not
been able to reach the pain or the imbalance (her sixth house
Pluto-Moon conjunction indicates that the cause of disease is
subtle and the roots go deep). Her chart showed issues around
the use of the Will (Saturn-Mars) and her Chiron placement
indicated that she was still attached to past suffering through
her body (the Earth element). When she stopped trying to force
through the issue, and worked instead on visualisation (utilising Jupiter skills) and on letting go of the pain and past suffering,
she was able to deal more constructively with the problem.
However, she commented that had she not had to deal with
this difficulty personally, she would never have studied so hard
and become so successful a catalyst for the transformation of
others (Uranus opposing Chiron).

The Crosses of Incarnation into Matter

Esoteric astrology sees Cancer as the 'Gate into Incarnation'
whereas Capricorn is the 'Gate into Initiation'. On the cardinal vibration, the urge to manifest (Aries) finds a home and
takes root (Cancer), balance is reached (Libra) and the will-to-
be takes form (Capricorn). In esoteric astrology, and
particularly that based upon the work of Alice Bailey, the
qualities of cardinal, fixed or mutable energies within the chart
represent three basic levels of human development. The low-

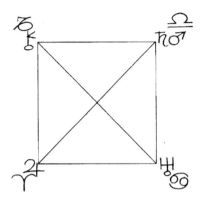

Fig 5

est level is an unconscious unity that is personality centred.
Then there is a conscious duality, composed of personality and
soul entering into a relationship, the life of the soul. The highest level is a conscious unity that is soul, or Self, centred. In the
cardinal cross, the personality is a vehicle for the soul and experience is based on spiritual attraction and intent. So, for
someone following the cardinal vibration, the path is usually
one of sacrifice and service which will manifest according to
the sun-sign, but the sign does not have to belong to the cardinal element. Capricorn follows the path of Initiation, Aquarius
of World Service and Pisces of World Saviour for instance. In
the fixed cross, aspirations are the motivation, and in the mutable one, desire.

In Soul Centred Astrology[24], Alan Oken stresses that anyone can be working on any of these vibrations, it is not just a
matter of an aspect pattern in the chart being located in a particular quality. A self-professed New Age Guru with a fixed
Taurean Sun, could be working on the fixed or mutable cross
just as much as on the Cardinal Grand Cross in his chart, which
is in mutable houses (see Fig. 6). The Cross is formed from Saturn and Neptune in Libra opposing Mercury in Aries, squared
by an opposition of Uranus and the Moon in Cancer to Chiron in Capricorn.

The Taurean potential is liberation from attachment to
matter, but his Chiron wound is in Capricorn, the gate to ini-

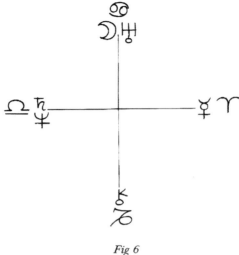

Fig 6

tiation. When Taurus is on the mutable cross, the will is likely to be used for personal desire. On the fixed cross, Taurus seeks an active transformation of desire, a release from attachment. Here the Scorpio polarity is at its strongest and the lesson is a transmutation of desire (in keeping with Mars placed in this sign). The sacral energies (related to the lower chakras) have to be lifted up into a creative fire and come under the control of the throat centre (ruled by Taurus). On the cardinal cross, Taurus 'stimulates the presence of the light in any form of matter'. Some of the karma of Taurus and Scorpio can be glimpsed in Alan Oken's statement that the personality-orientated Taurean will use the magnetism of these two signs to bring about opportunities for satisfying unbalanced sensuality and a desire for material possessions. The potential is, however, 'the establishment of one's true spiritual identity and direction', which may be the result of a painful process of transformation. He points out that the 'measure of darkness that accompanies these changes is also, in much greater measure, the expression of the light'.

The principle of the cardinal, fixed or mutable vibration can also be applied to the Nodal axis. On the lower vibration, the Leo-Aquarius axis has a desire for personal influence over others. Leo domination includes a desire to rule and impose personal values. Aquarius adds in the dimension of as large a group as possible. When the personality has become soul-centred, then the strength and force of the personality can be used as a vehicle for the good of the whole 'shining brightly with true spiritual radiance, using will and determination for impersonal, creative purposes'. Soul-centred Aquarius becomes the World Server, creating unity and wholeness.

Trines and Sextiles

Trines and sextiles represent old problems which have been worked on in past lives and show that an understanding has emerged towards the end of life or in the period between lives. In the present incarnation the soul with these aspects needs to strengthen the integration of the energies and put them to work constructively. The difficulty can be that these aspects are 'lazy' and take time to flow properly, often requiring the trigger of a major transit to start them off. Stephen Arroyo points out:

> There is some evidence that trine aspects correspond with wasteful or problematical conditions in far more cases than traditional teachings about the 'beneficial' effects of trines would indicate. For example the trine of Neptune is often found in charts of people who exhibit rather negative Neptunian tendencies: drug problems [etc.] ... or simply the inability to deal effectively with the material world. Uranus ... trines are almost as common as the more dynamic Uranus aspects in the charts of people who are particularly self-centred, unable to co-operate ... Jupiter trines often seem to indicate little more than a tendency towards lazy self-indulgence and a preference for relying on anything other than one's own hard work.[25]

A client of mine described sextiles as 'the quickest road to hell because they are so smooth and easy, you don't realise how quickly you are getting there'. Her chart comprised 'disjointed sextiles, which didn't quite connect to each other'. She had problems making choices and decisions, 'things just seem to happen to me regardless of what I want'. It was only when she began to be conscious that her Sun sextile Pluto gave her the potential to handle her own power, and Saturn sextile Mars the potential to use her Will to direct her life, that she began to make progress.

The Grand Trine and the Kite

The Grand Trine is formed by three trines connecting to each other in the form of a triangle, usually but not always in the same element. A Kite formation (Fig. 7) incorporates a third planet which is opposed to one of the planets in the trine, and sextiles the other two. The Grand Trine has enormous potential and the element in which it is placed can indicate the area through which the energies will manifest: Fire through the intuition and initiation, Water through feelings and contact with others, Earth through the senses and environment, and Air through communication and the mind processes.

Metaphysician and writer Douglas Baker had a Water Grand Trine (Fig. 8) Pluto-MC-North Node trine Uranus-Mars trine Jupiter-Venus. A formidable, larger-than-life personality, the university he set up teaches the use of power and esoteric thought. The Grand Trine shows an old skill in manipulation, vibration and healing forces, and the addition of Pluto forming the Kite configuration indicates considerable occult ability together with karma concerning the use, or abuse, of power.

The Inconjunct

Inconjuncts (the quincunx 150^0 and semi-sextile 30^0 aspects) are powerful karmic aspects indicating conflicting energies or experiences from the past which need to be synthesised and balanced in the present incarnation. The planetary energies involved are a major challenge in life and anyone with more than one inconjunct in the chart has a deep need to question the purpose behind incarnation. The inconjunct aspects will provide an answer and a pathway forward. Alan Epstein[26] sees this as an aspect which requires 'the balancing of the desired against the practicable, the ideal against the real'. He sees one side of the inconjunct as 'what is desired' and the other as 'the price that must be paid to attain it'. Although people may endeavour to live out only one end of an inconjunct, as with any aspect, ultimately there has to be an integration of the basic principles, a creative compromise which offers both a resolution and an expansion of the energies involved.

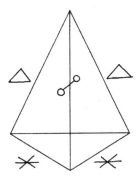

Fig 7

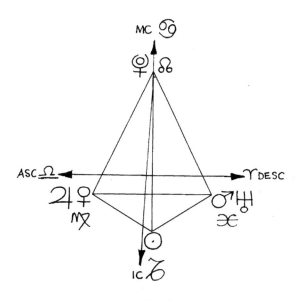

Fig 8

The quincunx (150⁰) relates to personal experience of the planetary energies, whilst the semi-sextile (30⁰) aspect frequently indicates the soul who projects the problem by attracting a partner (who often has the same planets in hard aspect) who acts out the difficulty. A client asked why he always seemed to attract Scorpionic/Plutonian women. He had the Moon semi-sextile Pluto in his chart and on examining the charts of his last three relationships, all the women had hard Pluto-Moon aspects. His own interest and karma lay in what he described as 'the rape of Mother Earth' (Moon in Virgo) and how mankind could best utilise and conserve the limited resources available whilst still advancing through technology (twelfth house Uranus). The company he ran was concerned with alternative technology and he was planning to write a book on this subject. I believe that everyone with a Pluto-Moon connection is here with the potential to aid the healing of the earth in some way.

Certain inconjuncts run as a karmic theme in charts. With the Sun inconjunct Uranus the soul is seeking its own individuality and self-expression; the Moon inconjunct Saturn is seeking to overcome a fundamental lack of self-worth and a block on the expression of feelings; Mercury inconjunct Saturn has a long-standing block on communication; Venus inconjunct Pluto is dealing with an inner 'black hole' which is insatiable for emotional nourishment and never feels loved enough; Mars inconjunct Uranus is suffering the effects of old wilfulness and unpredictability, whilst Mars inconjunct Saturn is restricted by a sense of powerlessness and helplessness, a blocked Will. The Sun, or Mars, inconjunct Pluto is dealing with old power issues and learning how to handle its own power rather than use it to force and coerce, either as victim or perpetrator. Neptune inconjunct the Moon or Venus is working on spiritualising relationships in a realistic way through unconditional love; rather than through an old pattern of idealisation and illusion.

The Finger of Fate
When two inconjuncts radiate out from a central planet (Fig. 9) to two other planets sextile each other, the result is a Finger of Fate which indicates karmic energies the soul must integrate into itself through the present-life experience. As its name suggests, the Finger of Fate is indicative of a 'fated' life script and the soul will repeatedly meet the energies represented by the planets until it achieves wholeness. Integration and release of the energies is facilitated by the opposition of a planet to the

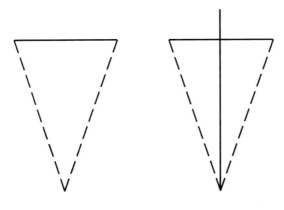

Fig. 9

central point, as this can act as an outlet. Configurations without the outlet need to use the energy of the opposing sign and house to form a point of release.

Unaspected Planets

In my experience, a planet with little or no aspects usually signifies where there can be a breakthrough either of a seemingly new 'personality' but which is actually from the past, or from the collective (archetypal) level of experience. Archetypes are universal forms, embodied in myth, which ring true for all of humankind. These archetypes, such as the saviour, victim, martyr, are extremely powerful and can appear to take someone over, although the potential has to be within that person in the first place. They are a part of the collective karma of humankind. When unaspected planets are activated by stress in the area of life they represent or by a transit, something breaks through and takes over with great force – the person acts in a totally unrecognisable way. Sometimes a past life personality manifests with unmet needs and desperate yearnings. At other times a competent personality may emerge who has the ability to handle the situation because the skill has been developed in the past. The karmic challenge is to integrate an unaspected planet, and the personality pattern, into everyday life.

3

Credits and Deficits

Attached to each planet is a specific karmic vibration – and a
lesson for the present life

Judy Hall, Karmic Astrology

The planets and their relationships with each other show credits and deficits, almost like a kind of karmic credit card. Some
map out areas of potential, other dilemmas that have been
played out through many lifetimes. Any planet, house placement or aspect can be seen as potential if it is worked with
constructively. However, hard aspects usually indicate a struggle to manifest that potential as the reaction to those specific
planetary energies is deeply ingrained.

KARMIC POTENTIAL

Conjunctions, trines and sextiles can be seen as indicators of
karmic potential, as can planets in compatible signs and houses.
Some planets 'fit' more naturally into particular elements. Mercury, for example, is at ease in the Air and Fire signs. Such a
placement will point to a natural talent for communication,
analysis or interpretation – unless hampered by Saturn aspects,
in which case there is a struggle to manifest the positive side.
It can also indicate an inherent intelligence which has nothing to do with being intellectual or passing examinations. The
dictionary definition of intelligence is 'quickness of understanding' and it is this alertness and ability to make intuitive leaps
that can be so helpful in dealing with challenging situations.
Similarly Mars in the Fire signs can indicate a natural courage
and assertiveness when confronted with a challenge. Venus is
a changeling planet, taking on the quality of the element and
sign in its relationships. In Libra it is naturally 'nice', getting
along with everyone, and it has the ability to provide a harmo-

nious atmosphere in which everyone can flourish. In Scorpio Venus is more suspicious, but loyal, intense and passionate when it learns to trust; in Sagittarius that trust is a natural feature of relating.

Saturn in Capricorn can illustrate the difference between a positive and negative manifestation of the planetary energy. When operating negatively, Saturn in Capricorn can indicate a soul who is particularly fearful, repressed and drawn to conventional religious practices or ways of organising society; a pillar of the Establishment, consistently refusing to move forward to learn new lessons. However, when Saturn in Capricorn has worked in previous lives on developing inner discipline and authority, it has the potential to use these skills in business, teaching or counselling – not in an authoritarian manner (which is the negative function of Saturn), but in a way which encourages the same qualities in others. It offers the possibility of moving from an external locus of control – that controlling voice from somewhere outside oneself which imposes rules and regulations through 'oughts' and 'shoulds' and is often confused with a judgmental God – to the inner voice which directs in accordance with what is best for the Self and its spiritual purpose. Saturn in Capricorn thereby attains inner authority and status which reflects who, not what, it really is.

Neptune aspecting Venus, Mercury and/or the Moon (or Moon, Mercury or Venus in Pisces)

Neptune contacts with Venus, Mercury and the Moon can indicate an artistic, musical, visionary or psychic-intuitive potential which is carried forward from other lives. At times, as with all karmic contacts, such potential is indicated through extremely wide orbs of aspect. Claude Debussy (fig. 10) had Sun/Mercury inconjunct Neptune, and Neptune trine Venus, and was something of an infant prodigy, with considerable talent as a pianist. His father believed him to be a second Mozart (who had Neptune opposing fifth house Mercury) and had plans for him to give concerts around Europe at a very young age. His bullying tactics unfortunately destroyed Debussy's talent for playing but he went on to compose music which was revolutionary for its time, and controversial in both form and content.

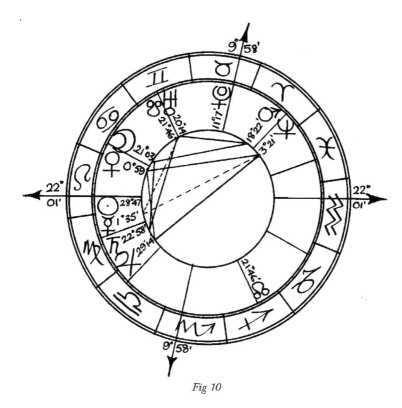

Fig 10

Debussy's Uranus-South Node conjunction in Gemini, square Saturn, indicates old karma around the revolutionary ideas of the airy Uranus coming into conflict with the established convention and form of the existing Saturnine structure. Throughout his life he alternated periods of intense creativity with stormy love affairs and the deepest despair. He had a wide Jupiter-Saturn conjunction opposing Neptune, Saturn squares the Nodes and Uranus conjuncts the South Node, indicative of the manic depression and genius which would pull him apart unless he could reconcile the warring energies within his psyche. Using conventional orbs and the major aspects his chart is 'split' into two parts linked by the wide Saturn conjunction to Jupiter, plus an unaspected Pluto. One pattern involves Saturn-Moon-Uranus-Mars (issues around the feelings and use of the Will). The other involves Jupiter-Venus- Sun-Mercury-Neptune (his creative potential and issues around love). One of

Debussy's most contentious pieces, *The Afternoon of a Faun*, is based on a poem about a faun who spies a nymph asleep on the grass and makes love to her. It was composed in the reverie which followed his own love-making. The two parts of the chart are linked by a quintile from Mercury to Uranus, which indicates the evolutionary potential of his original and inventive powers of creativity, but also his inability to live in the everyday world.

Debussy's life follows the stereotype of an artistic genius who somehow cannot have an ordinary existence. Born into a family which he felt was alien to him, the young Debussy was 'rescued' by his aunt who was described as 'totally besotted with him from the first meeting and determined to make him the child she had never had'. Debussy had the Moon in Cancer inconjunct the North Node in Sagittarius, an aspect indicative of stress and destiny connected with unconventional mothering (the Saturn- Uranus- Moon part of the chart) and of the need to find a new way of nurturing, and of being, himself. His aunt educated him to a standard far above that possible for his parents and encouraged his early musical talent. However, she died of cancer when he was still young, after his father had forcibly taken him back to the natural family in order to capitalise on that talent. Debussy's talent only flourished when he left his family and went to study abroad, but he always experienced great difficulty with the discipline required for music. He lived out the extremes of the Jupiter-Saturn and Neptune energies and was constantly in debt, depending on other people for support and having to prostitute his art by becoming a piano teacher and writing songs to pay off his creditors. He died from cancer and loss of hope at the age of forty-six.

Singer/songwriter Julie Felix, who has never had a music lesson in her life and cannot read music, and Bob Dylan, her contemporary and fellow-protester, have Uranus in-conjunct Neptune-North Node, and Neptune-North Node square Mercury. They set out not only to communicate with the world through their music (Mercury in Gemini) but also to change it (Uranus) by pointing out its injustices and failings. Julie Felix did this by taking an active part in demonstrations for peace and by developing an interest in the healing power of music.

This would have come naturally to her through the subtle awareness of vibration that Uranus offers to Mercury in aspect to Neptune.

Neptune contacts to Mercury, the Moon or Venus can also indicate the potential for attuning to, and focusing, spiritual vision. The soul with such aspects has a sensitivity which reaches beyond the vibrations of earth and is capable of raising its level of consciousness to the eternal, cosmic Self, thereby receiving guidance and wisdom. It is also one of the indicators of psychic potential and healing power, Pluto contacts with the Moon being another, and of clairvoyance. Such aspects are indicative of training received in the ancient temples in esoteric work such as out of body experiences, sleep healing, dream interpretation, trance, prophecy and telepathy. These ancient arts are now finding their place anew as the Age of Aquarius dawns in the evolution of human consciousness.

Neptune contacts to Venus have issues around love (as discussed elsewhere) but the potential is to practise unconditional love; the love that sees the beauty and uniqueness in every soul, allowing them to be exactly what they need to be. There is no enforced change or pressure to be something different. However, unconditional love does not mean being abused, deceived, colluded with or hurt by another, nor is it about being walked over. It is about having firm boundaries and being centred, so that if someone else behaves badly or not in accordance with what the soul would wish, it can simply step away and say: 'I love you, and I allow you to be yourself but I will not in any way, shape or form allow you to divert me from my path, nor will you trouble my peace of mind'. Those who are able to love unconditionally in this way can help the cosmos to evolve and, by offering loving acceptance to another, may create exactly the right space for that other soul to change and grow.

KARMIC DILEMMAS

Conflicting past-life experiences produce specific karmic dilemmas for the incarnating soul. These can be illustrated by the examples of Jupiter-Saturn and Saturn-Neptune contacts, but we will meet many others throughout this book. How difficult the dilemma is to deal with will be indicated by the aspect.

'Hard' aspects generally produce more problems with the resolution of the conflicting energies than the 'soft' aspects, although, in the case of a sextile aspect, the speed at which someone can change from being 'fine', to being totally immersed in the dilemma can be bewilderingly fast. The same dilemma can also apply to planets placed in corresponding signs or mutual reception. For example, Jupiter in Capricorn, ruled by Saturn, and Saturn in Sagittarius, ruled by Jupiter; or Neptune in Virgo (Neptune is then in the opposing sign to the one it rules and is given shape and a boundary by the earth which is its antithesis). The same dilemma is also represented by Neptune in Capricorn, ruled by Saturn (where once again Neptune finds itself confined by the earth), and by Saturn in Pisces, ruled by Neptune, (where Saturn undergoes the discomfort of the boundless deep of the water energy).

The Mystic/Pragmatist – Neptune in Aspect to Saturn

The 'Mystic/Pragmatist' dilemma represented by Neptune (the Mystic) and Saturn (the Pragmatist) brings materialism into conflict with spiritual urges. Neptune wants to find un-bounded bliss, while Saturn wants to stick to the rules. This dilemma can also apply to Saturn in Pisces and Neptune in Virgo. The aspect has appeared in so many chart readings for those drawn to Eastern practices such as Transcendental Meditation that such a chart now produces an instinctive assumption that 'this must be a meditator'. Such an assumption has to be put aside, however, as the person may well be living out the Saturn half of the aspect and resisting the seductive lure of Neptunian bliss. Readings are frequently requested at a crisis or changeover-point when it becomes apparent that the – so far – unrealised planetary energy has to be incorporated in order for the incarnating soul to achieve the impetus for new growth and wholeness. Meditators may find that, although their spiritual growth has moved forward, their career, relationship or health problems are subtly (or not so subtly!) holding them back from their goal of enlightenment. Similarly, materialists may come to feel that a dimension of life is missing: They say: 'There must be more to life than this.'

The past lives represented by an aspect between Saturn and Neptune involve on the one hand the mystical Neptunian approach which can range from the highest spirituality, creative inspiration, and states of consciousness, down through the escapist realms, the spurious ecstasy of drink or drugs, and into fantasy and imagination, madness and disintegration. Saturnine lives on the other hand embody religious experiences of strict discipline and an emphasis on guilt and repression, or materialistic experiences which leave no room for spirituality and are based on security and temporal power. In terms of spiritual development, Neptune is attunement to the immanent God-within, Saturn the emanation of a God who is wholly other.

The fundamental opposition between Neptune – the unbounded urge to merge and be one with the cosmos, and Saturn – the planet of boundaries and separateness, can only be resolved through a recognition that we are an eternal spirit (the Self) clothed in a body, a microcosm living on the earth and yet part of the macrocosmic universe. To live out only one end of the dichotomy by withdrawing from the world is as unproductive in terms of spiritual growth as is the totally materialistic approach. An integration is required which pays due attention both to the practical matters and lessons concerned with living in a physical body, and to spirituality. The evolved person is able to live in the world but is not burdened by its troubles. The truly enlightened being is a fusion of spirit and matter.

Positive aspects between planets, in particular the conjunction, sextile and trine – although it should be remembered that all aspects have the potential to become positive when the energies they represent are being used constructively – and planets in compatible elements and houses, indicate old skills to draw on, potentials to be explored. For example, a person with a Saturn-Neptune contact who has worked on resolving the Mystic/Pragmatist dilemma in other lives and is now ready to make the shift into integration has the potential to live as a truly enlightened man. President John F. Kennedy had Saturn in late

Cancer conjunct Neptune in Leo in the ninth house; in his public life he tried to put the strength of Saturn and the idealism
of Neptune into practice, although privately he seems to have
reflected other aspects of the Neptune-Saturn conflict through
his extramarital activities. His brother Robert had a fixed Neptune in Leo square to Saturn in Scorpio. It is interesting to
speculate on how many of his brother's ideals he would have
shared and put into practice had he lived, and also to consider
the karma which cut short two such promising lives. In her
book *A Case for Reincarnation* Christine Hartley explored the
idea of a family group incarnating together life after life:

> Take for instance that amazing family of the Borgias. Hardly
> anything good is said of them, yet in spite of the viciousness by
> which we chiefly remember them they were great patrons of
> the arts ... and above all they are distinguished for the immensely
> strong family ties which bound them together at a time when
> brother was frequently ranged against brother.
>
> Then look further ahead and you will see the same basic
> characteristics, the same abilities in the great House of Guise
> at the time of the last of the Valois kings ... (they) resemble in a
> marked degree that preceding family of the Borgias even to their
> violent and untimely ends. Could we look around today and
> find another family with the same fundamental loyalties, the
> same tragedies at their heels ... one has the idea that so strong
> and vital a group will return again and again in much the same
> proximity and circumstances until they have perhaps learned
> the lesson of the futility of worldly power.[1]

Although she did not answer her own question in the
book, in several conversations Christine and I explored the
possibility of a link to the Kennedy family from the Borgias and
Guises, or the Medicis, who were an equally powerful family.
It could certainly explain the peculiarly tragic and 'fated' life
of this New World family: a repeating pattern of nemesis balancing hubris and illustrating, as Christine points out, 'the
futility of worldly power' and the inability of wealth to buy long
life and happiness. We were particularly intrigued with the
notion of Jacqueline Kennedy as Lucretia Borgia. The daughter of Roderigo Borgia, who was elected Pope and became
Alexander VI, Lucretia is reputed to have poisoned her en-

emies, and possibly one or two 'friends' as well. She was used as a political pawn by her father, who contracted several powerful marriage alliances for her. On the other hand her father, who was a firm believer in nepotism, handed over control of the Vatican to her on two occasions complete with the authority to open his correspondence.

This idea certainly throws a new light on the 'suffering' Jacqueline Kennedy Onassis underwent in her Kennedy incarnation. She incarnated with a need to explore the more taboo areas of life and gain insight from them (Scorpio Ascendant). She had first house Saturn opposing Venus in the seventh house and therefore incarnated with a burden (first house Saturn) and the feeling of being unlovable (the opposition), with karma around relationships (seventh house Venus). The Saturn-Venus opposition also indicated her marriage to the much older Onassis. She had Jupiter in the seventh house of relationships and expected partners to be a source of wealth and expansion for her. Her companion in her later years was another immensely wealthy man but the relationship was somewhat secretive and Scorpionic. Her Pluto in Cancer concerned issues of power and manipulation and its placement in the eighth house, together with the Sun and Mercury in Leo, related to how she shared herself and her power with another. Her twelfth house Scorpio South Node signifies she had experienced considerable drama and trauma in past lives on the collective level (see Chapter 5). In the recent incarnation there was a need for her to move to the security of the Taurus North Node and away from the emotional games of the South Node. Her chart could well reflect a soul who had been married as a pawn in a power game in the past but who nevertheless held power behind the scenes. (See *The Hades Moon* for a much deeper discussion of Jacqueline Kennedy Onassis).

A resolution to the Mystic-Pragmatist dilemma is found in someone who is aware of eternal spirituality at the same time as being able to function in the everyday world.

The Optimist/Pessimist – Jupiter in Aspect to Saturn

The past life patterns connected with aspects of Jupiter (the Optimist) and Saturn (the Pessimist) involve the profligate and the miser, the person who lives on hope and the person who lives in fear, over-indulgence versus self-denial, and self-expansion against repression; they are exemplified in the extremes of the manic depressive. The Jupiter-Saturn square in particular indicates that the soul has had many opportunities to advance in past lives but failed to take advantage of them, and must now struggle with adverse 'circumstances'. The karma can be one of greed, which an old Indian wise saying perceives as 'a disease of the heart':

> The miser's money,
> which causes uneasiness, hardship,
> blindness and sleeplessness, is not money but a disease of the heart.
> Greed is not stilled with money,
> any more than is thirst with salt water.

The dilemma can also be found in Saturn in Pisces or Sagittarius and Jupiter in Capricorn, or both planets in Pisces.

Liz Greene describes the Saturn-Jupiter conflict as a 'sharp dichotomy between intuitive perception and practical observation' and one which 'symbolise[s] a choice between the faith which stems from an intuitive recognition of purpose in life, and the fear which stems from identification with and consequent control by the forces of one's environment.'[2] Her book on Saturn, read from the karmic perspective, affords many penetrating insights into the working of karma through this planet – who is after all, as she points out, the Lord of Karma – and into its interaction with the other planets.

The challenge of Jupiter-Saturn aspects is to integrate the intuitive perception of the oneness of life with the personal responsibility and self-discipline which Saturn has to offer, and thereby to find both meaning and inner direction. One of the saddest sights life has to offer is the depressed, purposeless Jupiter-Saturn individual who has taken refuge in over-indulgence or comfort-seeking addiction to food or other substances. One client, a Virgo Sun with Jupiter in late Sagittarius in a wide trine to Saturn in Virgo, and a wide opposition from Jupiter to Uranus in Cancer, was seen in the past as an enormously fat man, too huge to move and then, in contrast, as an ascetic indulging in total self-denial with the result that he died a lingering death from starvation. The client afterwards commented that he had experienced both extremes already in this life. He had been a gross teenager, stuffed with food by his mother as a substitute for love. Then, when he had gone to university to study Calvinistic theology, he had become anorexic and almost died. His life was saved when he abandoned his training for the priesthood, discovered the discipline of astrology, and the possibility of joy entered his life. He found a belief which was based on hope, trust and optimism of the future, and abandoned a faith founded upon control, repression and fear – which neatly resolved the karmic dilemma.

Change-Maintenance, Revolution v the Status Quo – Uranus in Aspect to Saturn

When Uranus and Saturn meet it is like driving flat out with one foot on the gas and the other on the brake. Uranus stands for chaos, change, reform and revolution; it is a catalyst for growth. Saturn wants to maintain the status quo and is concerned with keeping rigidly within the bounds of convention. The individual with these two planets in aspect, or who is strongly Aquarian or has Uranus in Capricorn or Saturn in Aquarius, is held between an irresistible force and an immovable object. He or she needs to be a catalyst for change, and yet must also learn to accept that everything is fine as it is. I have this contact in my chart and at my first consultation with Howard Sasportas he described an urge to put my foot behind people and propel them into 'what they might be'. He also spoke of the resistance other people might have to this. As he predicted, I had to learn in my therapeutic work to allow the impetus to change to come from my clients. My energy could be used as a catalyst, but only when they wanted it to be. Otherwise, I had to learn to stand placidly by while they remained stuck in the pattern of the past.

Past lives connected with this aspect always have elements of the reformer and the revolutionary who forces change, and the opposite – the person who remains rigidly fixed by fear in an old pattern of behaviour. This is often because of a memory of the persecution and punishment the world can inflict on someone who is ahead of his, or her, time. Change is never easy and 'is not made without inconvenience, even from worse to better' (Richard Hooker).

Howard Sasportas, one of the key movers in the transition to psychological astrology, pointed out that in mythology, Uranus was castrated by Saturn. Some of the blood fell onto the ground and became the Furies ('envious anger, retaliation and neverendingness'). The phallus, on the other hand, was cast into the sea and Aphrodite (or Venus) the goddess of love was born. Howard pinpointed a 'cleft stick' into which we all fall when confronted with the Uranian need for change and the Saturnian need for conservation. If we outwardly side with Saturn, then the Furies erupt internally, our blocked creativity and need for change boiling around inside ourselves with consequent psychological and physical damage. If, on the other hand, we opt for Uranian change, then the Furies appear to come at us from outside. Howard suggested that Uranian changes should therefore be made in a more Venusian way, smoothing the path of change and gentling the conflict.

He also identified another problem with making Uranian changes – guilt. When guilt and the expectation of punishment for independent thought are ingrained, any kind of breakthrough, whether to joy or pain, is likely to be accompanied by situations that bring the soul face to face with its guilt.

Karmic resolution comes in knowing when it is appropriate to act as a catalyst and when to stand back placidly and allow time to do its work.

POWER, WILL AND KARMA

Another karmic issue which is clearly outlined in the natal chart, and which can offer the opportunity to capitalise on a past skill or to make a creative use of a previously blocked or undirected energy, is that of will, and the use of personal power and assertion. The will may be an unconsciously expressed, inhibiting and controlling force, very much at the mercy of another person's assertive or aggressive power. Or it may be a consciously aligned self assertive energy which directs life in accordance with the needs of the Self, the Skilful Will.[3] There are many different types of will and ways of using it, as can be seen from a few of the dictionary definitions: 'faculty by which person decides or conceives himself as deciding upon and initiating action, power of deciding upon one's action independently of causation, control exercised by deliberate purpose over impulse, self-control, what one ordains, affecting one's intention or dominating other persons'. The outer planets in aspect to Mars indicate how the incarnating soul experienced the will in the past, how it will function in the present incarnation, and the changes it needs to make in order to develop its positive use of the will energy.

Jupiter in Aspect to Mars (or Mars in Sagittarius or Pisces and Jupiter in Aries or Scorpio)

Jupiter in aspect to Mars has an inner urge to expand which may manifest through a well-directed will or, as with all Jupiter aspects, it may indicate that the soul is out of control and may go over the top in its need to assert itself. It does, however, have the potential to harness the will and to use its assertive power to achieve its aims and objectives. The Jupiter-Mars will has the capacity to bring into being whatever it conceives. It has learnt in the past how to visualise, affirm and bring things into manifestation. It can be one of the greatest of karmic gifts or the biggest handicap. It brings into being the deepest, strongest programme – or pattern from the past. If this is unconscious it may well be in direct opposition to what the conscious mind thinks it wants, in which case the old pattern has to be brought up into awareness so that it can be reprogrammed into something that positively supports the needs and wishes of the Self.

Affirmations are a powerful tool for anyone with these planets in geometric relationship. This aspect, like Jupiter in the twelfth, often delineates the old priest or priestess who was taught abundance and many other skills in the temples of the past. Jupiter-Mars has the quality of a courageous will, it acts with integrity from the heart and is able to go forward in the face of fear because it has a basic trust in its power and purpose through its link to the cosmos.

The power of Jupiter-Mars visualisation was brought home to me most graphically when I sat with Justin Carson as he was dying. Justin taught affirmations and his powers of creative visualisation were unparalleled. He had an exact Jupiter-Mars opposition from the fourth to tenth house, and I have second house Jupiter sextile Mars in Gemini close to Justin's Sun. Together we made a formidable team. One day we were visualising a ladder up to the next dimension – Justin believed in doing things the easy way. The next morning the house next door had sprouted high scaffolding which from Justin's bed, looked just like a ladder to heaven. He had wanted to see snow again for the last time, and it obligingly snowed. Then he wanted sunshine, and there it was. There were many other incidents, both before his death and afterwards, but the most wonderful thing was how he communicated that he was alright after his passing. He had independently agreed with both myself and his partner, David Lawson, that the signal would be 42: the answer to life, the universe and everything. Justin had greatly enjoyed *The Hitchhiker's Guide to the Galaxy* and a taped version had been his gift to me whilst I was in hospital with pneumonia. When David and I went to register Justin's death, we were aware of him skipping along beside us giggling. We were first in. The registrar booted her computer and there on the screen was a large 42. It was the number of his entry on the register. When we explained to the registrar, she was: 'Gobsmacked and all goose-bumpy.' The gales of laughter were no doubt considered most inappropriate by those waiting to register other deaths but we knew that Justin had without a doubt communicated that he was still alive.

Chiron in Aspect to Mars (or Chiron in Aries or Scorpio)

When Chiron aspects Mars, the karmic challenge is to heal old wounds in the will. Due to past experiences, the soul feels that it cannot will things into being. Its assertion has been damaged and may have been compensated for by over-aggression, masking covert feelings of helplessness and loss of power. In my own chart, Mars in Gemini squares Chiron in Virgo. When I handed the original *Karmic Journey* over to the publishers, little did I know that the manuscript would be given to a Virgo to edit – who was French by nationality and a non-astrologer. When I saw the manuscript some months later it was covered in tiny, meticulous Virgo writing. Virtually every line had been rewritten and all my carefully chosen words had been changed – and she even altered the names of planets! I was furious. Transiting Chiron was conjunct my natal Mars, transiting Mars my natal Chiron and I had recently had a chart reading that said old anger was about to erupt. This was the moment! I rang Penguin, almost incoherent with rage. The editor-in-charge said: 'Don't be hysterical, everyone gets edited.' 'But not re-written', I replied. 'Tough' was the rejoinder as he put the phone down. I felt totally powerless and yet for one of the few times in my life, murderous. It was fortunate that 100 miles separated us. That he later phoned to apologise when he saw just what had been done did nothing to ameliorate the situation. He had triggered old pain, and, as has been reiterated time and again with my books, publishers do have a knack of bringing up will and assertion issues – and my publishing karma!

As Howard Sasportas, the series editor at the time, had persuaded me not to put my own name to several experiences in the book 'because they are too raw and powerful for the reader to deal with', I really felt I was being prevented from speaking with my own voice – classic for someone with a Gemini Mars sitting between Uranus and Saturn and that square to Chiron in the third house of communication. I know that, in the past, I have been burnt at the stake for 'heresy' and there have been other situations where both my will and my words had been squashed.*

At the time of rewriting *The Karmic Journey* transiting Pluto and Chiron are sitting on my natal Mercury and opposing Mars and transiting Mars is inconjunct natal Chiron. The wound, and the wounded book, is healing. And, as one of my publishers said the other day: 'Well, you are always very firm with us about what you want', so I guess my assertion skills are being honed by these experiences, and I am finding a resolution for the karmic wound to my will.

---

* *See* Deja Who? *for more details.*

Saturn in Aspect to Mars (or Saturn in Aries or Scorpio and Mars in Capricorn)

Although in conventional astrology Saturn-Mars contacts indicate a strong will, in karmic terms this is a potential strength to be developed in the present incarnation and the aspect denotes a blocked will, an inner feeling of powerlessness and helplessness which stems from a previous experience of being at the mercy of someone else's will or aggression, or of having had one's own will systematically broken. How far one has progressed in dealing with this is represented by the type of aspect concerned: hard aspects indicating a struggle in the present life, soft aspects that it will be a little easier this time.

In a television interview some years ago, ex-nun Karen Armstrong, (Saturn-Mars-Uranus), now a writer on religious matters and TV presenter, described her experience when she entered a convent in this life. She was put to work treadling an empty sewing-machine for days on end, so that she 'would learn obedience to God's Will'. Many people incarnated into this Christian/monastic experience specifically to learn about inner discipline; it required them to hand over their will to an external, controlling God who demanded nothing less than total obedience. However, as Stephen Lawhead puts it: 'True religion ennobles, it never debases.' Spiritual discipline was sometimes taken to pointless extremes and merely inculcated a deep sense of powerlessness which was carried over into future lives. Similarly, slaves, servants or some employees, experienced a negation of their own will as their master had total power and control. People with Saturn-Mars aspects need to learn how to use the will, to find their own, considerable, inner strength and discipline in order to direct their life.

Uranus in Aspect to Mars (or Mars in Aquarius and Uranus in Aries or Scorpio)

Uranus in aspect to Mars has issues concerning extreme wilfulness and the need to learn the 'right' use of force and vibrations. I met a man who 'remembered' blowing himself up not once but twice. He had Uranus square Sun-Mars in Cancer. The first time he blew himself up experimenting with kundalini power, against orders, when he was a magician in ancient Egypt. The second time he was a Victorian music-hall artist who used gunpowder in his act and thought he knew how to handle it. In the present life he was using the healing power inherent within the aspect as an osteopath, although still exerting 'force' in order to realign the body.

The chart pattern (Fig. 11) shown here is for a woman who 'remembers' being present when places blew up, another facet of Uranus-Mars contacts. The first time was in Atlantis when she refused to heed warnings to leave in time, believing that she was invincible and could control the situation through the use of crystal power. The second time, on Thera – ancient Santorini – she was a little wiser in recognising that nothing could prevent the natural forces manifesting. The issue of power is graphically displayed in the chart, there is the full force of that Pluto energy erupting from the depths, an energy which she found difficult to control or direct in the present life; and a Uranus-Mars trine indicates that she is still working on finally resolving the issues of extreme wilfulness in her current life.

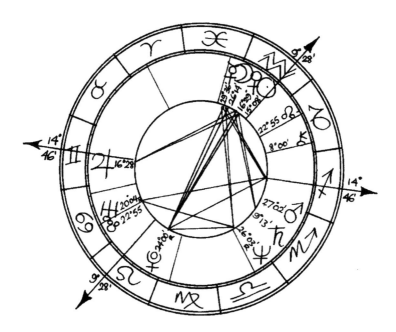

Fig 11

Resolution of the dilemma comes when the Uranus-Mars will is aligned to the needs of humanity as a whole.

Neptune in Aspect to Mars (or Mars in Pisces and Neptune in Scorpio or Aries)

Neptune-Mars contacts also offer a lesson about the will but this time this involves aligning it with the Self – that inner divine part of our being – and using that inner attunement and intuitive knowledge of its spiritual pathway as a life direction. Often this aspect seems to be linked with experiences of drug or alcohol addiction. It is as though the old, egotistical will has to be dissolved through total dependency and helplessness over one's actions. The person then has to learn that addiction is something which cannot be overcome by willpower.

'Willpower' is the use of force in order to exert control, either over oneself or over another. It is not the skilful use of will, which involves alignment with the direction one's Self chooses to take and willingly - rather than wilfully - following the spiritual pathway of the Self. The various 'Anonymous' programmes are successful because the first step includes an admission of powerlessness and the second a handing over to 'God as we understand him' which involves a surrender, not submission, to the divine force – a force which manifests within each one through the attunement to the Self. 'Alcoholics… are individuals driven to the point of deciding to live or to die. At this point in the life of any individual sudden insight and vision are possible. If this experience eludes most of us it may be because we are not sufficiently motivated to surrender our ego into the hands of a spiritual force'.[4]

Other steps for both the alcoholic and the Mars-Neptune contact include a deep, introspective examination of oneself; seeking forgiveness, and making reparation for the past – steps on the spiritual pathway towards the 'perfection' which the Self is seeking. One of the most important karmic lessons for the soul with Neptune-Mars is to forgive oneself for the past in order to be released from it, then finding a spiritual path of self-transformation to which one can dedicate one's life. So often there is something from the past that the soul is flagellating itself for, some 'misdemeanour' it cannot allow itself to forget, but forgiveness is essential if the past is to be left behind. When the situation is confronted in past life therapy, the soul usually finds anyone else involved has long since forgiven and forgotten.

The Neptune-Mars aspect has also been linked to a 'disguised lust for conquest' and to the 'missionary' lifestyle. With Neptune there is little violence in the conversion. The truth, as the missionary sees it, is taught by example and emanation in true Neptunian style. However, the gentleness of Neptune can be deceptive – thousands of people have been killed in holy wars fought in the name of a man who preached love and another who taught submission to the will of Allah.

Resolution comes when the will is aligned to serve the Self rather than the ego.

Pluto in Aspect to Mars (or both planets in Scorpio)

When Pluto contacts Mars the karmic issues centre around use, abuse and misuse of power and will. The person is often afraid in the current life to use their strong will as they have an innate fear of misusing it – or having someone else use their will against them. With this aspect one can have been victim or perpetrator in the past. It has often been involved in forceful conversion to a set of beliefs.

The influence of Pluto in conversion is rather different to that of Neptune as Pluto, although it can be equally devious, is rather more forceful. A client, Mac, who became a friend over the many years we explored karma together, had Jupiter-Saturn square Mars-Pluto. He was regressed to a life in which he had been a fanatical (Pluto) Jesuit priest who was involved in forcibly converting a country and then teaching the children, through the use of harsh discipline, the 'true' religion. It is a Jesuit who is reputed to have said: 'Give me the boy up to the age of seven and I will have the man.' Coincidentally, a woman to whom this client had a compulsive, and mutual, unlikely attraction (her Sun-Pluto conjunction conjoined his Mars-Pluto conjunction) did not know of this regression. When she regressed she went back to the same incarnation and was terrified of his 'cold eyes'. She commented afterwards that she would not have thought him capable of the fanaticism he displayed at that time. It did, however, explain why, on her first meeting with him in this life, although she was inexplicably pulled to him, she also felt a deep fear. However, in that first meeting he totally turned her life around and helped her to find a new, spiritual, pathway. His way of making reparation for that Jesuit life was to go to Africa on voluntary service, following a past life confession and absolution from a priest who believed in reincarnation. In the process he absolved his karma around power – and forcible conversion – represented by his Sun conjunct Mercury and Pluto in Cancer.

Some ten years later when he contracted lung cancer, Mac attributed it to his Jesuit life. During his time in Africa, he had contracted testicular cancer, but had used his powerful will and self-healing abilities to cure himself within the six week period of grace the hospital granted him before he underwent castration. When the lung cancer was diagnosed he declined treatment. He explained it was 'time to leave the planet', which happened to be his second Saturn Return. He stated that his good karma 'resulted in being in a comfortable nursing home with good friends around him'.

I spent time with him and we worked both on releasing his personal karma and also on the Tibetan Buddhist idea of clearing pain and suffering for others through his actions. Almost up to his death, he was positive and joyfully looking forward to his new life, but then he became mortally afraid. By then he was on morphine for his pain and the nurses attributed his visions of hell fire to his medication, but when I went into his reality with him, it was his strong belief in hell that had taken over. He was surrounded by flames. We worked on forgiveness and letting go. I tried to 'talk him through' his death and twice he stopped breathing for fifteen minutes only to start again as the fear took hold. He clung to life with a tenacity only Pluto-Mars could muster when unconscious, but a day or two later I took his hand and said, 'OK Mac, you've always wanted to firewalk. How about the two of us give it a try? I'll come with you as far as I am able'. Holding hands we walked together towards the fire. It parted, leaving a path over which the fire arched. As we walked through the fire, it burnt off and purified the remnants of his karma. On the other side his guide awaited him – someone with whom he had been in strong contact for many years and who had been particularly close in the last weeks. However, as his guide told me: 'The fear had kept us apart, I couldn't reach him'. Now with the two of them reunited, we all three went up through a tunnel of light to a much brighter place. My work done, I returned – most reluctantly!

Resolution of the Pluto-Mars will dilemma is achieved when the soul becomes empowered to use its power wisely for the collective good.

Pluto-Saturn-Mars

A Dominican monk (Saturn opposing Pluto-Mars), who had left his order, called it blasphemy when I suggested he should take back the projection of his will from God and learn to take control of his own life using the extremely strong Will energy indicated by the Pluto-Mars conjunction. The problem he had approached me about was intimately connected with (Saturn opposing Mars) feeling helpless and fated and with his projection on to another of that powerful Pluto-Mars will. He had gone into a monastery for many reasons, not the least of which was to escape from his sexual feelings. On his first night he was brutally raped by another member of the community with whom he had a strong past-life connection, of which he was intuitively aware. The savage, sado-masochistic sexuality and power struggles of the Pluto-Saturn-Mars combination were projected on to and unleashed by another person who acted out his inner conflict for him. This enabled him to disown the dark (Plutonian), shadow (Saturn) sexually aggressive (Mars) part of himself. The subsequent violent homosexual affair lasted for seven years and after he left the monastery he still felt that this man had power over him. He could not control his life in any way and he had completely lost the ability to do even simple things like travelling on a train and ensuring that he had sufficient money for the journey.

Gradually he began to learn to live in the world again, but was paralysed by his lack of will and his inability to assert himself. He did not know what he wanted to do, or where he wanted to be. He kept praying to God, but received no answer.

He was offered a job running a venereal disease clinic (Pluto and Mars are connected to the sexual organs), which he found fulfilling as it brought him into contact with people again and also gave him the opportunity to organise a small department. Ultimately, after a couple of other encounters with powerful people, he did learn to use his will, not to control but to direct his life, and just as importantly, he learnt not to hand his power over to someone else who would then control him. He had learnt the karmic lessons of Pluto and Saturn aspecting Mars.

Pluto in Aspect to the Sun (or Pluto in Leo and Sun in Scorpio)

When Pluto is in aspect to the Sun an old pattern is indicated where power was projected onto another person – usually, but not always, a man. Personal power was not owned or used because the other person was seen as more powerful. In the present life, the pattern tends to be repeated with power initially being projected on to the father (or other dominant male). In a woman's chart, this projection may remain with the father or be transferred to a partner, but for both men and women with this aspect, power struggles are likely to be a dominant theme throughout life as the soul fights to regain its power. Resolution comes when power is owned and utilised for soul-empowerment, but not used for 'power-over' purposes.

LOVE

The other major set of ingrained patterns relate to Love in all its manifestations. Outer planet aspects to Venus carry ingrained karmic messages that have been absorbed throughout many lifetimes:

Chiron-Venus	'Love hurts'
Saturn-Venus	'I don't deserve to be loved'
Uranus-Venus	'I don't need love'
Neptune-Venus	'Love has to be perfect'
Pluto-Venus	'There will never be enough love'

The companion volume to this book, *Karmic Connections*, explores these expectations in much greater detail, but we need to understand just what is involved here as many people incarnate to deal with 'love' issues. Some will have just one set showing in the chart but others may well be trying to heal and integrate all of them, whilst some unfortunate souls remain trapped within these conflicting voices.

Chiron-Venus or Chiron in Taurus or Libra

Chiron-Venus contacts indicate old pain around love and relationships. This may have to do with rejection or abandonment, loss or abuse. The soul is wary of relationships and needs to heal the expectation that love will hurt. If this pattern is operating, particularly unconsciously, in the present life, it can draw highly destructive or painful situations – which may well be a repeat of old interaction with the same person or persons involved. Someone with this aspect often hurts others before 'it is done to me'. Healing comes from a loving relationship with someone who can be there regardless of what happens – the old cleaving together 'for richer, for poorer, in sickness and in health'.

Saturn-Venus (or Venus in Aquarius or Capricorn)

With Saturn-Venus the soul has learned, often through several lifetimes, to believe that it is unworthy of love. Relationships are often based on a kind of 'prostitution'. The person settles for being taken care of, having a home and food provided, being little more than a servant or a chattel, and other such dismal scenarios. There is a lack of real love. Sometimes the soul may find itself in a life where actual prostitution is the only way to keep body and soul together – and this does not only occur with a female body. Other relationships may be cold, highly restrictive and unloving. The soul tends to believe: 'Well, that's all I can expect, I don't deserve more'.

There can, of course, be a scenario previous to this where the incarnating soul has acted badly within a relationship and therefore feels that it deserves to be punished or to lack love. In an aware soul, the situation may have been taken on to learn to be a foil for someone else who is learning a difficult lesson.

So often with Venus-Saturn, the soul falls into the pattern of rejecting before it is rejected, leaving before the partner can leave, or behaving appallingly badly and then saying: 'There, I knew it' when the other person cannot take any more. Such an aspect may also indicate an old vow of chastity that has not been rescinded, or a promise to be faithful 'for ever' to one person and one person only. In which case, the healing comes through rescinding that vow and reframing it to the relevant life only.

The healing for Saturn-Venus in general can only come from learning to love oneself. Only then can love be received from someone else without feeling somewhere in the depths 'Well s/he can't be much good if they love worthless me'. When the incarnating soul can love and accept itself, then the pattern of loving turns into deep commitment – and the ability to love in turn.

Uranus-Venus (or Venus in Aquarius)

This is the aspect that has considerable difficulty with intimacy and commitment. At the extreme, the soul will have chosen celibacy. Less extreme is the person who had a relationship but who split off sex from love and remained detached, in effect, never giving the heart to another. On the other hand, it could have been unwise and left its heart in another's keeping so that part of the soul and heart need retrieving. The soul believes that it doesn't need love – and may shun or fear it.

This aspect can also indicate ambiguity and ambivalence around sexuality and gender. It shows up in charts where the soul has taken on a lesbian or homosexual lifetime to learn a different approach to sexuality (or who is repeating an old pattern of sexual behaviour). This is particularly so when the eighth house is involved. It may be an indication that the soul has switched gender for the present lifetime – and may well feel that it incarnated into the 'wrong' body. Transsexuality or transvesticism may result. Learning to be intimate and share thoughts and feelings can be the process of many lifetimes but gradually the soul learns to trust, and learns that intimacy goes beyond fear and into an expression of soul love.

Neptune-Venus (or Venus in Pisces)

Neptune-Venus is a challenge to practise truly unconditional love. But the past life patterns include the 'madonna/whore dichotomy' when the soul asks 'how can I be spiritual and sexual at the same time' and the deep-seated feeling that love has to be perfect (usually instantly!) or it isn't good enough. The tendency is to put the beloved on a pedestal, to idolise and idealise, and then feel totally disillusioned when they act like a mortal, fallible, human being.

The healing comes in realising that unconditional love means loving someone 'warts and all', being prepared to work at a relationship that has enough going for it to be worth working on, but not becoming caught up in a snare of illusion and delusion. Unconditional love sees the pearl in the heart, but loves whether or not this manifests. It also knows how to set appropriate boundaries and does not collude.

Pluto–Venus (or Venus in Scorpio)

Incarnating with Pluto in aspect to Venus, the soul brings back an expectation of trauma in connection with relationships, and a deep need for intense emotional closeness. This is the emotional black hole which sucks in all the love and affection it can get and yet still demands more. It is 'insatiably greedy for emotional nourishment'.[5] Its old patterns of relationships have been predatory, symbiotic and demanding – but it is not only in the sexual relationship that the manipulative pattern is apparent. For example, clients who respond to my telling them how far down on my waiting list they are by pressurising, however gently, for me to give them priority, or who ring, 'Just to see how you're getting on with my reading,' will inevitably have Pluto in aspect to Venus. As Stephen Arroyo points out this placement is 'prone to use one's attractiveness or friendliness to gain power, money, or simply to inflate one's ego.'[6]

The Pluto-Venus attuned soul must learn to totally change its way of relating, to fill itself up from the source of 'divine' love which emanates through the cosmos. This divine love will provide the endless source of nourishment it craves and which no mere human can provide in such abundance. The soul will then be able to give of itself, knowing that its own store of love will always be replenished. And in giving, it will also learn to receive.

Stephen Arroyo also mentions the repeating pattern of Pluto-Venus conjunctions or oppositions in which a fiancé or lover dies or disappears. I see this 'loss' as a characteristic of all Pluto-Venus aspects. At times the cause of the loss is physical death, and at other times it is the death of a relationship which produces the grief and pain. It is as though the relationship cannot continue in its present form and, in order for the soul to learn a new, non-symbiotic way of loving, it must learn to let go entirely of its old patterns.

A woman with fifth house Venus in Aquarius opposing Pluto in Leo fell in love with a much younger man who was from different cultural background. Their Moons were conjunct and she called him her 'soul friend' because they understood each other so well. There appeared to be an old contact between them but one which raised several issues aligned to her Pluto-Venus. Initially the relationship was wonderful, although it had to be kept secret as they were living in a Muslim country, but she did meet his family (in addition to the secretive Pluto energy, his Neptune was sextile her Venus, her Neptune squared his Mars). She arranged for him to get a job with prospects, which he had been unable to find for himself, but did not at the time realise that this was not acceptable to a proud Muslim man. He had a Grand Cross in his chart which indicated a conflict between his expansive ideas and ambition and his family duty: South Node-Sun opposing North Node-Jupiter, Moon-Pluto-Uranus opposing Chiron-Saturn. Her twelfth house Moon and Saturn was conjunct his Moon-Pluto-Uranus. They had planned to marry and go away to another country together. However, his father said that if he continued the relationship he would be cut off by his family. The young man chose his family, but she would not accept this decision and kept trying to pressure him into seeing her again. Although she said that she understood that he had no cultural acceptance of marrying for romantic love, she still could not understand how the 'soul friend' with whom she had been so close could cut her off and 'become so cold'. She flew home and insisted on an immediate counselling session (Pluto-Venus). I suggested to her that she should practise cutting the ties with him, setting him free to be himself and allowing him to make his own choices. When she tried to image the two circles, with herself in one and him in another, tears rolled down her cheeks. She said that all she wanted to do was to be in the circle holding him. The Pluto-Venus aspect of herself could not let him go.

The Pluto-Venus attuned soul will often find itself in an addictive or co-dependent relationship and its lessons are epitomised in an Alcoholics Anonymous handout aimed at abrogating the controlling nature of the alcoholic partnership. The lessons are, however, pertinent to all Pluto-Venus contacts:

To 'Let go' is not to care for, but to care about.

To 'Let go' is not to fix, but to be supportive.

To 'Let go' is not to be in the middle arranging all the outcomes but to allow others to effect their destinies.

To 'Let go' is not to be protective, it's to permit an other to face reality.

To 'Let go' is not to adjust everything to my desires, but to take each day as it comes and cherish my self in it.

To' 'Let go' is not to regret the past, but to grow and live for the future.

To 'Let go' is to fear less and love more.

It is only through the pathway of loving more and loving unconditionally without strings, giving love without expectation or demand of it being returned, that the soul who is attuned to Pluto-Venus can grow beyond its 'black hole' and learn the true power of love.

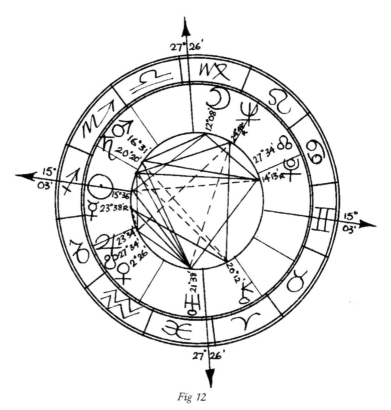

Fig 12

WILL-LOVE-POWER

The chart for a karmic Will-love-power dilemma is shown here
(Fig 12). The Saturn-Mars conjunction in Scorpio in the eleventh house forms a Grand Trine in the Water element with
Pluto and Uranus; squares Neptune, sextiles Jupiter conjunct
the South Node, and inconjuncts Chiron. Venus in Aquarius
is unaspected, indicating that love is not integrated and that it
has been experienced as separate from will and power. This
is the child of missionary doctor parents (the ninth house 'belief system' of Neptune squaring Mars in the eleventh house
linking to the medical missionary lifestyle), born into a long
line of missionaries. She said of her Chiron in the fourth house,
which represents her experience of home: 'As a child there was
no home. My parents were always there for other people, never
there for me. We always had nannies. At seven; having been

120

sent to boarding school, I never went 'home' again. And as an adult one doesn't know how to make a home because one has never experienced a home.' As a child of four her father explained to her, while teaching her the Lord's Prayer, that she 'actually had two fathers, one of whom loved her and she must love Him. He was an extremely stern, authoritarian, all-powerful God who could see her every move' (a manifestation of her Capricorn South Node energies, see Chapter 5). She was not at all comfortable about this, especially as her own father was strongly Capricorn and lacking in emotional empathy with her.

> At about this time I was told the story of Abraham and Isaac (by my father). I identified very much with Isaac and I was the first born - so God became a rather frightening figure as at any time He might request that I be sacrificed so that God should know that my father loved HIM above everyone else. He (my father) would have to do this (and with hindsight, knowing my luck there would be no ram conveniently caught in the thicket!!).

She grew up literally fearing the love-power of God and the control He had over her (Saturn-Mars). All she could do was obey this external locus of control. At the age of seven she was sent to boarding school in England and farmed out to an uncaring Aunt for the holidays (Venus in Aquarius incarnates with the expectation of cold and unemotional 'relationships'), seeing her parents once a year when they came home on leave. She felt totally abandoned, rejected and powerless. Later she married a Capricorn army doctor and carried this pattern over into her marriage, living in married quarters wherever he happened to be posted or being left behind in England when it was 'too dangerous' to accompany him. At the age of fifty her husband left her for another woman. She divorced him, taking up her old career and becoming a paediatric physiotherapist (a Neptune-Mars 'rescuer') quickly rising to the top of her profession, and advancing to a position of authority (the Pluto-Mars contact representing 'power'). Inwardly, however, she still felt helpless and powerless, at the mercy of 'fate' (Saturn-Mars). At the age of sixty she danced over a long-dead, sun-dried goat in Greece, symbolically laying to rest her Capricorn South Node. At the age of sixty-two, in an unknowing preparation for the conjunction of transiting Pluto to her natal Mars activating the Grand Trine, she began training in psychosynthesis - having been told she would live to be ninety-seven she decided to 'prepare for a useful old age'.

She was still exploring her will-power issues and identified a pattern of victim-persecutor-rescuer within her present life which directly related to a regression she underwent several years earlier to an Italian life. In that life she was the brother of a rather simple-minded boy who was taken off by the local lord for a minor infraction of the law. (S)he followed and tried to argue for his freedom (an action represented by the aggressive Mars energy in contact with the liberating Uranus) but was also imprisoned. Subsequently they were both sent to the war galleys as slaves (Saturn-Mars indicating constraint and powerlessness). (S)he was intelligent and quickly rose to be the slave master, a position (s)he abused (the power of Pluto-Mars) by demanding homosexual (another Uranus-Mars manifestation) relationships with the slaves for sensual self-gratification (Jupiter-Mars). Crisis point was reached when (s)he demanded intercourse with her own brother (third house Uranus signifying somewhat unusual sibling karma). (S)he committed a murder; possibly of the brother but this was not clear, and was imprisoned again. Before the trial the town was razed by a volcanic eruption (Uranus and Pluto energy) and fire. (S)he escaped from prison and went around the town rescuing women and children and putting them in boats. (S)he sacrificed her own life in a truly Neptune-Mars action, and died in the fire.

In a regression to a later life, linked to her fourth house Chiron, she was in colonial America as a sickly, 'Anne of Green Gables type child' and died at the age of eleven rather than taking on the issue of owning her own power; As she went through her death she 'skirted round a cloud instead of passing through it' – she found it impossible to meet death head-on as represented in the present life chart by the wounded Chiron inconjunct the grim-reaper, Saturn. Prior to her birth into the present incarnation she decided to face the issue of her will and her power. However, this was delayed until the action of Pluto transiting Scorpio propelled her into her own depths and activated the potential of the Grand Trine for the power to bring about transformation. Her dilemma was unresolved until she was able to integrate the power of love, represented by the very wide conjunction of Venus to Jupiter, into her expression of will, which came about through her perceptive abilities as a counsellor and the work she carried out in her profession.

SELF WORTH

We have already examined the expectations around love that can be carried over into the current life. The soul has also had experiences that affects its self worth. Aspects of Saturn in particular indicate old patterns of constriction and repression, of long-standing inadequacy and fear. People with Saturn-Sun and or Saturn-Moon contacts benefit greatly from recognising that they have chosen to incarnate with difficult childhood experiences so that they can heal the patterns from the past.

Much will depend on the stage of consciousness reached by the incarnating soul, on how much it sees itself as at the mercy of 'fate' and on how much awareness it has of its inner dynamics. When it recognises that it is creating its own reality, the aspects are likely to manifest as more internally centred experiences leading to psychological and spiritual changes. It may be necessary for the soul to reconnect to a particular feeling or emotion, to reiterate its past experience and to accept it as its own before it can be released. In such a case the experience of lack of self worth may be intense, but it may also be short-lived as acceptance will bring release, integration and change.

It must of course be borne in mind that the planets and the aspects represent the part of the psyche which derives from the past-life experience, and although the word 'soul' has been used to describe the principle which carries these patterns, it should perhaps more properly read 'the part of the soul'. It is necessary to examine all the aspects in the chart in order to ascertain the underlying emotional themes which may be in conflict with one another. For example, the Moon square Saturn in Capricorn and Mercury-Venus in Virgo both carry constriction on recognising and expressing self-worth. The second placement reiterates and emphasises the problem in the present life through its expectations of unattainable perfection. The incarnating soul's behaviour at any one time will depend upon which planetary faction is in ascendancy over the others, but the overall behaviour patterns will present all the underlying themes.

Saturn-Sun (or Sun in Capricorn or Pisces)

An aspect of Saturn to the Sun is indicative of a lack of self-esteem arising out of a fundamental block on the sense of Self and its worth and value. This frequently manifests through an early experience of emotional coldness from or loss of a parent, usually the father. The challenge is in learning to parent and nurture oneself, providing self-validation. The soul can only experience only being loved and approved of when it conforms to a set standards – individuality being positively discouraged. There is no intrinsic acceptance of who the incarnating soul is. This lack of validity of itself is connected to the old pattern which gives the message: 'I have no value, I might as well not exist.' The soul lacks confidence as it has not had the vital experience of receiving unconditional love and affection. Its energies are channelled into inner defences against deep feelings of vulnerability and into its outward need to succeed to prove to the world that: 'I am here, I do exist, I have worth and substance.' At some point in its journey this soul will have to meet its 'shadow' and integrate all that it has denied for so long into itself. It must develop self-esteem if it is evolve beyond the past life blockages that created the lack of worth in the first place.

Saturn-Moon (or Moon in Capricorn or Pisces)

For Saturn in aspect to the Moon the difficulty tends to lie in obtaining nurturing and affection from the mother but the effect is the same. The incarnating soul lacks self-esteem and a sense of self-worth and this is reiterated by childhood experiences. It assumes it is unlovable. The past-life pattern is one of emotional isolation and difficulty and the soul is cut off from emotional nourishment because it does not know how to receive it; and the family into which it incarnates may well also not know how to give it. The soul may not 'fit' into the family as a result of having had poor, or no, previous contact with family members. Liz Greene[7] points out that someone with this aspect has to learn that the security of family ties is an illusory one, the only security being within oneself. The soul yearns for love like a small child, but is unable to make the contact or feel the warmth needed for mutual interaction. As an adult, it will often settle for a 'safe' relationship rather than risk exposing its vulnerability. At its heart, it does not believe it deserves a 'good' relationship. Here again the challenge is to nurture and validate oneself.

A client with a Saturn-Moon-South Node conjunction in Cancer in the fourth house conceived a child during the Second World War, following the death of her first husband, at a time when she was destitute and homeless. The child, a girl, had to be adopted although the mother later married the father and brought up his teenage children. The mother incarnated with the expectation that mothering would be a source of sorrow and difficulty to her, anticipating rejection (Saturn/Moon/South Node), and she needed to learn to let go of her child, overcoming past possessiveness and a tendency to 'smother' (fourth house Cancer Moon). She had also incarnated with six planets in the twelfth house, including Chiron, and was working on her karmic issues in an extremely intense way.

When the client's daughter was thirty her adoptive parents died and she traced her mother. The daughter had Moon in Virgo semi-sextile eighth house Saturn, tenth house Neptune square Venus, and Chiron inconjunct the Sun. She also had four planets in the seventh house, indicating that she had considerable relationship karma. Her tenth house Neptune expected elusive mothering and her eighth house Saturn had karma regarding how she shared herself with others. Her own lack of self-worth echoed that of her mother but was more difficult to see because it was a semi-sextile.

The daughter already had a young child and shortly after meeting her mother again she gave birth to a son. She went into severe post-natal depression and rejected him, and he was subsequently fostered, made a ward of court and eventually adopted. The daughter 'remained in torment, unable to love or make meaningful relationships'. The mother 'tried to help, but was filled with guilt and could find no solution'. At a later stage the daughter refused to see her mother.

Her mother asked whether this, was karmic restitution. The interaction between the charts was not heavily karmic and showed few contacts. There were personal planets to Uranus inter-aspects, indicating a freedom/commitment dilemma, and reflecting the daughter's own Sun-Uranus conjunction opposing Jupiter – an aspect which indicated that she may well have grown and expanded rather more through her adoptive parents than her biological ones. A Neptune square to the mother's Moon indicated illusions, guilt, and perhaps idealisation of mothering. Saturn opposes Uranus, a change/maintenance dilemma. It appeared as though the daughter had needed to learn a karmic lesson about relationships and had chosen a mother who expected to 'lose' her child, but not a mother with whom she had intense personal karma to work out. It could, of course, have been that they were part of a soul group who had incarnated to help each other with some difficult lessons although I saw no indication of this in the charts (the usual indications would be repeating Neptune-Moon or Venus aspects and nodal contacts). It was more that they both shared similar issues and that basic loss of self-worth that had to be healed. With the Sun inconjunct to Chiron it also appeared that the daughter may have had direct karma with the father, although this was not explored as he was dead and the mother was more concerned with the immediate effect of the interaction and the prospects for the future. She found it difficult to accept that, having once given up her child, the child should return to her and then reject her. This, however, was the expectation and lesson expressed in her Saturn/Moon/South Node which needed to move beyond the confines of the biological family and into a wider understanding of the meaning of relationship. As she had developed her own self-worth, it was also possible that through the unconditional love offered by the Neptune-Moon inter-aspect and the empathy from her own experience, she could in time help to heal her daughter's wounds.

Saturn-Mercury (or Saturn in Capricorn or Pisces)

Saturn in aspect to Mercury incarnates with a fundamental difficulty in communicating itself to others. The soul may feel that it lacks intellect or a quick intelligence, or it may reflect fixed patterns of thought from the past in which it may have experienced perceptual, speech or hearing blocks. When lack of confidence and loss of self-esteem are part of the equation, it may well feel that there is nothing to communicate. It therefore can find communication within a relationship difficult and may incarnate into the kind of family in which children are 'seen and not heard', in which great emphasis and value is placed on intelligence and ability, rather than on who the child is; or in which individual expression is discouraged or forced into a channel unnatural for that soul. The soul must learn to communicate itself out to the world and to express its own uniqueness in its interaction with others, as a way of valuing both who it is and what it has to say. It is often around the time of the first Saturn Return, or even later, that the soul discovers that it has something to say. A delayed return to education may well reveal unrecognised intellectual depth, or the soul may learn to express itself in other ways. A strongly focussed and disciplined mind may emerge once it is freed from the constraints placed upon it in the past.

Saturn-Venus (or Venus in Capricorn or Pisces)

As we have already seen, with Saturn in aspect to Venus the soul can have an inherent sense of being unlovable. Because of its past experiences, it does not believe it can be loved, and it may also feel deeply vulnerable and open to pain through the emotions. It tends to incarnate into a family which will support that perception of itself and experience emotional deprivation and conditional 'loving'. As a result, it may well retreat into being 'good' in order to obtain what passes for love. Again it is an aspect with which the soul may well settle for 'safe' relationships. When the soul learns to love itself, self-worth is raised and the soul naturally enters into life-enhancing relationships.

PLUTONIAN ISSUES

Pluto Aspects

The karmic lessons for Pluto centre around power, symbiosis and separation and long-held feelings of guilt, resentment and rage, as well as underlying issues of rejection and abandonment. These often show up in childhood around parental interaction. As Susan Forward points out: 'Parental love is the only kind of love in which the ultimate goal must be separation.'[8] However, for many incarnating souls who are attuned to Pluto the insidious strangulation of the psychic umbilical cord pervades relationships far into adulthood. Mother or Father takes on the archetypal role of dominance and authority, acquiring the willing or unwilling projection of power from the child who must later struggle to regain it.

Pluto–Sun (or Sun in Scorpio)

Aspects of Pluto to the Sun involve overt power struggles with the image, if not the actuality, of Father in order that the incarnating soul may regain its lost power. A client, a twin, (Sun in Gemini inconjunct Neptune and square Pluto) was most concerned about her fear and dislike of her father. She described a 'creepy feeling' about him and was sure that he had abused her as a very young child. Now in her twenties she was still experiencing 'interference' from him in the form of a strong mental power over her and deliberate participation in her dreams. Her twin did not experience difficulties to the same extent and she had married and become the powerful partner. It was suggested that both girls should work on cutting the ties with the father, particularly the one who first consulted me, as there were strong past-life links to him. Shortly afterwards she moved out of the family home, something she had found impossible to do prior to this despite her problems with her father.

This aspect is particularly difficult for women, who have traditionally handed over all their authority to a man: first father, later husband. They may well find themselves incarnating into families where powerful, authoritarian fathers still demand absolute obedience, with the consequent enfeebling of the soul's ability to exert itself, and risk of abuse of the child. Repressed rage and anger will then fester into resentment, an energy carried over into so-called adult relationships which may well in turn be abusive or parasitic. It can be equally difficult for men who misplace their power.*

Pluto–Moon (or Moon in Scorpio)

The power struggles involved in Pluto aspects to the Moon are more subtle and covert, but no less damaging, and are linked to old traumatic experiences which programme the incarnating soul to expect emotional issues such as rage and resentment, abandonment, rejection, and guilt which are carried over into childhood and adult relationships. It is as though the incarnating soul carries a tinge of paranoia relating to a certain powerful, but frequently unspecified, 'they' who are 'out to get me', 'won't let me be happy', etc., which causes the soul to metaphorically look over its shoulder in fearful apprehension whenever it is aware of things going well or of being happy. This is not an imaginary fear as, in the past, persecution will undoubtedly have come 'out of the blue'. Pluto has great difficulty in letting go and also stores up resentments and hurts which can well up from the depths of the unconscious with a force which has nothing to do with the present-life trigger event. In particular these negative emotional expectations are linked to karma around mothering and being mothered which the Pluto-Moon soul anticipates will be life-threatening and devouring. The most appropriate symbol for the Moon-Pluto mother is that of the Indian goddess Kali who holds the power of life and death. Many souls attuned to the Moon-Pluto energies face death in childbirth at some stage in their journey. So much karmic material has surfaced over the years on this aspect that I wrote *The Hades Moon*. It is the longest book I have ever written – I did not so much finish as have to stop. There simply wasn't room to say more. The following story which was included in *The Karmic Journey* is typical of what must by now be hundreds of Moon-Pluto experiences I have worked with astrologically and through regression and counselling. This, however, is my own story:

I was born into a family in which for at least five genera-

---

* *(See* Karmic Connections *for further insights.)*

tions the Moon-Pluto women's husbands had died or disappeared, leaving them to bring up the children and to look after their own elderly mothers. By the time I incarnated the pattern was beginning to change in that my father was physically, although not emotionally, present during my childhood. Whilst giving birth to my daughter, I was deeply unconscious and in danger of dying (Pluto conjunct Ascendant square to Moon in Scorpio). I experienced a spontaneous regression to a past life in which I was giving birth on a straw pallet in a hut. I had deliberately chosen to die in that incarnation as I could not face yet another mouth to feed in an already over-large family, worn down by grinding poverty. Recently, in past life therapy, I returned to that life and discovered that my husband had died, leaving me with several children. I had been given a house on his farm by a young man who fathered the last child. But I was 'not good enough for him' and his sister and mother broke up the relationship so I experienced rejection. Not only that, the birth was a difficult one (shoulder first) and yet the sister refused to allow a doctor to attend. No matter what, I would have died even if I had not decided to give up the struggle. In the present incarnation I was told by the wise being who was with me at the birth that I had to decide whether to opt out or to deal with my karma. I chose life, and both I and my daughter survived although my husband died shortly afterwards and I brought up my daughter alone. My daughter does not have the Moon-Pluto aspect in her chart, thus breaking the family pattern, although Pluto/Uranus was on her Ascendant, with a Saturn-Moon opposition also present in the chart.

In this life I met a man who told me he had been my son, but that I had abandoned him and his brothers and sisters by dying young. I have been regressed to several lifetimes where there were mothering difficulties. As Pluto began by transit to approach my Scorpio Moon I was told by psychics, palmists and astrologers that should I have a child, it would probably be handicapped or die. Determined to circumvent this, I was sterilised. On the first pass of Pluto over the Moon my daughter informed me she was pregnant. Her baby was stillborn; the Saturn opposition to the Moon had its own lessons to learn. Although she was not taking on my karma, I did work through some of my own lessons by seeing my daughter suffer in this way. As a result of the baby's death, I had to face up to many issues I had hitherto been unaware of concerning separation. The symbiotic nature of Moon-Pluto contacts was illustrated by the fact that I started menstruating, in the middle of a cycle, as soon as the baby was born. On the final pass of Pluto over the Moon my own mother suffered a life-threatening, although not fatal, disease – issues of abandonment also lie buried deep within the Moon-Pluto contact – and at the same time my daughter conceived again. When she conceived her next child, menopause was upon me (which led to yet another book!). The Moon of change brought about a deep healing within the family dynamic. I am hopeful that my granddaughters will not have to go through the same Moon-Pluto issues in their lives.

The challenge with a Pluto-Moon aspect is to be creative, although not necessarily on a biological level. Many women with this pattern are expected to conform to what their mothers have always done or to live out the unlived life of a deeply frustrated mother and, although they may inwardly feel deeply rebellious, some comply. A considerable number of them, aged around thirty-five to forty, ask for readings as they have to face making a decision on whether to have children or not 'before it is too late'.

> Too often women get caught in a restrictive, single vision. Instead of realising, a woman will concretise. Instead of admitting everything into her totality – waiting, accepting, ripening, transforming and being transformed – a woman will literally conceive and bear a child.[9]

These women have to break free from the past and from their mothers, or from archetypal expectations of their sex. When women perceive that there are different ways of becoming creative and that their karma may necessitate moving away from the biological level, new choices will open up together with the possibility of overcoming the old, destructive cycle.

As the act of birth can often be traumatic, it can bring up a great deal of the emotions and pain from the past which the

Moon-Pluto carries. Pluto signifies that it will be hard to let go on many levels, but especially of the past. It has issues such as guilt to confront – particularly if Neptune aspects are also involved. This guilt is usually all-embracing, non-specific, and cannot be pinned to anything in particular. When analysed, this guilt is found to be partly related to the mother in the present life and partly to the soul's interaction with the mothering energies and emotions in past lives. Psychotherapy may be necessary to deal with this old pain, but the positive side of the Pluto-Moon contact is a healing of those old wounds in the psyche and a release of the inner creative energy.

The possibility of creating anew, without fertilisation by external male energy, is one of the issues explored in the literature of the feminist movement, particularly that written whilst Pluto was transiting Libra and Scorpio:

> Rites of Passage have turned inward where they can be lived out as stages of psychic transformation.
>
> A woman need not literally have a daughter to bear witness to the mystery of continuity ... a child is as much the offspring of the body of your imagination, the treasure hard to attain, as it is the blood fruit of your womb.
>
> It is essential also to let these daughters of imagination go from you - there are mothers in myth who would kill their own children if they proved a threat to their own individuality and passion. It takes great strength to let go of a thing you have created: a child, a work of art ... but the estrangement, the giving up, the separation are often necessary in order for something fundamentally new to emerge ...
>
> Perhaps that flowering of women, that gathering of women in our time who choose not to conceive literally, those who choose at a young age to be (paradoxically) past the age of child-bearing, are those to whom the burden of a cultural labour has fallen. Like the vestal virgins who tended and carried the public fire, these women might be the bearers of a kind of illumination that we have not known before ... [but] if the mothers who conceive of new forms of language and culture forget their connection to the body, to the real female depth of tissue, to the earth (their Mother), the life they create will be sterile.[10]

However, the impact of Moon-Pluto aspects is not restricted to girl-children. This combination represents the 'devouring mother' in all her awesome power, who will swallow her boy-child whole rather than allow him to separate from her. Roger Waters (Mercury and Moon quincunx Pluto, and Moon square Saturn) articulates the underlying fear of the Moon-Pluto aspect in the Pink Floyd song 'Mother', in which he perceptively points out that mothers have a habit of making their children's worst nightmares come true. Susan Forward links the misogynist, the man who hates and abuses women, to this 'devouring mother' figure:

> The mother who validates her son's striving for independence and encourages him to separate from her when he needs to, gives him some very important tools with which to deal with life. When the mother is willing to let her son establish his own identity, by permitting him to take risks on his own and by allowing him to make mistakes, yet being there for him should he need her, she helps to build a man who is confident about himself and his abilities. The suffocating mother, on the other hand, restrains and constricts her son's development by over-controlling him and by making him feel inadequate and helpless.[11]

It is this symbiotic dependence in infancy, and beyond, which ultimately forces the incarnating soul to face up to the separation issues and the prospect of abandonment which so terrify it. If these issues are not confronted in childhood, they will arise on the death or loss of a parent, partner or child, propelling the soul back to explore roots either in helpless infancy, or beyond, into the previous incarnations which have contributed to this desperate fear of letting go. The challenge for the Moon-Pluto soul is to own its creative power and find a new outlet for its emotional energies. It will then have great healing potential and be able to become a powerful force for transformation and regeneration. I personally believe that people with Moon-Pluto aspects are able to draw on their skills as partakers in the Great Mysteries and to heal the earth – the Great Mother.

PATTERNS OF THE PAST

4

Mansions of the Soul

The Houses represent unfolding spheres of life. They are the 'where' of a chart, indicating the area in which things will happen or through which planetary energies will be expressed … It is a journey into expanding awareness.
Judy Hall: Astrological Images

The houses are the 'where of a chart'; they show the area of life in which karma will manifest. (If the birthtime is not known, then using a sunrise chart will give a symbolic picture.) When examining the birthchart in the light of karma, certain houses have stronger karmic implications than others and planets placed here point to particular areas to be worked on during the present life. Other houses may indicate skills and abilities that are karmic, or relationships that stem from an old interaction or which will bring up old issues. Aspects to the rulers of these houses can further illuminate the nature of the karma.

House System

Placidus house cusps are used throughout this book. The amount of 'space' allocated to a house, and the number of planets which a house thereby incorporates, is significant for karmic work — despite the difficulties encountered in extreme northern latitudes where the restriction of a particular house may well indicate an area of life which is not relevant to the present incarnation and the expanded house will indicate an important area to be worked on. It would appear that for some souls part of the karmic experience is connected with finding balance within such extremes: the darkness and isolation of the period of perpetual night, and also the effect on the pineal gland (a spiritual linkage point) of being bombarded with constant light during the period of the midnight sun. As a Finnish commentator said: 'In winter, the darkness creeps into my mind and depresses me. But in March, when light conquers dark, you almost go out of your head with joy.'[1]

FACING UP TO INCARNATION:
THE ASCENDANT AND FIRST HOUSE

The first house is the house of the Self and the Ascendant is the persona or mask the soul dons to face the world. The Ascendant and planets in the first house indicate how the incarnating soul will view the prospect of incarnation, birth and nurturing, and how it will interact with the other souls it encounters.

There is a theory which postulates that the womb is the most wonderful place in the world. The incarnating soul floats in mystical unity with the mother, cushioned and nourished by its own integral life-support system. However, there is another line of thought which considers the uterus threatening, hostile, non-supportive and a most unsafe place to be. To which school of thought one belongs will depend on one's experiences prior to birth and on the sign and planet(s) on the Ascendant.

Neptune, Venus, Taurus, Pisces and Cancer will usually be identified with the five-star womb, and Pluto, Saturn, Scorpio, Aquarius and Capricorn will probably recognise the no-star variety. The attitude of the Libra or Virgo Ascendant towards incarnation will tend to depend on whether or not Pluto, Saturn and/or Neptune also feature in the equation. With first house Neptune in Virgo on the Ascendant, the soul is likely to incarnate with the dualistic view that incarceration into matter is separation from the divine and birth into an 'abode of the damned'. In other words, hell. Saturn in Virgo may well agree that it is 'a place of misery'.

The first house Neptune in Libra, however, all other things being equal of course, is likely to enjoy the uterine experience and may continue the symbiosis and non-separation from the mother, and the rest of creation, a long way into incarnation. The umbilical cord of the psyche being much harder to sever than the physical structure. On the other hand, this being Neptune and Libra, it may be ambivalent, but ultimately it must decide whether incarnation was or was not such a good idea after all, and either fully incarnate or withdraw. A typical scenario for this dilemma is the baby who is born with the cord around its neck or the child with breathing difficulties in the first few months of life. (This script can apply to anyone who has Neptune, Pluto or Saturn close the Ascendant.)

The Ascendant

The Ascendant is where the soul meets the environment; it is both a mask with which to face the world and an inbuilt perception based upon past experience which will colour that world. The Scorpio Ascendant, for example, tends to view the world with inherent suspicion and hides behind a mask of secrecy, while the Sagittarius Ascendant is naturally optimistic and open unless mitigated by mistrustful Saturn. The Ascendant is a way of interacting with others – it is what is first perceived but may be totally misleading. For instance, an Earth-sign Ascendant may appear to be practical, a good organiser who is well grounded, and yet, if there is no other Earth in the chart, this may be a protective outward projection to cover feelings of being totally out of touch with the practicalities of daily life. 'The world' demands that these be handled efficiently, and so a competent facade is erected. The Ascendant can be seen in karmic terms as representing the compensatory, balancing, positive qualities available to be built into the persona and projected out on to the world. (If you do not know the Ascendant, put the Sun on the first house cusp to make a sunrise chart):

The positive **Aries** Ascendant can develop individuality, leadership, ego strength and a pioneering spirit. It can balance out previous procrastination, egoism and selfishness, or too much giving up of itself.

The positive **Taurus** Ascendant, being grounded in the body, can use sensory perception and practicality to interact with the environment. It has the opportunity to develop the quality of endurance. It compensates for previous fixity, indulgence, materialism and possessiveness, or for ignoring the physical level of being.

The positive **Gemini** Ascendant is concerned with communication, information-gathering and the processing of knowledge. It can develop an adaptable approach to the world in order to compensate for over-rigid beliefs held in the past. Its difficulty is that it can fall back into hypocrisy or lack of concentration, inattentiveness and superficiality.

The positive **Cancer** Ascendant has the ability to offer nurturing, protection and sensitivity to the world. It can overcome any previous tendency to smothering, manipulation and insensitivity. However, it needs to guard against possessiveness and sentimentality.

The positive **Leo** Ascendant can be powerful, empowering, authoritative, and heart-centred. It compensates for previous autocracy, dominance, self-centredness and intolerance.

The positive **Virgo** Ascendant is rational, learning to give discriminating service, and to become fruitful. It can balance out a previous undiscriminating acceptance of life. Its difficulty can lie in being overly fastidious and hypercritical, suffering from perfectionism and impossibly high ideals.

The positive **Libra** Ascendant is concerned with relating, harmonising, balancing, compromising and adapting. It balances out selfishness and self-centredness, but may fall back into indecision or the lethal niceness of the people-pleaser.

The positive **Scorpio** Ascendant can develop the qualities of penetration, insight and healing. It can either fall into the trap of, or compensate for, suspicion, hostility, vindictiveness and destructive emotions.

The positive **Sagittarius** Ascendant is philosophical, optimistic and expansive, it is the eternal seeker after truth. It balances out previous narrow-mindedness, bigotry, moralising and insouciance.

The positive **Capricorn** Ascendant can develop a personality which is responsible, authoritative, successful and prudent. It needs to avoid old patterns of control and repression in order to overcome emotional isolation. Its difficulty may lie in confusing material success with spiritual fulfilment.

The positive **Aquarius** Ascendant can be far-sighted, detached, perceptive and humanitarian, initiating social change. It compensates for too much attachment, but may fall back into an old pattern of amorality, anti-social behaviour and eccentricity.

The positive **Pisces** Ascendant has the potential to develop mystical, intuitive and empathic qualities. It is offered the opportunity to balance out a previous pattern of untrustworthiness, insincerity, lies, immorality or opportunism and victim mentality.

The First House

The first house, and the planets located in this house, indicate how the incarnating soul will face the world in which it finds itself. **Mercury** is enquiring and communicative. **Mars** is assertive, hasty and impatient and can have an underlying, deep-rooted anger, while **Venus** on the other hand is concerned with creating a beautiful environment and harmonious relationships. **Saturn** brings with it a burden, a sense of responsibility which the soul meets when young. **Neptune** wears a veil of illusion which can be difficult to penetrate, a longing to be back in the spiritual realms and no sense of itself as a separate, unique individual. The **Sun** is highly aware of its own individuality, but the **Moon** is reflective of the feelings of those around it. **Pluto** is intense and secretive, whereas **Jupiter** is expansive and naturally expects the world to provide for its needs.

Jupiter

With Jupiter, or the Sagittarian Ascendant, the soul incarnates trusting the process of growth and expecting good nurturing from the cosmos. It has an inherent faith and optimism in this process, which can overcome poor nurturing from its biological parents. The incarnating soul may well have within the family one person, a grandparent or aunt, for example, who will ensure that it receives the nurturing it needs.

The lesson for Jupiter is that of disciplined expansion into fullest consciousness and integration of all the parts of its being into a totality of Self and God. It must recognise that ultimately there is no separation, but for Jupiter, unlike for Neptune, this is a process of expanding awareness, a function of self-consciousness not self-immolation. Neptune is at one with the cosmos and unaware of separation. Jupiter is at one with the cosmos, encompassing both separation and integration, whilst maintaining its own integrity.

Saturn

Saturn, or Capricorn on the Ascendant, on the other hand, can indicate that the soul has been too closed during previous incarnations. It may be repressed and constrained and needs to open up its boundary to interaction with someone else. The soul incarnates with the sense of duty or responsibility of a task to be done. It is only when the process of maturity brings the soul to an appropriate age that this can be discharged. In the meantime, the soul can feel it carries the world on its shoulders. Later in life, considerable karmic wisdom emerges.

The first house Saturn incarnates with the expectation that life will be difficult as the soul is already carrying a heavy burden. Saturn, or Capricorn on the Ascendant, can indicate fear and resistance to birth. The soul often experiences a difficult struggle to be born which necessitates forceps or Caesarean section delivery – a process which confirms all the soul's worst fears. Or it may undergo a premature birth which necessitates separation from the mother and time in an incubator. The soul feels isolated and alone, and the baby is often met with the hostility or indifference of a mother worn out by the pain of a protracted delivery or who is falling into post natal depression. This may well have been an unplanned, unwanted pregnancy or the mother may have been experiencing her own fear and isolation during the gestation period. Either way, soaking up these emanations from within the womb, the incarnating soul is acutely aware of its discreteness; it feels unwelcome and uncared for. Incarnating with the expectation of coldness, rejection and poor nurturing, it inevitably meets physical or emotional deprivation – one can, of course, be physically well cared for and yet emotionally deprived, and vice versa. This may be the child of an elderly, inadequate, chronically sick, depressed or 'absentee' parent.

The soul with a first house Saturn tends to face responsibility early, meeting hardship with fortitude or resignation because it expects nothing else. A woman with Saturn on the Scorpio Ascendant was born shortly after her sister died. Her mother grieved for the lost child continually and paid no attention to the new baby, who received no nurturing from her mother throughout her childhood – which was exactly what she had expected when she incarnated.

The first house Saturn may also need to explore its 'shadow', all those facets of itself which it does not wish to own or acknowledge and which are pushed down into the darkness of the unconscious, from where inevitably, sooner or later, they will demand attention. Such a demand may be expressed as a projection of the undesired quality or emotion 'out there' to another person, which is the dynamic operating in most relationships. On the other hand, it may continually surface as emotional tension until it has to be acknowledged and integrated. A Saturnine soul is therefore prone to incarnating into a family which has carried forward an ancestral 'shadow' pattern and an unspoken edict forbidding certain feelings. This is referred to by family psychologist Robin Skynner[2] as 'screening off' unacceptable thoughts and emotions. The child quickly rediscovers that a specific response or emotion, for example anger, is simply not allowed to exist. It consequently re-learns to repress what it has found difficult to deal with in its past lives, and ultimately does not even notice it. Nevertheless, not to acknowledge one's unacceptable facets does not make them vanish into thin air. Anger which has been ignored, for example, will remain located deep within the psyche or stored in the physical body as 'disease'. And, from time to time, given sufficient stimulation, it will surface, countered by such thoughts as: 'This is not me, I am not like this.' Part of the lesson to be learnt from Saturn is to acknowledge that: 'Yes, this is me, I can tolerate and accept the darker side of myself.' These are Saturn's greatest gifts: the possibility of integration and the inner strength which follows acceptance of the totality of the Self.

Uranus

The incarnating soul who is attuned to the vibration of Uranus, or the Aquarian Ascendant, expects to meet chaos and disruption and needs constant stimulation and acceptance of itself as an individual, rather than conventional mothering, which is usually experienced as smothering. It is naturally independent and anticipates nurturing that will support its urge towards self-determination and individualisation. Its karmic lesson is to evolve steadily, rather than undergo periodic revolution and total change as its means of growth.

Neptune

With first house Neptune, or Pisces on the Ascendant, the soul can experience the difficulty of being born to a mother who either has an undefined boundary of her own or who is knocked out by drugs or anaesthetic and unaware of having given birth. Such an experience may mean that neither the child nor its mother are able to separate psychically. The child may itself be suffering the effects of the drug – a difficulty which may later be recreated through drug or meditation experiences in which the 'child' seeks to regain its lost unity with the mother and the cosmos.

Whenever Neptune falls in the first house, or Pisces is the Ascendant, the incarnating soul is unsure of its boundaries and needs to learn where 'it' ends and another begins. As with the twelfth house Neptune, the lesson is to distinguish: 'Who am I? Who are you?' whilst retaining a fundamental sense of interconnectedness to the whole of the cosmos. Neptune can be the planet of the highest spirituality or of the deepest escapism. The incarnating soul can be naive, too trusting and open to deception. It is the cosmic sponge, soaking up emanations and taking on pain indiscriminately, without separation into 'mine' and 'yours'. The soul with first house Neptune is capable of great sacrifice and yet must learn how to protect itself and how to say 'No' when appropriate, learning that atonement is more apposite to its spiritual functioning than atonement. Neptune is the planet with integral oneness, but the lesson is one of discriminating unity. The incarnating soul must cleanse and strengthen its aura to provide a protective barrier as in past lives it has been too open.

Pluto
Pluto in the first house, or Scorpio on the Ascendant, indicates that the soul has incarnated with the expectation of trauma, intensity and issues relating to death, as does the Scorpio Ascendant. My Pluto is conjunct my Leo Ascendant, and when I was hypnotised and taken through the conception-to-birth experience, contrary to my expectation of being a soul lightly attached to the foetus from conception onwards, I found that I had been instantly compressed to the size of a pinhead and held in the womb. I experienced gestation as a traumatic imprisonment, acutely aware of my mother undergoing the emotional frustration and fear of an unfulfilling wartime marriage. Towards the end of the pregnancy I endured an intense feeling of constriction and suffocation, and a long process of fighting to begin the birth. My mother is deeply Plutonian and held on to me until the birth became a power struggle and a survival issue, which, at a deep level, was exactly what I expected because of my past experiences with birth.

Many incarnating souls with Pluto or Scorpio on the Ascendant face the issue of death through the loss of a parent, sibling or grandparent, either whilst in utero or during childhood. It is part of the Plutonian lesson of the need to let go. Death may also be faced more directly, either at birth or during the early years of incarnation through a life-threatening illness. The soul may also have to deal with rejection, abandonment, guilt and resentment at an extremely early age. Usually unspoken, but nevertheless clearly heard, the parental message is: 'If you did not exist, I would be free to be something different,' or 'I am trapped within this situation,' a message which induces guilt, and resentment in the child, triggering an old pattern. Pluto on the Ascendant indicates that the soul is also peculiarly open to abuse by one or both parents. Abuse can be defined as: 'Any behaviour that is designed to control and subjugate another human being through the use of fear, humiliation and verbal or physical assaults.'[3] With Pluto, it is just as likely to occur on the emotional level as on the physical.

Pluto near the Ascendant expects birth to be traumatic and life-threatening. Pluto on the Ascendant of the mother and an exact Pluto-Uranus-Virgo Ascendant conjunction of the child to the mother's Chiron featured in a birth by vacuum extraction. The mother's contractions had almost ceased and the baby's heart was slowing. Both were near to death (Pluto). The baby had been conceived during a civil war (Uranus) and the mother had been coping with the breakdown of her marriage. The child had incarnated with the expectation that birth would be life-threatening and that the world was, in any case, an unsafe, unpredictable place to be (Pluto-Uranus). This was reinforced both by the toxic state (Pluto) of her mother's body (Virgo) and the way in which she herself was suddenly sucked out into the world (Uranus). She also had an eighth house Saturn opposing the Moon, showing an inbuilt expectation of rejection and isolation. Owing to the trauma of her birth, she had to be cot-nursed for forty-eight hours and was denied the comfort of physical contact with her mother. The family moved house constantly during her childhood and she experienced continual disruption in her environment. Her father died early and she was briefly abused by her stepfather. However, she overcame her difficulties around power and abuse, learning to own her power whilst still young. She was then able to move on to dealing with her other karmic lessons, and to face the prospect of change and growth with equanimity.

A channelled being gave a graphic description of one man's task as shovelling shit to make space behind him for others. It was an apt description of that man's tenth house Pluto and first house Scorpio. All of us with powerful Pluto or Scorpio placements find ourselves doing just this. We have to work on our own darkness, and to ensure that our past produces fertile compost for the future. If not, we create havoc in ourselves and those around us. We can also aid other people to go down into their own blackness as we are not afraid to shine a light into the darkest recesses of the psyche. It is only when such a light is present that we can resolve our psychological or emotional conflicts, thus clearing the karma. And, of course, we have to work on moving the karma which is expressly composed of the collective rubbish of generations.

Pluto – in any house – has the lesson of finding and owning its power and authority. In the first or twelfth house the incarnating soul may in the past have misused, abused or given away that power. Now it is time to reclaim it and use it wisely.

Chiron

When Chiron is in the first house, the world is viewed as unsafe and wounding – or wounded. The soul may be on a mission to heal and many powerful healers and shamans have this placement. Other life experiences may well have been traumatic and painful and the soul carries forward an unhealed wound. Early life may be dramatic as a 'shamanic test' brings out the wound and provides the opportunity for it to heal. It is as though the pain has to be reiterated so that the soul is pressured into learning the lesson or regaining the skill that will do something about it:

> 'A Shamanic Test is a challenge we have created for ourselves because we see the opportunity for using and integrating negative force to leap into a much higher level of consciousness, power and vision .... To experience a Shamanic Test is to die to your old self. You can either move forward to a whole new level, or you can crash and burn. If you fail (or have failed) a Shamanic Test, typically you may have buried the pain and it will be affecting you negatively. But you still have the opportunity to learn the lesson, past the test, transform it, and receive all the benefits from having been successful. The test is on-going if it is not passed the first time. (Chuck Spezzano)'[4]

I have seen many children with first house Chiron incarnate into families where their birth created problems of one kind or another, or where there were already difficulties so that the family environment was wounded. Children born in such circumstances facilitated the healing of the problems or exacerbated them.

A child with Chiron in Scorpio right on the Ascendant was the product of an 'on-off' relationship that had torn the mother apart emotionally. She had left her husband for a man she recognised from the past and who was 'the only person who understands me' but he found it impossible to commit to her. He denied the child was his and walked out of the relationship yet again a month or two before the birth was due – provoking premature labour. The child was born by caesarian section and so was separated from the mother for an hour or so afterwards. His parents got back together again soon after the birth but, in the process, the grandmother who had born the brunt of supporting her daughter and her two children was told not to visit the family again. Harsh words were exchanged. This was extremely painful for the two children who had a close relationship with their grandmother, particularly as the mother refused to discuss the reasons. The children, not unnaturally, attributed it to the return of this man. Eventually their father, recognising the pain that was created, brought the children to visit the grandmother. The grandmother was careful not to say anything to the children that turned them against their mother's new partner, but they intuitively recognised the truth.

The child's Chiron was exactly conjunct the grandmother's Moon and square her Pluto. It was also conjunct his elder sister's Pluto. His Pluto-Moon-Venus-Mars conjunction was conjunct the grandmother's Sun. His North Node was conjunct the grandmother's Chiron and his Mercury-Sun conjunction (opposed Saturn) was on her Neptune. This was clearly a karmic connection, but it was also reflecting a family pattern carried through that Pluto-Moon connection. Both the mother, the grandmother and the great-grandmother had been separated from a beloved grandmother after the birth of a brother. This child could well break the line with the potential to heal an ancestral pattern as well as his own.

A year later the child severely burned his hands, necessitating a long stay in hospital. The relationship with the grandmother had to some extent healed prior to this although it was still tenuous and she had not seen her grandson. She was able to help the burns by providing complementary therapies which were so successful that skin grafts were not required. She visited regularly and her relationship with her grandchildren was healed.

One of the tools I use in addition to astrology is Chuck
Spezzano's *Enlightenment Pack*. It pinpoints underlying issues
and shows a way of healing situations. When the grandmother
consulted me shortly after the child was burnt it was clear from
the chart that this was an extraordinary child. This was confirmed by the first card picked for the birth: Child of God:
Grace. This is the card of the Buddha Child. In the illustration,
the person has just been helped over a chasm by a hand, leaving chains behind. The card for the situation with the
grandmother was Shamanic Test. For the burnt hands it was
Forgiveness: Healing. The image here is a soul embracing its
image in a mirror with another figure waiting in the background. As Chuck Spezzano says, forgiveness is a core healing
principle:

> 'If the world is simply a reflection of your own mind, all blame
> and judgement are projections of your own guilt and self-attack,
> then forgiveness of others releases both the others and the sub-
> conscious guilt within you. ... One of the core dynamics of any
> problem is broken bonding, or separation. Guilt is the superglue
> of life which keeps us stuck in painful patterns and situations,
> while forgiveness is the solvent which releases us not only from
> our guilt, but also from our withdrawal, unworthiness and sac-
> rifice, and from the feelings of deadness, exhaustion, difficulty,
> being stuck, valuelessness and overcompensation.'[5]

The final card for the outcome of the situation was Freedom:
Gift. Pictured here are a woman bending down to offer a
chironic key to a shackled woman. If the grandmother could
forgive and move on without holding guilt or blame, then everyone could be set free from the patterns of the past.

What struck me forcefully was the image for the child.
Before he was born the grandmother had done some soul work
with a powerful shaman. Her daughter had had great difficulty
with all her births and the grandmother wanted to heal a family pattern around this. The grandmother intuitively felt a
powerful connection with this soul but knew he needed help
to incarnate. When she went to meet his soul she travelled to
'the outer deeps' where his soul had been consigned a long time
ago. She brought him back with her, leaving him at a point

where he could make his own decision about incarnating. She had been that helping hand who lifted the soul over the chasm and freed him from the shackles of an ancient curse.

Personal Planets in the First House

The personal planets, whilst not carrying such a heavy karmic charge, also indicate how the soul will meet incarnation, and describe the dominant energy in its interaction with the environment. For the Sun, development of the ego or the Self is paramount; Mercury works through the mind and understanding; Mars meets its challenges with courage, impatience or anger, Venus with an urge towards unity and harmony.

The Moon carries with it the opportunity to learn the twin lessons of mothering and emotional equilibrium. A young man incarnated with Capricorn on the Ascendant (conjunct twelfth house Chiron). The Moon in Aquarius in the first house opposed Venus in Leo in the seventh, forming a T-square to Saturn in Scorpio in the ninth. He was an unwanted, unplanned pregnancy and the third child in four years born to a middle-aged mother. His father had left home some days before his birth to live with another woman, but was forcibly brought back by his mother's family. Shortly after the birth his mother experienced severe post-natal depression (Saturn square the Moon) and entered hospital, returning there periodically over the next four years so that his early nurturing was intermittent and on the whole poor (the expectation of the Capricorn Ascendant). His Aquarian Moon indicated detached, unpredictable and unstable mothering and yet, paradoxically, he was deeply attached to his mother, living with her until his thirties. He was unable to break away from what had become a suffocating bond, formed through fear, isolation and idealisation (Mercury-Venus square Neptune-Saturn opposing the Moon).

He was initially very much disliked by his elder brother and sister, who blamed him (a Capricorn scapegoat) for the 'loss' of their mother, teasing and tormenting him throughout his childhood. The children were brought together by the early death of the father, but, even as adults, they remained fixed in a pattern of childish interaction. He had incarnated with an inner sense of worthlessness and lack of confidence (Saturn-

Moon) which was reinforced by his uterine and childhood experiences, and the development of a repressed personality. The emotional impact of these experiences was internalised – at one point in his childhood he was hospitalised for chronic constipation, a psychosomatic manifestation of his inner constriction. At the age of eleven he became a Buddhist, finding his nourishment and sustenance in his contact with the cosmos (Sun conjunct Jupiter trine Neptune), and rejecting worldly matters (wide Saturn-Neptune conjunction, ninth and eighth houses). In his mid-thirties he underwent the progressive transits of Saturn-Uranus-Neptune to his Sun, Jupiter and Mars, which enabled him to overcome the past conditioning and to leave home.

The Second House

The second house indicates resources and abilities which have been brought back to help in dealing with the present incarnation. The **Sun** in this house indicates that the inner Self has been developed in the past. The **Moon** in this house signifies that the soul has good experience around mothering and nurturing, although this may be offset by difficult aspects which indicate areas still to be worked on. It has worked on the emotions and feelings and often has psychic abilities that can be employed in empathising with other souls. **Mercury** has developed the mind and the innate intelligence and this can be utilised in understanding the world, and other souls, around itself. **Venus** has worked on relationships and the creative energy in the past, and **Mars** has developed will, courage and assertiveness.

   Jupiter is at its best in the second house; it indicates an inate skill of visualising and manifesting that which is needed to sustain life, just as the old priest/ess knew that the cosmos would provide. In the past the soul has learnt the laws of creative manifestation and now whenever there is a need it is provided for. When the energy is being used unconsciously, a beneficent 'fate' provides. When the utilisation of energy is conscious the pattern of putting out the request and receiving the answer is understood, as is the maxim 'as we think, so we are'. This understanding can then be passed on to others.

My own experience is perhaps the best example I can give of this. When I was ready to begin working full-time on karmic counselling and to write my first book; a friend said, 'I've got an old cottage that would be perfect for you'. It was exactly what I had always dreamt of even down to the walled garden and inglenook fireplace. And it had room for seminars and workshops together with a wonderful healing earth energy just waiting to be plugged into. Exactly what I needed in order to proceed with my work – which includes teaching creative visualisation and reconnection to the past.

Saturn in the second house shows wisdom, self-discipline and integration; this is the gift of a Saturn whose limitations and difficulties have been overcome. **Uranus** is creative thought, with a marvellous understanding of vibrational forces and a natural affinity for change and transformation. **Neptune** in this house offers the gift of imagination and spirituality, while **Pluto** brings forth a deep understanding of the cycles of life: the knowledge of healing and regeneration that comes from intimate contact with the old mystery/fertility religions and the wisdom of the Mother Goddess. Chiron is a powerful healing ability carried forward from the past.

The Third House
The third house indicates karma with siblings: both the planet and the sign need to be examined in order to understand fully the manifestations of this karma.* If the **Sun** or **Moon** are located in the third house, then in a past life the father or mother was most probably a sibling. **Mars** or **Pluto** often indicate quite a violent karma with a sibling and issues of sibling rivalry and power struggles are also common.

With **Neptune** in this house the incarnating soul feels that it must have been adopted because it is so alien to the rest of the family. A third house Neptune is frequently misunderstood and miserable; it feels unique and separate from the rest of the family but isn't treated as such. The karma may perhaps result from having been too close to the family in the past, now

---

* *See* Karmic Connections

the implications of the wider 'family of man' have to be recognised. This placement has also been seen in the charts of people who under regression have felt themselves to be 'aliens' from another galaxy – now incarnated into the earth environment specifically to learn their own karmic lessons whilst helping in the evolution of mankind.

The third house also indicates karma around communication and with **Saturn** in this house the soul frequently finds that it does not fulfil its intellectual potential until the mid-thirties owing to a fundamental block on learning or communicating what it knows or who it is. Such a block is at times linked to perceptual and conceptual differences, to speech or hearing defects coming forward from the past, or to an inability to fit into the conventional education system: the child simply does not see the world in the same way. On the other hand, the child may have been forced by parental pressure into specific academic pursuits and may develop a different mode of communication when it matures.

The Fourth and Tenth Houses

The fourth and tenth houses indicate parental karma, what the soul expects to meet within the context of the family, how it expects to be parented and, when the **Sun** and **Moon** are involved, whether the parent has been a parent in another life. With **Chiron** placed here, the soul expects 'home' to be an unsafe place, with wounded or wounding parents; **Uranus** too expects things to be unsettled and chaotic. **Neptune**, on the other hand, has the most wonderful illusions about parents, until the soul needs support when the elusive parent slips away. The Lord of Karma, **Saturn**, indicates stern, authoritarian parenting karma whilst **Pluto** shows that there have been many power struggles around parenting and being parented in the past.

The Fifth House

The fifth house can indicate both karma with children or creative karma, and that with love affairs. The **Sun, Mercury, Venus, Mars** and **Jupiter** placed here are naturally attuned to the creative energy which will flow with ease and manifest through the energy of the sign on the cusp, unless there are difficult aspects to be overcome. For example, with the Sun in Cancer the incarnating soul will naturally produce children, in Gemini it will produce words but if that Sun, or Mercury, is aspecting Saturn then finding a publisher may be difficult or it may lack the confidence to try.

Saturn in this house often experiences a delay or difficulty around physically producing a child, or with creating things. It arises from not, in the past, having taken advantage of the opportunities afforded to be creative, or in not having valued the products of creation/creativity. The result in the present life is that the struggle offers the opportunity to develop a sense of value concerning the ability to create on any level. The fifth house **Uranus** is naturally inventive and capable of extremely original thought which may find some opposition to being accepted as art because it is so far ahead of its time. **Neptune** in the fifth house offers a creative imagination which is the manifestation of previous work in developing and using this ability. Neptune may, however, need some constructive, grounding aspects in order for the potential to manifest as otherwise it may produce someone who is the eternal dreamer, not the doer.

The Sixth House

The sixth house offers pointers to both bodily karma (see Chapter 7) and career possibilities as it shows the area of work through which an energy may – or may not – manifest and can point to the resumption of an old vocation for healing. **Saturn** in this house often brings a need to confront the energy behind chronic illness and to understand psychosomatic dis-ease. This may be dealt with in the body into which the soul is incarnated or it may be dealt with through professions such as nursing, osteopathy or social work.

Uranus may manifest through subtle disruptions of bodily rhythms, causing dis-ease or leading into careers concerned with realigning the energies. It may indicate a karma with technology, sometimes going back as far as Atlantis, the present life often being the first opportunity since that time for the soul to reconnect to the same level of technology. The soul with the technological karma symbolised by Uranus in the sixth now has the opportunity to make ethical choices connected with how it will utilise its abilities and knowledge in careers such as electronics, computers or alternative medicine.

A client (Sun in Taurus with Uranus in Cancer in the sixth) had both health and technological karma. She had been the subject of medical experiments in Atlantis, including transplants and replacement of vital organs by synthetic ones. She ended up as a head controlling a body which was mostly a machine. Her experience included:

> A most unpleasant replacement of most of the digestive system with clear, plastic-like tubes and the abdominal cavity being left open so that its working could be viewed by the scientists. As they 'progressed' more and more of the organs were replaced including the reproductive system. A foetus was introduced into the artificial uterus, fed by recycled blood. This produced violent rejection symptoms. The brain was intact and conscious during this time, although it had electrodes and monitoring equipment implanted.

The client had expressed her problem as 'extraordinary health problems'. As a result of that previous life, and of an initiation experience which went wrong, the neural connections within her present body misaligned between the etheric and physical body causing a malfunction manifesting as allergies and colitis, and continuous 'astral travelling' which did not allow for recharging of the physical body during sleep. The client later commented that her bowel condition had been so bad that a colostomy had been proposed, which was why she had requested the reading. She had also experienced migraine and menstrual problems from a early age. Complementary medicine and aromatherapy were recommended in view of the karmic carryover and this cleared the imbalances. Her experience with the Uranian energies from that life, and the fact, that she had five planets in Fire led her into a present-life career in psychological and physiological research into the condition known as 'burnout'.

The Seventh, Eighth and Eleventh Houses

The seventh, eighth and eleventh houses are indicators of relationship karma. The seventh and eighth houses relate to
one-to-one relationships and how the soul gives and shares of
itself in relationship. Planets placed here show the karma within
any close relationship, not just 'love' or marriage. If the **Sun**
or **Moon** is located here, then the partner of the incarnating
soul could have been the mother or father in a previous relationship; or the current life parent could have been a partner
in a past relationship. A man with a seventh house Aquarian
Moon (opposed by Pluto) had a powerfully dominating and
controlling mother. His father had died when he was 13 and
at the funeral his mother turned to him and said: 'You'll have
to take your father's place'. She made him a surrogate husband
and was obsessively jealous of any woman with whom he became involved. Consequently he did not enter a stable
relationship until his mid-thirties – a relationship to which his
mother was violently opposed. In regression he went back to
a life where his mother was his wife. But he was a detached,
non-intimate husband who spent his time in scientific studies,
leaving his wife to control the family and the estate he owned.
She never had from him the emotional commitment and intimacy she craved. Small wonder then that the scenario played
itself out yet again with slight variations. The power-struggle
in which she engaged was typical of **Pluto** in the seventh house
also.

When **Neptune** is in the seventh house, old illusions, delusions and deceptions surface sooner or later; although the
relationship may well seem ideal for quite some time. With
Uranus placed here, the splits tend to become noticeable
rather quickly. The souls grow apart, reflecting an old 'free-
dom/commitment dilemma' resurfacing.

Wherever **Chiron** is placed, there is an old karmic
wound but eighth house Chiron in particular seems to meet
loss and grief in the current life that is a carryover from the past.
The soul has to heal the pain, and then put the experience to
constructive use. When **Saturn** falls in the eighth house, old
vows of celibacy may be intervening in the current life, and
with **Uranus** placed here, ambivalence and ambiguity around

sexuality and gender have their roots in the past.

The eleventh house centres on karma connected with friends and groups, in the widest sense of the word. If **Pluto** is in this house then there is karma around dominance, manipulation and other power issues, and power struggles are likely to manifest within group situations. **Saturn** and **Uranus** both have karma with authority figures and control versus freedom, and may in the past have been too attached to dogma and ideas, whether conventional (Saturn) or revolutionary (Uranus), rather than to the underlying wisdom or understanding. In the present life both Saturn and Uranus must come to accept that each incarnating soul is entitled to maintain its own views on life without judgement or challenge.

For example, many souls still need the guidance of a conventional religion, others have moved into an understanding of karma, and yet others have moved on to create their own reality. To each his own, without interference from Saturn or Uranus manifesting through another soul – although Uranus has the potential to act as a catalyst for another soul when appropriate. Saturn has to learn to let go of the past and allow change to occur naturally. Uranus has to develop evolution and not revolution, and the soul with this placement must learn to preserve the best of the past and incorporate it into the future. The tendency is to 'throw out the baby with the bath-water' by jettisoning everything from the past and undergoing radical change. Uranus is a planet of transformation but the choice is between change through chaos or orderly evolution.

Again a personal example may best serve to illustrate how Saturn and Uranus in the eleventh house work. I have both these planets in Gemini. My teacher, Christine Hartley, told me that I tried to fit into conventional society in some lives (Saturn), and in others attempted to bring in new ideas and new ways (Uranus). She 'saw' me, amongst other confrontations with the establishment and authority, as being burnt as a witch and suffering at the hands of the Inquisition – an experience which several million souls share as the Inquisition and the witch-finders were active for several centuries. My chiropractor is convinced that I was hung for insubordination in a previous life.

In this life, as a mature student at college I rarely said anything during a class (the inhibition of Saturn). However, as part of my religious studies course I insisted (Uranus) on doing a thesis on Spiritualism with special emphasis on the eternal existence of the human soul and, by inference, reincarnation. It did not go down at all well with the college. My Mars sits between Uranus and Saturn and occasionally manifests conflict in order to teach me to stand up for myself and to highlight my need to explore different beliefs. After three years of Saturn being in the ascendancy and me biting my tongue, Uranus broke free. One of the tutors, a United Reform Church minister, said in answer to a question concerning healing, 'I don't think it has any value. I don't know anyone who has been healed'. I asked him since when had his ignorance been the criteria for judgement? I had used his tutorial room for spiritual healing sessions all the time I was at college (the subversive activities of Uranus). The room happened on that day to contain several of my patients and they all leapt to the defence of healing.

I was undergoing teacher training and my college record card stated 'Has very peculiar ideas and should not be allowed near children'. I fought long and hard for that comment to be removed (Uranus-Mars-Saturn) although I had no intention whatsoever of actually teaching. (It was later pointed out to me by Howard Sasportas that there are many ways of teaching.) Although I have never seen a clear connection from that tutor to myself and did not feel there was personal karma between us, I always instinctively felt that his bigotry and narrow-mindedness stemmed from a life as an Inquisitor. Several years later this same tutor pulled up at a bus-stop where I was standing in the rain. He told me he owed me an apology, he had become a healer. He then got back in his car and drove off, leaving me still standing in the rain!

The Ninth House

The ninth house shows karma around beliefs, ethics – and publishing! When the outer planets are placed here they usually relate to religion: **Pluto** to fanaticism, coercion and enforced beliefs, **Neptune** to mysticism, **Uranus** to revolutionary ideas, and both Neptune and **Chiron** to suffering for one's beliefs in the past. Such karma may be as victim or perpetrator.

The Twelfth House

The twelfth house is the main house of karma and planets in this house always have heavy karmic connotations. Many people ask: 'I have an empty twelfth house, does this mean I have no karma?' The answer is that there is no such thing as an empty house. If there is no planet located in the twelfth, or in any other house, then the sign on the cusp of that house, the placement of its ruler and its aspects will give indications of the karmic pattern:

The **Sun** in the twelfth house indicates a soul who has been an important, prominent person in a past life, or lives, and may now have to work behind the scenes rather than be in the public eye, and have to content itself with less recognition than it deserves.

This was clearly demonstrated in the chart of an opera singer (Sun conjunct Pluto in the twelfth close to the Cancer Ascendant, opposing Jupiter and trine Saturn in Aries) who had not found the fame which her voice merited. Somehow she always seemed to miss 'the big chance' through a series of mishaps. One day she opened a Russian book about a nineteenth-century singer and found that she was looking at a picture of herself. In that life she had received considerable acclaim and adulation. In the chart for the old incarnation, she also has the Sun in Cancer conjunct the Ascendant, but this time in the first house, squaring Jupiter-Saturn in Aries and trine Pluto on the MC. She also recognised her present-life family as part of that old interaction. In this life she had tried to persuade her son to be a violinist, but he insisted on becoming a singer (his Pluto-Mars conjunction had a strong will). In the past life her son had been a violinist and her present-life husband a devoted friend, who never married and had, it appears, suffered from unrequited love (twelfth house Neptune inconjunct seventh house Venus). In the present life she has Venus conjunct the South Node in Gemini, indicating the possibility that she may marry an old friend or lover, and her husband's twelfth house Neptune inconjunct seventh house Venus indicated an old idealisation, or soulmate contact, with karma returning through a relationship.

Delay or lack of recognition can be a hard lesson to accept, particularly if in the past the soul has demanded everything immediately, the 'I want it now' syndrome (often linked to the Fire or Cardinal signs), or who had taken identity from a public role (Libra and the Mutable signs) and now has to learn who it really is. The karma can also be one of pride or egoism (particularly for Leo, Aries, and Capricorn), ruthless ambition (Cancer) or cruelty (Scorpio) so the lesson for the present life would be that of leadership without arrogance or false humility. The soul with this placement must learn to do the job not for the sake of reward and adulation, but for the sake of 'a job well done'. This applies not only to the working environment but to any sphere of life.

With this placement there may also be karma with the father and aspects to the Sun and the sign on the cusp will indicate the past pattern. For example, a man with Aries on the cusp and an aspect from the Sun to Pluto was in the present life subordinate to his ageing father who ran the company where they both worked. When he regressed to a past life, he found that the positions had been reversed – his father had then been his son, whom he had held back and who had ultimately fought him, winning control of the country in which they were then living.

The **Moon** in the twelfth house has karma with the mother and around mothering and being mothered. It could have been overprotective and smothering (Moon in Cancer for example), or too withdrawn and detached (Aquarius). Equally there may be karma to do with over-sensitivity (Pisces, Cancer and Neptune aspects), feeling out-of-control with erratic mood swings (Uranus aspects). The sign in which the Moon is placed and aspects to the Moon will further clarify the past pattern.

A client with a twelfth house Moon in Leo regressed back to a time when her mother was her slave. She later commented that she was still treating her mother exactly like a slave. Many people with the Moon in the twelfth house find that they have been through a whole series of incarnations which involve their mother - a pattern which is repeated and carried over into the present life. Another client was aware of being much disliked by her mother in the present life. In regression she explored three other such incarnations but was able to let them go and to begin the process of mothering herself, releasing herself from the chains of the past.

The karma attached to the twelfth house **Mercury** relates to how the mind and the ability to communicate have been used in the past. The pattern can vary from simple gossip (Gemini), sarcasm (Sagittarius), slander and destruction of a reputation (Scorpio), forcing ones' own ideas onto others (often linked to a Pluto aspect), to being coerced into a particular way of thinking by outside pressure. It can indicate a refusal to use innate intelligence (aspects to Saturn), or a rigidity of ideas (Taurus or Capricorn), and too much analysis or criticism (Virgo). In the present life the soul is tested as to how it uses the mind and its ability to communicate. Actual blocks on communication stemming from past lives such as deafness or speech defects may manifest through this house or the third and sixth houses, particularly if the chart includes difficult aspects to Mercury from Saturn, or Gemini on the cusp of the house and/or aspects to planets in Capricorn.

Venus in the twelfth indicates karma connected with relationships. The sign on the cusp tells the history of the connection and any other sign sharing the house will give further clues to the karmic past. Aquarius indicates too much detachment; Cancer too much attachment; Capricorn that something is holding the soul back from relating to others; Scorpio old passions, intrigues and jealousies. The dual signs of Gemini, Sagittarius and Pisces, can have problems with commitment and faithfulness, or may exhibit promiscuous behaviour. Venus now has to deal with the consequences of these actions and may experience considerable difficulty in finding the right partner whilst these old issues are being resolved. Relationships can change dramatically once the karmic implications are understood, particularly when a more appropriate choice of partner is made rather than old patterns and consequent disappointments being endlessly repeated.

Venus in the twelfth may also indicate that the soul has had incarnations as a woman, or close past-life links with the women with whom it has relationships in the present life. In the latter case there may be difficulties as a relationship that feels so 'right' on one level is in fact founded on the past. A great deal of adjustment may be necessary as often the new personality is not so compatible as the old and this may cause friction. On the other hand, if the old pattern was one of discord, it may be necessary to adjust to the fact that the new persona is more agreeable. The old animosity can then be overcome and the past forgiven, thereby opening the way for both souls to grow through the relationship.

Mars has karmic issues around will, aggression, assertion, violence and war. It should be borne in mind that a war undertaken out of duty to one's country with no hatred for the enemy will produce different karma from a moral crusade. Mars in the twelfth often involves having been a soldier in at least one incarnation, usually several, and may indicate the positive qualities of leadership, discipline and self-reliance. Alternatively, Mars may have been drawn back endlessly into violent confrontation instead of developing the Will and assertive qualities. There may be karmic issues of cowardice and courage – the soul may have to learn that discretion can be the better part of valour and that it can sometimes be foolhardy to attack when a strategic withdrawal would enable the fight to continue another day. The twelfth house Mars placement may also indicate that the soul has had strong male incarnations and that it needs to integrate the masculine energy, particularly if Mars is in the twelfth house of a soul incarnating into a female body or if its previous incarnation was a 'macho' male. It now has the opportunity to learn the qualities of gentleness and sensitivity. Where war and confrontation have been the old pattern, the present-life lesson may involve developing the softer, more artistic side.

A soldier with twelfth house Mars in Cancer became a major at an unusually early age, following the family tradition, but was increasingly unfulfilled and disillusioned with his life. He had always been interested in photography and he decided to take the risk of abandoning his 'safe', if somewhat dangerous, lifestyle in order to start again as a photographer. He had learnt his assertive lesson well and was able to put a great deal of drive into promoting himself and his career. He utilised his past experience and contacts by specialising in military subjects, but branched out into his other interests of people, places and words through travel books.

Jupiter in the twelfth can indicate karma centred around over-indulgence and expansion or mistakes in the handling of assets, particularly when coupled with Saturn, or placed in Taurus or Capricorn. A woman with Jupiter conjunct Saturn in the twelfth house had a seven-year battle with her ex-husband over control of her family business after they divorced. Her background had been to squander her inheritance, and in the present life she had to work hard to preserve it.

Jupiter can, on the other hand, have a close connection with the priest/ess and the temple and indicate a soul who has a long association with Egypt. There is often a karmic need to put that old knowledge to work, utilising inherent wisdom and skills to alleviate the karmic suffering of mankind.

Saturn, the Lord of Karma, is at home in the twelfth house when there are easy aspects, but rarely displays his wisdom and gifts before middle age is reached. Prior to this the emphasis is on releasing the burdens carried over from the past – which may involve past feelings of separation and isolation – and on confronting the fears and restrictions imposed on oneself by those burdens. A Saturnian past-life blockage can only be released through following the injunction, 'Know thyself.' When the past has been confronted and the soul released from bondage to old inadequacies and karma, twelfth house Saturn offers up its gifts of self-reliance, confidence, discipline and strength. This is the planet of karmic wisdom.

Uranus is a subversive planet and this placement may indicate karma coming back in a far from straightforward way. With Uranus in the twelfth the soul often has strong memories of past lives which may surface through dreams or deja vu. Such memories can involve a cataclysmic event, as in the case of a girl with twelfth house Uranus, whose recurring nightmare of being buried alive unexpectedly found its source when she visited the Pompeii exhibition in London. Uranus also has links with man-made revolution and chaos, as in the case of the Aquarian with Sun square to Saturn-Uranus in the twelfth house who uncovered, during a regression, a life as a Puritan in the Roundhead-Cavalier conflict, and then another life as a peasant during the French Revolution who became a leader of the people. Similarly, a workshop participant who had Uranus exactly on the Ascendant had a scar across her throat from ear to ear, and a terrible recurring nightmare of which she could only say: 'It's the Terror'. During regression she too went back to a life in the French Revolution, but as an aristocrat who lost his life to Madame La Guillotine. In the regression (s)he was pulled from bed in the middle of the night, summarily tried and executed at first light.

Twelfth house Uranus also indicates that the soul may have links going back to Atlantis and now has to deal with technological karma stemming from the use, and misuse, of science and technological knowledge at that time. The present age is the first time since Atlantis when the technological advances present the same type of opportunities and dilemmas.

With this placement the soul knows instinctively what it took science hundreds of years to rediscover; that this seemingly solid and stable earth and everything on it is a mass of vibrations open to manipulation and change; that chaos ensues when human interference disrupts the fragile balance. However, Uranus has the ability to synchronise vibrations and restore harmony. The twelfth house Uranus also has insights relating back Atlantis, and is naturally drawn to areas like astrology, music therapy, massage, acupuncture and polarity therapy - all of which utilise the subtle Uranian energies.

Neptune in the twelfth is one of the most challenging karmic placements. It has been variously described as 'divine home-sickness' and 'a leaky aura'. It indicates the soul's longing to return to the more celestial realms. The following quote is from fiction I believe, but it sums up the peculiarly Neptunian ambivalence to life on earth: 'I came back because I wanted to, of my own free will. No one forced me to return. But now that I am here I want to take flight; to hide again in obscurity, to put this vast ocean between myself and this place. It bodes me no good.'

The lesson to be learnt from Neptune is one of surrender, rather than submission, to the divine; of at-one-ment not atonement. The challenge is to develop unconditional love. In the past the soul may have failed to face up to suffering in a realistic, practical way – a pattern frequently accompanied by an escape into religion, mysticism, drink, drugs, meditation, or some kind of institution. Alternatively, the soul may be repeating a pattern of endlessly sacrificing itself as the archetypal martyr, victim, scapegoat or saviour. The lack of boundaries lead to it absorbing pain almost by osmosis – there is no marker between its own emotion and that of others. There is a great need in this case to establish boundaries and strengthen the protective aura whilst maintaining the ability, when desired to merge with others. On the other hand, twelfth house Neptune can have taken up residence in a cold and lonely ivory tower because it cannot handle the feelings of others. Its boundaries act as a barrier to 'suffering' and yet, paradoxically, it is constantly presented with the state it so wants to escape from.

A middle-aged woman (Neptune in Libra) had a Near-Death Experience after taking more cocaine than she intended to 'in order to get closer to God', although 'He had told me that I would never get closer than I was already'. Prior to the experience she had felt very loving and totally connected to the cosmos, but not earthed, and had a pattern of compulsively giving away all she owned. After a three-day coma she felt totally alienated and overwhelmed by the pains of the world, having to withdraw inside herself. It took two years to regain her equilibrium and begin to restructure her life. She decided to utilise her channelling abilities and began what she described as 'a life of service to suffering humanity', although she still found it difficult to commit herself and displayed an unfortunate, unconscious Neptunian tendency to 'use' people and then move on without taking responsibility for her actions. Compare this with the experience of another client who wrote:

> I am aware of an unconscious skill needing to be brought out and used, and I think it is connected with 'seeing' but more, perhaps, 'far sight'. Certainly seeing past and future. I look at Moon inconjunct Neptune in the twelfth, mutual reception Mercury, sextile Jupiter and trine Uranus in the eighth. I feel that when I've learned to handle the exact Saturn opposition Moon, I'll be able to use that sensitivity more effectively. Someone described me as a psychic sponge. Indeed, I've had to learn to examine myself when strong emotions overtake me. Is it me? Or is it someone else's? And of course I've had to learn about cleansing.

In a workshop guided meditation she experienced 'a time of joy and harmony, a sort of Garden of Eden' when asked to go back to a pleasant, happy life. Her description beautifully conveys the sense of Neptune in harmony with Being:

> I go through the door and find myself in a simple robe with woven sandals on my feet. I'm in a steeply mountainous country. Although we are in the Tropics it is pleasant since we are at seven or eight thousand feet. The mountains go much higher and I'm aware that the highest is a pinnacle, like a beacon, shining with crystal or perhaps ice.
>
> I find myself going down a path, and am met by a boy and a girl. There is joy and happiness in meeting them: we jump and hug. Perhaps I am their older sister. We continue down the path and come to a low graceful stone house from a veranda outside. There is an astonishing feeling of no anxiety, no responsibility. A sort of unthinking innocence of being, as though I've never had to face a dilemma or a moral problem. Happiness and a feeling of at-one-ness with my surroundings and the people I meet seems to be the normal state. Life feels as if cut from one piece: not the complex problem of reconciling opposites and disparate sub-personalities I experience now. The surrounds are always simple and harmonious too. I think 'what about relations with men?' and a man appears, and picks me up with great love

and a sense of fun. My father? I think I must be somewhere between 14 and 16.

A woman comes. It is time. We are dressed in simple white garments. We go from the house down another path and rejoined on our way by other women. We come to a round 'temple' building. The atmosphere is calm and everyday. Inside there is a pool of water in the centre of the building. I dip my hand in this and touch my forehead. It is a sort of cleansing. With my scribe, the person who writes down what I say, I go to one of many separate alcoves. I am a seer [the Neptune-Moon-Uranus configuration has psychic abilities]. This is matter-of-fact [the pragmatic Saturn-Moon], it's like being part of the Civil Service. I have an area of country which I know well by 'seeing'. Every day, like this, I look in my silvered mirror and report what I see. I'm looking for the condition of the crops; the state of the roads, the occurrence of pests, etc. My perception and ability to look at things in the normal way is slightly different. As well as normal seeing I see what is like swiftly moving coloured mist around everything. The colours of the mist indicate the process through which an apparently solid object is moving - how it is changing. As I see, I speak: and my scribe writes everything down. Afterwards all the scribes report back to the 'priestess' in charge, and the seers listen to make sure the report is correct.

The soul incarnating with **Pluto** in the twelfth house has to face the archetypal, evolutionary forces hidden deep within the darkness of the human psyche. Pluto in the twelfth, or on the angles of the chart, can also be a key to obsessions, compulsions and phobias stemming from other lives. (Saturn may also be implicated, as a phobia is really fear of the fear one feels on encountering the phobic object.)

A client came for consultation about a relationship problem but mentioned, in passing, that she had a phobia (Pluto in Leo in the twelfth house square Moon in Scorpio). She could not bear to be in a crowd of people because of her overwhelming fear that she would loose control and would either pass out or throw up. She also had great fear of other people vomiting. Part of her fear went back to a past life when she had been in contact with typhoid and had been locked away with the sufferers for several weeks. The dead bodies were not removed and she had a great fear of passing out because as soon as anyone did they were thrown onto the heap of dead and decaying bodies. It appeared that one or two of the survivors resorted to cannibalism and, therefore, staying in control was vital for self-preservation. She did not contract typhoid and lived for many years with the nightmarish memory of her ordeal. The stench in the room had been unbelievable, there was no fresh air and no water and she had had to listen to the typhoid sufferers literally retching their life away. As Pluto is incredibly deep and devious, however, this was not the only root of the phobia and it has still not been released; although it was eased to the extent that she is now able to take part in meditation groups, which would have been unthinkable prior to reconnecting to that past experience. This fear of vomiting, of something coming up from the depths, is a surprisingly common one. In all the cases I have seen there were Pluto-Moon squares involved.

The twelfth house Pluto also represents karma connected with using, abusing, and being misused by, power. The soul has to deal with control and manipulation issues and has a deep fear of letting go. When in contact with Mars and Saturn it links into the karma of collective power and many people with these aspects 'remember' being involved in events like the Holocaust. A client (Leo Pluto-Saturn-Mars in the twelfth) regressed to a concentration camp. Although she survived the camp, she later committed suicide as a result of her guilt at surviving. She felt at that time that she 'could not live in a world which had allowed such a thing to happen'. She was intuitively aware of the collective karma of mankind and of the Jewish 'scapegoat' karma in particular as she was born, in the present life, into a Jewish family.

The idea of a 'chosen people' who suffer through the capricious acts of an authoritarian God demonstrates clearly the effect of 'as we think, so we are'. In other words, when a people expect to suffer, they are wide open to abuse by those exerting power as they are not 'programmed' by their belief system to resist. On the other hand, those who believe they are chosen' in the sense of favoured, for example in their divine right to rule, are much more likely to strongly defend their position when it is threatened and not to allow that abuse of power.

Pluto in the twelfth is also connected to healing power and it is frequently seen in the charts of those who become doctors, nurses or therapists out of some kind of compulsive necessity, the unconscious repetition of an old pattern, rather than out of the conscious desire to heal. The ability to heal is real, however, as is the ability for trance mediumship and clairvoyance, which also has links with the Pluto twelfth house placement, particularly when Pluto is in Cancer or Scorpio or has links to the Moon. The placement represents an old skill coming forward, and can become an asset when consciously utilised.

In his book *Pluto, the Evolutionary Journey of the Soul*[6] Jeff Green explores at length the twelfth house Plutonian need to let go of egocentric control and surrender to the universe, and this book is recommended for further study of the placements of Pluto, as is my own *Hades Moon*. Howard Sasportas in *The Twelve Houses*[7] gives an in-depth exposition of all the planets in the twelfth and other houses, and includes a karmic perspective.

5

Soul Intention

Our life purpose is our own personal path of evolution.
Tracy Marks, The Astrology of Self

The karmic purpose of incarnation can be seen in the lunar
Nodes. Unlike the planets, the Nodes are not physical bodies.
They are spatial and perceptual points in space – which is perhaps why they are able to hold the past so powerfully and yet
are places of purpose and potential. The North Node is concerned with purpose and evolution, new energies to build into
the life, the South Node with deeply ingrained patterns of
behaviour. The South Node of the Moon indicates that which
has been learned in previous incarnations and carried over,
and the North Node that which is to be developed in the
present incarnation. The South Node represents behaviour
which is instinctual, unconscious and compulsive. It operates
from a deep survival level, overriding intellect and logic. It is
a paradigm constructed from all that has gone before, an endless cycle of repetition and reaction to emotional and
environmental stimuli. It is as it is because it has always been
that way: fixed, rigid and unyielding. That which has been
found to work in the past is relied upon, even though it may
no longer be appropriate or relevant to the life plan. The result can be the negative manifestation of energies which were
once positive.

A client in her mid-thirties complained that she was always being offered – and accepting – top level, high-powered
management jobs which entailed jetting around the world and
taking ruthless decisions (South Node in Aries in the eleventh
house), when all she really wanted to do was settle down, preferably within a relationship, and apply her considerable but
unexplored artistic talents to the development of a mystical

tarot pack (North Node in Libra conjunct Neptune in the fifth house). The aggressively assertive quality of her South Node in Aries, which she had carried over from previous male lives, had been helpful to her in reaching the top of her profession. However, the constant repetition of the South Node pattern was stultifying her growth and interfering with the development of her Libra North Node potential for harmony, beauty and creative relationships.

When challenged by circumstances which demand change, the incarnating soul's initial reaction is to retreat into what is known and familiar – the South Node. However, the relentless inner pressure of the North Node towards growth into new modes of behaviour insists upon modification of the old inbuilt pattern. The predisposition towards instinctive behaviour eventually comes to be recognised as a block on progress, and the potential for change is acknowledged.

It is at this point that the energies of the North Node can begin to manifest, awkwardly at first, but gaining in competence as attunement to the karmic purpose progresses and old fears and inhibitions are left behind. The relapses which may occur from time to time are not necessarily detrimental to progress; a falling back into old patterns may initially feel comfortable and give temporary respite from the struggle. It is also an opportunity to reconnect to the positive qualities of the South Node, and qualities that can be taken into the future. Not everything has to be left behind as evolution progresses. The impetus towards transformation is renewed when the old patterns are suddenly experienced as confining and suffocating, and the resultant surge of growth heralds a new stage of evolution with all its attendant possibilities. Tracy Marks says: 'The nodal axis is like an alchemical factory through which we are capable of transforming the raw material of past lives and deeply ingrained behaviours into new sources of energy.' Change is of course never easy, but those who follow willingly find the way smoother than those who resist every step of the way.

It must be remembered that the nodal axis is an exact opposition and that, as with all oppositions, there are several approaches to working with the opposing nodal energies. One way is to allow the conflicting pull from each end to indiscriminately tear the structure of life apart, swinging wildly from one extreme to the other as each Node has its brief, transit-induced moment of power. Or, slightly less destructive, living out each end in totally unconnected compartments of life. The second approach is a variation on the same theme, living out one end, usually the South Node, and rigidly excluding and repressing the other. In both these approaches the flaw is in experiencing the 'ends' as disparate, and having no connection or flow other than conflict between the two points. The tension embodied in an opposition aspect is dynamic, and the possibility of action, compromise and resolution is inherent within it.

If the ancient Chinese perception of the Nodes as a dragon is utilised, the North Node representing the head and the South Node the tail, then another possibility emerges, that of synthesis and integration. The positive skills and energies incorporated in the South Node can be harnessed to the growth and development of the North Node potential. And the dragon's tail can perform its function of eliminating that which is outgrown and ready to be discarded.

In the example given at the start of the chapter, the client was aged thirty-six and her second nodal return was imminent. The time was ripe to harness the courage and action of her Aries South Node to find a positive outlet for her creative energies. She located a publisher who was interested in a new tarot pack, resigned her job, moved out of a destructive relationship into a supportive one, and gave herself the time for contemplation and reflection which formed the basis of her spiritually orientated designs for the new pack.

Moving into the North Node mode and attuning to the karmic purpose brings about a profound change in orientation, a major shift having been made from unconscious response to conscious choice. The soul no longer feels helpless, powerless, at the mercy of external forces. Awareness brings change. Change is empowering and creates new possibilities. The choice to respond to life in accordance with the karmic purpose provides inner fulfilment and a sense of integration and harmony.

There are many levels of meaning and experience within

the lunar Nodes and the house and sign placements must be synthesised to reach the core. The sign in which a Node is placed will indicate how the energies will operate, and the house where the energies will operate. For example, the energy embodied in a Cancer North Node is one of nurturing. In the fourth house that energy will manifest in the home and with children. In the twelfth house however, it will manifest on the collective level, perhaps through working in some kind of institution. All the different levels are a valid way of experiencing karma and can be perceived as a spiral leading from the superficial to the profound. During the course of a life, or a series of lives, it is possible to move between the levels many times whilst travelling to the core. Even those who are fortunate enough to attune to their ultimate purpose early in an incarnation will explore the multilayered Node in all its manifestations.

The following is intended as a brief guide to the behaviour patterns, both inherent and potential, of the lunar axis. House and sign placements need to be integrated in order to reach the deepest understanding of the karmic purpose:

THE NODES IN SIGNS AND HOUSES

North Node: Aries/First House
South Node: Libra/Seventh House
Karmic purpose: to develop the Self unselfishly
The primary aim for the Aries and/or first house North Node is to develop the Self and its own unique individuality, projecting this out through the sign on the Ascendant and/or the house and sign in which it is placed. The danger is that the new behaviour pattern may be egocentric and wilful, aware only of the needs of 'Me', although learning to be selfish may be a step on the path to being centred in the Self.

The past pattern indicated by the Libra and/or seventh house South Node is too much adjustment and compromise in meeting the needs of others, the incarnating soul always putting itself aside in relationships and being too easily influenced by what 'they' want. It lacks the confidence to accept its own fundamental need and right to develop as an individual, receiving validation from its interaction with another rather than from its own internal source of power (the Self). The Libra South Node often believes that to be good is preferable to being true to itself, and may retreat into people pleasing and a kind of lethal 'niceness' that is not at all to be trusted:

The Price of Nice

'Nice' behaviour eventually has a 'price' for both the 'nice guy' and the other person or persons involved. It is alienating, indirectly hostile and self-destructive because:

The 'nice guy' tends to create an atmosphere such that others avoid giving him or her honest, genuine feedback. This blocks emotional growth.

'Nice' behaviour will ultimately be distrusted by others. That is, it generates a sense of uncertainty and lack of safety in others, who can never be sure if they will be supported by the 'nice guy' in a crisis situation that requires an aggressive confrontation with others.

'Nice guys' stifle the growth of others. They avoid giving others genuine feedback, and they deprive others of a real person to assert against. This tends to force others in the relationship to turn their aggression against themselves. It also tends to generate guilt and depressed feelings in others who are intimately involved and dependent on the 'nice guy'.

Because of the chronic 'niceness', others can never be certain if the relationship with a 'nice guy' could endure a conflict or sustain an angry confrontation if it occurred spontaneously. This places great limits on the potential extent of intimacy in the relationship by placing others constantly on their guard.

'Nice' behaviour is not reliable. Periodically the 'nice' person explodes in unexpected rage and those involved are shocked and unprepared to cope with it.

The 'nice guy', by holding aggression in, may pay a physiological price in the form of psychosomatic problems and a psychological price in the form of alienation.

'Nice' behaviour is emotionally unreal behaviour. It puts severe limitation on all relationships, and the ultimate victim is the 'nice person'.

(source unknown)

The pattern of compromise and adjustment begins early in life and is particularly expressed through the parental relationship. One client reported that her first house North Node had tried to manifest early and that, as a small child, her constant cry had been 'I onts' ('I want'). Needless to say, she did not get what she wanted. Any aspiration to individuality and independence were firmly quashed by a mother who thought she 'knew best'. Her seventh house South Node pattern quickly came to the fore: 'Whatever you want, I'll be a good girl', she whimpered. It took the client another forty years to accept that she had her own rights, and several more before she felt comfortable about asserting her needs – a period which corresponded to the transiting North Node conjuncting her South Node and stimulating the integration of the nodal axis.

The development of the Aries and/or first house North Node may entail facing difficulties within a relationship as the partner or parent is thwarted by the unexpected refusal to gratify every whim. The demands tend to be increased as the partner meets opposition and believes that, if enough pressure is applied, the newly emerging autonomous being will cave in and the compliant status quo will be restored. All the Aries will, energy and courage are called for at this point. Self-assertion classes, martial arts or other means of channelling the Aries or Mars energy can be helpful and supportive. The incarnating soul at this time seeks constant reassurance that it really is 'OK' for it to assert itself and that it is now time for others to adapt to the changes taking place. In this situation group therapy or a self-help group can provide the support family or friends could be unwilling or unable to give owing to an unacknowledged conflict of interest. The Libra South Node ability to find balance and harmonise with others can be used to smooth the way to an expression of personal competence and power.

North Node: Libra/Seventh House
South Node: Aries/First House
Karmic purpose: to relate harmoniously to oneself and others

The karmic purpose of the Libra and/or seventh house North Node is to enter into relationship with the Self and to develop the ability to relate to others and to adapt as appropriate to external needs, rather than slavishly follow its own internal demands to the exclusion of all others. In other words, it has to learn the art of creative compromise.

Work will be needed to overcome the inherent wilfulness and self-centredness of the Aries South Node, and to see beyond the confines of individual needs. For this Node the demands of 'Me' have been of paramount importance, the individual believing that he or she alone is right and has the answers. An unconscious Aries South Node is arrogant and bombastic, its most used word 'I'. An aspiring politician (Ascendant conjunct Sun and South Node in Aries) said: 'Of course I will be elected', 'I know what they need', 'I've told them …', 'I can give them …', 'When I'm elected I'm going to …' etc., etc. He never stopped to listen to his prospective voters, and only ever told them what he could do for them. He was most surprised when he failed to get elected.

Learning to listen to others is the first step in becoming more open to the Libra North Node. Gradually an acceptance of wider needs and aspirations will develop, together with the ability to co-operate within a group to achieve common aims.

The aspiring politician, following his initial defeat, went to talk to a sixth-form college. After his carefully scripted opening remarks, even he could not fail to notice a certain restlessness among his young audience. He had the courage (Aries) to stop and ask them what was wrong. He was told: 'You are just like everyone else, talking at us. You don't care what we think or even what we want to know about.' He threw away his speech and opened up to questions. He learnt a lot from that confrontation and changed his approach, knocking on doors and asking: 'What can I do for you?' He was not elected the next time around, but it was close run. He continued to work for his prospective constituents, moving more and more into his Libra North Node and channelling all the courage and drive of the Aries South Node into fighting the local council on their behalf on a number of controversial issues.

It is within the field of personal relationships that the Aries South Node takes its worst toll, and the Libra North Node offers its greatest rewards. An understanding of 'Us' brings a closeness and companionship which the ivory tower of the Aries South Node has never before known.

For the seventh house Node (North or South) in particular, the soul may find that personal relationships are also the place for meeting old karmic associates and for striving to balance what has gone before. With the South Node, relationships may frequently be a re-run and it may take an extreme effort of will and determination to move out of an old, self-immolating pattern of relating. North Nodal relationships will be a particular focus for growth based not only on retribution or reparation for old wrongs but also on the development of loving harmony with another person as the North Node learns that two individual entities can come together to make a third whole - a relationship. Individuality is not sacrificed or repressed, it is brought into the relationship and offered, together with love and respect for the individual it is meeting. The two come together in integration and co-operation to form a harmonious partnership which allows for individual and joint growth.

North Node: Taurus/Second House
South Node: Scorpio/Eighth House
Karmic purpose: to find inner security

The North Node in Taurus and/or the second house indicates that the soul must develop the ability to live within the body, utilising its own resources to develop inner security rather than relying on others, possessions or the past to provide roots. It has to become centred within its own eternal being, the only kind of security that can be taken out of the world at death.

There is a need to move away from the manipulative, power-based emotional games of the Scorpio South Node and to free itself from the jealousies and possessiveness that arise out of insecurity. The past for the Scorpio South Node is full of resentment, trauma and upheaval, and the resultant suspicion and caution when it is faced with something new can make growth a time of drama and crisis. The Taurus North Node needs to experience the safety of feeling itself unfolding in tune with its own inner, inbuilt rhythm of evolution. It must learn that steady progress based on the slow accumulation of intangible resources such as stability and patience can lead to growth.

Taurus is an earth-based, practical sign and as such the North Node also needs to deal in tangible assets. The incarnating soul has to utilise the senses when interacting with the environment, in contrast to the Scorpio South Node which feeds on emotional interaction. Taurus needs to experience the unity between body and Self, to take pleasure in sensual rather than sexual contact. It has to be self-sufficient on all levels.

One client, who had a flourishing professional practice, was nevertheless terrified that her marriage was over despite the fact that she had hardly seen her husband for many years. Indeed, the setting up of her practice and the satisfaction of her Taurean North Node demands for self-sufficiency had meant that they had to live in separate countries most of the time. With the Scorpio South Node, however, she found it difficult to let go of the apparent and illusory security of the marriage. Moreover, she felt that as a divorced woman she would not have the same status and assets she enjoyed as a married woman, despite the fact that, on a purely materialistic level, she was well able to provide for herself. She also discovered that she had secretly rather enjoyed the Scorpionic games they had played with each other – lovers, fights, reconciliations, etc. As actress Sheila Steafel put it: 'Alone you miss the adrenaline of a bad relationship – there's nothing to complain about.'

Taurus, however, is rooted in survival, and that Scorpio South Node knows from way back that it has been down in the pit not once but many times, and survived. From there it has brought back insights and endurance available to very few people - resources which the Taurus North Node can apply to growing and everyday living.

North Node: Scorpio/Eighth House
South Node: Taurus/Second House
Karmic purpose: to regenerate

The Scorpio and/or eighth house North Node soul learns to share its own unique insights and resources with others. This is not a nodal placement that can be taken superficially; it penetrates where others fear to tread as it explores both the heights and depths of consciousness to bring back insights for the benefit of others. This nodal placement explores the dark side of the eighth house 'birth, death and rebirth' cycle. It is usual for the eighth house North Node to undergo several significant 'deaths' and new beginnings during the course of a lifetime as the quest for regeneration continues. The sensuality of the Taurus South Node can be used as a way of communing and sharing emotionally with another, leading the way into the intensity of the Scorpio North Node relationship. Many power issues will be raised and must be worked through before the regenerative energies can be freed. There is a need to overcome material possessiveness and to move beyond obtaining emotional security from possessions (Taurus South Node) in order to learn to share oneself fully with another.

A uniquely honest, penetrating and loving relationship is possible for the Scorpio North Node brave enough to open its heart to another. However, few souls with a Taurus or eighth house Node, whether North or South, can resist the temptation to look back longingly to the past and what might have been, or forward to the future and what might be, yet such a behaviour pattern does not express any dissatisfaction: Scorpio likes a little fantasy to add spice to life but will be genuinely bewildered if its partner expresses jealousy as a result.

The tendency to cling to what might have been is illustrated by a North Node in Aries in the eighth house. A man, then in his early thirties, met a woman whom he had known briefly years before. They went for a drink: 'I caught hold of her hand to help her cross the road and that was it, I just never let go again. There was an electric current between us.' His North Node conjoined her Sun and his Libra South Node conjoined her Neptune. The 'affair' was never consummated despite the fact that he 'could hardly keep his hands off her'.

He was unable to move from the sensuality of the South Node into the sexuality of the Aries eighth house North Node. Both were married to other people, and both had sexual problems within the marriage. They discussed living together and eventually, after four years, he left his wife: 'Someone had to make the first move.' (Aries Node beginning to manifest.) However, she never left her husband and the affair finally ended after another four years and much vacillation on both parts. In the meantime every new relationship he started ended as soon as it became sexual. He explained that it wasn't fair to the new woman, as his lady friend might decide to come to him. The beautiful illusion of the Neptune conjunct the South Node lasted longer than most, reinforced by the attraction of the Sun conjunct the North Node but he never managed to manifest the potential for a 'real' relationship.

Scorpio is on the path of self mastery. In esoteric astrology it is the Avatar who comes to bring spiritual knowledge. Part of Scorpio's challenge is to master the urges of the instinctual nature and fuse them with the spiritual self. This brings about a profound recognition of the soul's immortality and the spiritual responsibilities it engenders.

The eighth house North Node has far deeper and older links with the creative cycle than may appear on the surface. This is also the house of levels of consciousness and awareness, and there is a corresponding ability to go higher than anyone else as well as lower. There is a correlation with the old mystery religions and their deep understanding of the underlying cycles, seasons and forces of creativity. The North Node in the eighth house often denotes the artist, medium or mystic with access to different higher levels of consciousness, and sexual encounters can also lead to expanded levels of awareness.

The eighth house Node (North or South) can also lead to karmic sexual encounters. A man (eighth house North Node, Sun in Scorpio) met a woman (seventh house South Node) on a Greek island. He stood holding her beneath an olive tree, that age-old symbol of fertility, by an ancient church. There was no sexual contact and yet: 'A spontaneous cosmic super-orgasm occurred. Two beings fused together on all levels and reaching a point where past, present and future held no meaning. It was all Now, total awareness, total expansion. We were the cosmos.' His Libra conjunction of Neptune/Mercury/South Node was conjunct her Venus. They had worked the old Mysteries together many times before.

North Node: Gemini/Third House
South Node: Sagittarius/Ninth House
Karmic purpose: to communicate

The Gemini and/or third house North Node desires to develop the ability to communicate what it is, rather than what it believes in. The Sagittarian South Node has, in the past, developed a set of principles or ideals to live by and has available a wider vision which could be used to process information, to see beyond 'the facts' and to develop the intellect and mental abilities as a way of perceiving the world. However, the ideals of the Sagittarius South Node may be of the 'blind faith' persuasion, and the Gemini North Node needs to use the intellect to re-examine whether the precepts by which it now lives are really meaningful and in accord with what it has experienced. In the past Sagittarius has acquired knowledge, now Gemini must bring it into real life.

There is a duality about both the Sagittarius and Gemini Nodes which can lead to a 'double' life based on the nodal contradictions. A very old and experienced occultist had the North Node in Gemini in the third house. Outwardly she led a highly respectable, upper-class life; inwardly she was a high priestess. She wrote popular fiction under a pseudonym, serious works under her own name. Her nonfiction work on occult and mystical matters betrayed the deep knowledge which came from years of magical working. And yet she would not allow the autobiographical account of her occult life to be published while she was alive, or for several years after her death 'for fear of upsetting my conventional family'. She privately complained that she did not receive the public recognition to which her work entitled her, but what she did not recognise was that her own ambiguity and inherent contradiction, evident in the half-public, half-hidden airing of her knowledge, prevented acknowledgement of her contribution to modern occult understanding. Interestingly, her major impact, especially after her death, was overseas. There she was valued as an extremely wise women indeed – her ninth house Node being valued in a far country rather than closer to home, the third house.

Another facet of the Gemini and/or third house Node is that karma may be confronted through, or with, a sibling. The position of Mercury and its aspects in the chart will provide a clue as to the area of life in which this will manifest. For example, a Mars-Mercury conjunction in the fourth house, with an opposition to Saturn and an inconjunct (quincunx) to the third house North Node, indicated a long-standing rivalry between souls who had been born in this incarnation as twin boys. It manifested in the present life as a constant battle for their mother's attention and an inability to concentrate in school, with consequent disruptive behaviour. Separate schools proved helpful in allowing each of the boys to express himself as a separate personality and eventually they learnt to live in harmony with each other.

North Node: Sagittarius/Ninth House
South Node: Gemini/Third House
Karmic purpose: to seek meaning

The Sagittarius and/or ninth house North Node seeks principles to live by and asks the ultimate questions of life: 'Why are we here?', 'Who am I?', 'What does this mean?'. It synthesises information and makes great leaps of intuition to give meaning and purpose to life, but rarely stops questioning. It is an eternal quest.

The ninth house and/or Sagittarius North Node indicates the natural philosopher of the zodiac and the soul with this placement is drawn towards the religious, spiritual and metaphysical areas of life. It frequently travels long distances, both physically and mentally, in its search for truth and meaning. Rarely is anything taken at face value; knowledge is esteemed, as are morals and principles, not just for its own sake, but because it gives underlying structure and pattern to life. Life itself is often perceived as a giant mandala.

The South Node in Gemini can retreat into superficiality, busily gathering information and facts, rather than face the implications of the knowledge they impart. Knowledge brings responsibility and the need to live it, not just to believe. The Gemini South Node soul is not always ready to take the enormous evolutionary step forward into being what it believes. One becomes truly what one is when moving into the Sagittarius North Node. In doing so, one becomes a co-creator: '.....the birthright given each soul is that it may know itself to be itself and by choice become one with the Creator.' (Cayce, Reading No. 2571-1)

There may be karma to overcome with the ninth house North Node from having preached in the past rather than teaching by example – through Being – or from having been overzealous in carrying out religious duty, rather than attending to the meaning behind it. St. Paul placed 'faith', defined in the dictionary as 'spiritual apprehension of divine truth apart from proof', above 'works' in the hierarchy of desirable spiritual qualities. The Sagittarian North Node has to bring out inbuilt faith based on knowing rather than belief. A Benedictine monk, a fervent convert to the Catholic faith (ninth house North Node) was sent out of the monastery and back into the world by his fellow brothers 'in order that he could round himself out as a person by experience of living'. For him, blind faith was not enough.

North Node: Cancer/Fourth House
South Node: Capricorn/Tenth House
Karmic purpose: to nurture
The development of the nurturing capacity and emotional give-and-take is vital for the Cancer and/or fourth house North Node. The Capricorn South Node has an ingrained, restrictive, 'tightfisted' attitude to emotional giving, and a judgmental attitude based on an external locus of control (all the authority voices from the past whenever that might have been). 'Somebody out there' provides the authority, not the Self. With this placement, the soul is extremely uncomfortable with emotion and has not learnt how to provide emotional support, although it will probably be most proficient at providing the physical/materialistic necessities. When threatened, the Capricorn South Node can retreat into a strict, authoritarian 'Thou Shalt/

Shalt Not' type of response, and allow no opposition or inter-ference. A father (Saturn-Sun conjunct South Node in Capricorn) took out a court injunction against his sixteen-year-old son (fourth house Capricorn Chiron-North Node opposing tenth house Uranus-South Node in Cancer) to have him re-moved from the family home. His submission was that as the boy refused to remain a strict vegetarian, in accordance with the father's rules, he was no longer part of the family.

The disciplinary skills which the Capricorn South Node has developed in the past can be harnessed in a constructive way to the soul developing the ability to take a caring respon-sibility for itself and its family. 'Rules' could become a code of conduct which is based on an internal locus of control, the inward voice of the Self providing guidance and direction. And the inner strengths of Capricorn which include self-discipline, self-reliance and authority could be utilised towards the devel-opment of the Self and the expression of its loving energies.

With the Cancer North Node the soul has the potential to learn not only to mother, the traditional Cancer role, but also to move beyond this into nurturing both itself and a family in the widest sense of the word, supplying food and nourishment for the soul as well as the body. This arises from an intake and outpouring of love which is supportive and growth-inducing, not smothering as Cancer love can so often be in its all-embrac-ing relentless grip. It is rather like breathing. Spiritual nourishment is taken in from the cosmos, and breathed out as a gently nurturing cloud to fall wherever it is needed. Elisabeth Kubler-Ross had the North Node in Cancer (fifth house). No one who listened to her could doubt that she lived and breathed disciplined love. Her fifth house Node provided a creative outlet for her unique nurturing qualities through her patients, books, tapes and workshops. In *Death, the Final Stage of Growth* she provides a perfect example of the synthesis of the Capri-corn-Cancer, fifth-eleventh house Nodes:

> Humankind will survive only through the commitment and
> involvement of individuals in their own and others' growth and
> development as human beings. This means development of
> loving and caring relationships... You can become a channel and
> a source of great inner strength. [You must give up] all that is

not truly you, all that you have chosen without choosing and value without evaluating, accepting because of someone else's extrinsic judgement, rather than your own ... [You will gain] your own, true self; a self who is at peace, who is able to truly love and be loved, and who understands who and what (s)he is meant for.[1]

Karma may be experienced by the Cancer and/or fourth house Node through the family. It can be seen in placements where there is a difficult family relationship or family stress, or where there is a disabled child to be cared for. Planets, and aspects to those planets in the fourth house will further delineate the karmic patterns involved.

The wife of the Capricorn father mentioned above had Saturn conjunct South Node in Libra (fourth house), closely conjunct her son's Neptune-Mars conjunction. She saw her role as keeping the family together at all costs and providing a buffer between her children and her husband. She could not move out of her Libra South Node. Many years later she was able to obtain a divorce, but was unable to adapt to the situation as she felt she had no role in life. She believed that the karmic tensions in the family situation had not been worked out because of her husband's refusal to grow or change in any way. It would appear that her fears may well be justified and there may be a need for the family to continue to try to work out the old patterns in another incarnation. However, it will also be necessary for this woman to move into her Aries North Node in order that her own growth may proceed. She also has the choice to step into Grace: to let go the past and move on, freed from the karmic round.

North Node: Capricorn/Tenth House
South Node: Cancer/Fourth House
Karmic purpose: to gain authority

The karmic lesson for the Capricorn North Node is to control the excessive emotionality and possessiveness of the Cancer South Node in order to develop self-discipline and a corresponding authority in the outer world.

Cancer and the fourth house are concerned with the inner world of dependency and vulnerable emotions, Capricorn and the tenth house with the outer world of achievement and self-sufficiency. The Capricorn North Node seeks success through a career. From a secure material foundation an inner spiritual strength develops. Capricorn has to find within itself self-reliance, self-control, and its own autonomous Being. It can then contain and channel the nurturing capacity of the Cancer South Node and express this to the world in an ordered, disciplined flow. As a part of this process the Capricorn Node may take on the role of the 'scapegoat', one who suffers for, or on whom fall, the 'ills of the world'. This may be a part of the process of alleviating the collective karma of mankind, but it is approached in a less 'unthinkingly sacrificial' way than that of the Pisces and/or twelfth house Node. There is always the sense, with Capricorn, of deliberation before action, of weighing up all that is involved prior to incarnation, and then acting with commitment to the course decided upon. This was particularly noticeable in a client who had contracted Aids and felt that he was thereby partaking in a cleansing of the planetary energy, a choice that he took seriously and believed he had made prior to incarnation. He spoke of himself as a scapegoat, not in self-pity, but as a positive force for good.

On a deeper level the Cancer-Capricorn, or fourth-tenth house nodal axis is concerned with the integration of the male and female cosmic energies. The Earth Mother, boundless in her giving, has to unite with the stern Father-God to soften his heart with love so that together they will find an outlet for the universal love energy: just enough control and just enough free will to provide optimum conditions for growth. To reach this goal may involve exploration of the inner world of the psyche, of the archetypal energies invoked by the words 'Father', 'Mother', 'God', and of the anima-animus principles. These energies need to be recovered into consciousness and re-integrated into the Self in order to achieve wholeness. Psychoanalysis can be undertaken for many years in order to penetrate the core meaning to the Self of these archetypes and to attune to the energies they invoke. However, the language of the subconscious mind – the temporary abode of these energies whilst the soul is in incarnation – is symbolic and it is possible to remove 'negative conditioning' and replace it with a powerful attunement to these energies through the use of symbolism, imaging and affirmations.

Phyllis Krystal, in her book and tape *Cutting the Ties that Bind*, provides useful exercises for attuning to the cosmic parents and experiencing the balancing of these energies on the inner levels, and for nurturing the inner child – who may be a remnant of the Cancer South Node. She points out that 'unless the subconscious mind is impressed, no changes can be made in a person's life, no matter how much he may consciously desire to change and evolve'. A way through to the resolution of the Cancer- Capricorn nodal axis is offered:

> A major part of our work involves cutting the cords or ties connecting us to anything or anyone in whom we place our trust and which therefore become gods for us. Because these lesser gods are impermanent and can be taken from us, they are unreliable as a source of security. It is not important whether these bonds were forged by love, need, pity, fear, hate or any other emotion [Cancer South Node]. What is important is that they have the power to keep us dependent on the things to which they attach us instead of on the high C (Higher Consciousness)... When a human being is willing to reach up in consciousness to make contact with the indwelling source of wisdom and healing, his work [Capricorn North Node], whatever its nature, is necessarily refined and strengthened as it is raised beyond the domination of the ego.[2]

The integration of the male-female nodal energies takes the traveller a very long step on the evolutionary pathway towards wholeness and enlightenment.

North Node: Leo/Fifth House
South Node: Aquarius/Eleventh House
Karmic purpose: to be self-empowered
The impetus for the Leo and/or fifth house North Node is towards using its own power creatively, rather than operating through collective power (Aquarian South Node), and thereby to solve the head-heart dilemma.

The soul with the South Node in Aquarius sees power as belonging to the group or collective. It purports to have the detached perspective of love and power without emotion, operating from the head. Yet Aquarius can be one of the most emotionally motivated signs – although it is frequently cut off from awareness of that motivation, particularly when exhibiting an unconscious South Node reaction. Aquarius is prone to living in the head rather than using it, as it can inhabit a world of fancifulness. Greta Garbo was perhaps as well known for wanting to be alone as for her acting ability. Her Aquarian South Node is in the tenth house, representing her interaction with the outer world. She is quoted as saying: 'Even when I was a tiny girl, I preferred being alone... I could give my imagination free reign and live in a world of lovely dreams.'[3] And yet, through her Leo North Node, she was capable of portraying deep emotions so vividly that her audience were caught up and carried along with her, totally believing in the make-believe reality (Aquarian South Node) she was creating.

Aquarian detachment is frequently 'not-in-touchness' rather than impartiality. One of the dictionary definitions of detachment is 'selfish isolation' and this is a useful interpretation of the space inhabited by the unconscious Aquarian South Node. The conscious Aquarian South Node has a deep, universal love for humanity in the abstract, but the incarnating soul may find it difficult to apply this feeling in a one-to-one interaction. It may be too involved in solving the wider world issues to deal with the problem on its own doorstep. The Leo North Node can draw on this universal love and wider awareness, and refine and channel it to a point of focus.

Leo is connected with the heart, and the Leo North Node is impelled towards communicating itself through the heart energy. Part of Leo's purpose is to open both the heart and the higher-heart chakras. Loving, and keeping the heart open, no matter what. Used with love, power becomes empowerment. Recognition of the link between love and power, and taking back the projection of power from outside itself, is necessary in order for the soul to own its power. Until power has been retrieved from the external object on to which it has been projected, it cannot be internalised as one's own.

Power is an emotive word, wrongly associated with ego, manipulation and exploitation. And it can easily become this if we are not in touch with the higher purpose of power. True

power is inner authority, clarity, and total freedom. To be in touch
with power we have to be 'centred', a state when all of our being is aligned in balance... The state of being centred is one of
being connected to the universal forces and is essential for true
power to manifest. To be centred is to be powerful ...[4]

The Leo-Aquarius nodal axis encompasses one of the
most difficult dilemmas to resolve, that of the head versus the
heart, raising the questions: 'Do I do what I think is right
(Aquarius) or what I feel is right (Leo)?', 'Do I follow the con-
ventions of logic, upbringing and society, or do I act in
accordance with my instincts?', 'How do I move from an involuntary emotional response to one which I know will
promote my growth and well-being?', 'How do I operate from
a base of love without falling into the trap of mushy sentimentality?'.

The answer is found in the integration of the collective
with the personal, the Nodes becoming the focal point for universal love directed through the individual. St. Augustine
taught 'Love God, and do as you will'. When will, power and
love are aligned to the personal expression of the cosmic Self,
the dilemma is resolved; head and heart become one.

North Node: Aquarius/Eleventh House
South Node: Leo/Fifth House
Karmic purpose: to channel collective power
with foresight

The soul with the Aquarius and/or eleventh house North Node
must give of itself freely to humanity, working with the collective rather than exercising personal power. The Leo South
Node has already become competent in the exercise of its own
power and now that power must be aligned to the generic
purpose. There is a need to work through interaction with others for the common good.

An unconscious Leo South Node may become involved
in domination and power struggles, trying to take egocentric
control of the group with which it is working, and may share
the Orwellian 1984 view of 'real power' as 'power over men',
and perhaps extending as far as the Pluto-Mercury-Mars-
Saturn destructive power impulse: 'Power is in inflicting pain

and humiliation. Power is in tearing human minds to pieces and putting them together again in new shapes of your own choosing'.

In the past the Leo South Node has been the leader, 'the king'. 'Come to me' is now its innate response to life. It tends towards individualism and needs to learn that interdepend–ence is not weakness, that co-operation is not debilitating, that accord is not impotence. It will still lead as that antipodal Aquarian energy is always one step ahead, but when the Leo South Node energies are consciously utilised, benign autocracy is transformed into democracy.

The Aquarian North Node progresses towards a compre-hension of equality and coexistence founded on each member of the group contributing according to his abilities and poten-tial. Equality in this context does not mean uniformity, there is an acceptance and appreciation of individual difference which allows each one to develop and grow in accordance with one's own unique pathway. It is not, however, an insular pas-sage, progress is aligned to the group ideals and purpose. Coexistence is based on an appreciation of the parity of mu-tual essence – humanity. The whole of humankind is the extended family of the Aquarian North Node and its concern is for the progress and well-being of all. With the Leo South Node the soul is its own unique creation, the time has now ar-rived to offer that creation up as a part of the greater whole.

The Trappist monk and mystic Thomas Merton had the North Node in Aquarius in the fifth house (conjunct Mercury and Jupiter) and the South Node in Leo in the eleventh house (a reversed nodal placement). The conjunction of Mercury-Jupiter to the North Node in the fifth house demanded to be heard and, despite his vow of silence, be became a writer on mysticism and monasticism. Towards the end of his life he became concerned with Aquarian issues such as 'racial dis-crimination, the threat of nuclear war, the 'God-is-dead Movement' and with Catholic renewal.'[5] Suzanne Lilley-Harvey, in an article on Merton, summed up the man:

Thomas Merton ... was a man whose life was a living parable of [the] attempt to awaken and to find his purpose which was both individual and universal. He was a man who ... was attempting to achieve self-mastery over the lower desires and to give birth to the divine principle within himself ...During the latter part of his life he became known for his ecumenical views on religion and his active cultivation of universal tolerance for, and interest in the truth in all religions makes him in many ways a kind of harbinger of the Aquarian Age ... his gaze out towards the world again but centred in a new and illumined identity, whereas earlier he ran from the world and its intoxicating ways, he now embraced suffering mankind and the problems of the world. This is characteristic of the 'evolved' Aquarian who derives his sense of ego from an identification with the collective ... Throughout Thomas Merton's life and work the theme of unity winds its way to a resounding chorus: the unity of man with God and of man with man. And the interior resolution of the freedom versus responsibility dilemma [a Leo-Aquarius nodal dichotomy] was his most urgent need and goal.[6]

Merton himself wrote: 'God leaves us free to be whatever we like. We can be ourselves or not, as we please. We are at liberty to be real, or to be unreal ...But we cannot make these choices with impunity. Causes have effects.'[7]

North Node: Virgo/Sixth House
South Node: Pisces/Twelfth House
Karmic purpose: to serve with love

The Virgo and/or sixth house North Node calls for discriminating service to humanity as a way of expressing an inner attunement to 'divine' love. The soul with this placement does whatever is required of it, because it loves unconditionally. 'It's not how much you do, but how much love you put into the doing' (Mother Teresa, Sun in Virgo)[8].

All too often the Virgo Node, North and South, gets mired in a rut of servitude and obsequiousness, stuck with the 'dirty jobs' in life. This can manifest on many levels, Virgo can function as the hatchet man just as often as the janitor. One client summed up her nursing job as 'dirty, degrading and disgusting. We are the shit-shovellers of Daffodil ward'. She felt no connection with those she 'served', no pity or compassion for their pain, no instinct towards brightening their day. By contrast another client (Virgo North Node, tenth house), matron of an old people's home said: 'Everything we do is an expression of our love, nothing is distasteful, we have fun and laughter, we are a family.' She had developed the compassion and empathy which her Pisces South Node had brought forward from the past, together with a very real connection to 'divine love', and expressed this through her Virgo North Node as service which was an inner state of being.

The unconscious Pisces South Node has many negative patterns. This is the archetypal saviour-rescuer-victim- martyr, constantly pulled back into trying to save a person, or the world, and quickly finding itself yet again a victim or martyr. It can express sympathy but tends to wallow in another's suffering or pain, lacking the detachment of compassion which creates space for objective help. It is capable of great self-sacrifice but all too easily falls into the victim-martyr-saviour pattern. Its most oft-repeated cry from the heart is: 'I did it all for you.' It sees virtue in vicarious suffering and self-immolation, but never verifies whether the sacrifice is appropriate or growth-inducing. Indeed, such sacrifices can be deeply inhibiting for the development of the recipient, who can become the victim as guilt is a common by-product of the Pisces South Node oblation. Piscean guilt is all-pervasive, and those self-effacing individuals who feel they have no right to be alive are a good illustration of it. They perform constant acts of reparation under the name of service in order to validate their very existence. True altruism is a rare commodity but it is the positive expression of a well-developed Virgo North Node.

One of the most common manifestations of the unconscious Pisces South Node and its connection with 'family karma' is the mother who gives up everything for the sake of her children, and then tries to live out her own unfulfilled dreams through subtle manipulation of those children. An obsessively religious mother (twelfth house Cancer South Node), married late in life, gave up her much loved nursing career to care for three children and an alcoholic husband who quickly developed throat cancer. Her husband died when the children were young and she had to integrate her Cancer-Capricorn nodal energies by taking on the role of mother and father, and supporting the family. However, her unconscious sixth-twelfth house nodal axis pervaded and influenced the family. 'After all I've done for you' was her constant theme. Her eldest son (second house Libra South Node) became a doctor, against the advice of his school who said he was manifestly unsuitable as he disliked people; her daughter (fourth house Pisces North Node) became a nurse and felt 'called by God' (or Mother?) to devote herself to the under privileged; her other son (twelfth house Capricorn North Node) lived with his mother and worked at home, but felt a pull to the priesthood.

The sixth house North Node may also have to face karma through health and work. Bodily karma is indicated in the sixth house and may be a manifestation of psychosomatic causes, or a misuse or abuse of the body, carried over from previous lives. One of the lessons for the Virgo and/or sixth house North Node is to develop an understanding of the interaction of mind-body-emotions-spirit and the dis-ease that results from any disharmony. A client had the reversed nodal connection of North Node-Jupiter-Uranus in Pisces in the sixth house opposing Saturn-South Node in the twelfth. Past-life experiences with skeletal manipulation and healing had led him, unconsciously, into osteopathy where he was able to utilise these skills. He was held back by arthritis in his hands – a sign of locked-in anger, helplessness and frustration. He also presented problems of: 'herpes, over-eating, weight loss, mood changes and flatulence …obviously I am working out a lot of karma via my body …how can I shift my karmic workload into modes of expression which are not so patently self-destructive?' Among the past-life conditions which surfaced were torture, rage, unexpressed grief at the loss of a twin, religious conflict, fasting to produce hallucinations and visions, emotional frustration and a self-chosen wasting disease.

Clearly much work was needed to unlock his inner inhibitions and guilt. He had endured a difficult, emotionally conflicting and traumatic childhood and part of his problem was centred on the psychosomatic effects of a disharmony of the mind and emotions on the body which manifested as disease. Another factor was the blocked, non-flowing nature of the Pisces (and afflicted Neptune) energies within the chart, and of course within himself, which needed to be freed and expressed. His work was in a sense a reparation for that which had gone before, and he needed to move into being of true service. Liz Greene was quoted to him:

> Service, rather than 'good works' is an innate quality of the inner man. It is a state of consciousness rather than a planned act. Service of this kind is the result of inner integration, for once the body, feelings and mind of a man are in balance then he can begin to become aware, intuitively, of the purpose and nature of his inner psyche. He is no longer occupied in reconciling the battling components of his nature, but through an inner attunement ... he can listen to his real direction ... Service which is the result of inner balance is the potential of Saturn in Virgo when he is expressing in a conscious way and this placement is common among physicians, surgeons and those who tend the mental and emotional ills of others because it is a fulfilment of the inner needs of the group.[9]

An equally appropriate and apt exposition for the sixth house North Node and the Pisces-Virgo nodal axis.

North Node: Pisces/Twelfth House
South Node: Virgo/Sixth House
Karmic purpose: to attain enlightenment

The Pisces and/or twelfth house North Node explores the karmic lessons of the past on both the collective and the personal levels to attain enlightenment. It has the potential to move beyond the wheel of rebirth, to enter a state of grace and to attain release into the 'divine whole'.

The perfectionist Virgo South Node can fall back into an over-analytical, critical, judgmental mode of behaviour which restricts and inhibits the free-flowing, mystical and visionary expression of the Pisces Node. It therefore needs to develop detached, accepting, compassionate and unconditional love for all. However, the Pisces North Node has to utilise the constructive discrimination of the Virgo South Node, as otherwise it may give, or act, without thought, evaluation or restraint.

The exploration and expression of the twelfth house collective karma of humankind may involve taking on an archetypal victim, saviour or fantasy role. Film star Marilyn Monroe, whose portrayal of woman was the archetypal essence of the feminine and who was revered by many as a goddess, had a twelfth house Cancer North Node. Just how much of an illusion she projected came to light years after her death when the 'falsies' with which she endowed her cancerian bosom were auctioned. Pop star Bob Geldof, who initiated Band Aid to feed the starving millions of Africa, has a Pisces North Node in the second house. He identified the collective need, putting aside his own career (Pisces sacrificing itself) to raise money for practical aid (second house). However, when the famine crisis was repeated the next year, the scheme faced criticism and Geldof flew out to Africa to see for himself what had gone wrong. The answer to the crisis could perhaps have involved a little more practical Virgoan organisation and follow-through to aid the visionary idealism of Pisces. Band Aid became more successful in the years following as it broadened its base of operations, and was incorporated into a much bigger aid effort as time passed.

The investigation into personal karma may entail an enquiry into the hidden, darker side of life, and into the karma of the family into which it incarnates. This is the Node of hidden ancestral skeletons surfacing into the light of conscious awareness. A friend (twelfth house Sun in Scorpio conjunct North Node) was surprised when one day, having idly turned on the television, he was faced with a programme investigating the disappearance of his great-grandfather from a direct train between Scotland and London. The research had been meticulous and many details, previously unknown to the family, were brought to light.

For some twelfth house and/or Pisces North Nodes the descent into the darkness of mankind has to be faced in a very intense way. It would seem that, in order to have the prospect of release from the cycle of rebirth, some souls take on the daunting task of dealing with a 'huge chunk' of karma all at once. Much suffering may be involved, including experience of institutions and other traditional twelfth house areas of life. For many souls this includes descent into chaos, breakdown and disintegration of the old self in order to move beyond its confines towards a more esoteric level of incarnation and manifestation of the Self. For others, it may entail working with those who are undergoing the descent into madness and alienation, guiding their journey towards a new wholeness. Some evolved souls offer themselves in order that others may learn their lessons from caring for the seemingly disadvantaged and handicapped.

One brain-damaged child (reversed nodal placement, twelfth house North Node in Virgo and the sixth house South Node conjunct Sun and Mercury in Pisces) brought about a profound growth both in herself and in her parents. She unfailingly displayed love, patience and perseverance to overcome her disability, no matter how difficult and painful her life became. Her mother (tenth house Taurus North Node) developed her own healing talents through the Metamorphic Technique, applying it first to her daughter and then to a wide circle of disabled children. Mother and child became channels for unconditional love.

It is the pathway of unconditional love and the transmutation of atonement into at-one-ment with the divine which offers the Pisces North Node the opportunity to move beyond the endless round of birth, death and rebirth into a spiritual state of grace. 'Grace' is the point of karmic balance; all debts and obligations are cleared, through forgiveness or reparation. Evolution on this level of incarnation is complete, all possibilities are open.

Reversed Nodal Placement

The reverse nodal placement occurs when the sign of the Node falls in the opposite house to its natural zodiacal placement. For example, Virgo is the natural sixth house, the reverse nodal placement is a twelfth house Virgo North Node opposing a sixth house Pisces South Node. This placement indicates that the soul has already worked on both of the opposing nodal energies in the past. The purpose of incarnation now embraces a deeper integration and focused expression of the positive energies. The twelfth house Virgo North Node has, for example, to deepen its attunement with the divine (Pisces) and focus this through practical service (Virgo) to the collective. The sixth house Pisces North Node draws on its ability to channel the divine energies from the collective level and express this in everyday life and work.

A client who had the sixth-twelfth house Virgo-Pisces axis strongly emphasised in her chart, tried to live in a drifting, dreamy Piscean way but kept meeting the Virgoan need to pay the rent. She had Venus conjunct the North Node in Pisces, opposed to Saturn conjunct the South Node in Virgo and found herself 'somehow drawn back again and again into prostitution, actual and metaphorical'. However, she spent more time counselling her men about their problems than engaging in sexual intercourse. Eventually she made the transition to counsellor without the need for the intermediate stage. The unconditional love of her Pisces Node became expressed and earthed through the Virgo Node, which offered practical solutions based on a deep understanding of the psychological and spiritual malaise suffered by her clients.

The Sun or Moon in the Same Sign as the Node
In natal charts where the South Node is in the same sign as the Sun or the North Node in the same sign as the Moon, or the Sun and Moon are in the same sign, then the challenge and lesson is to do what has been done before but to do more constructively, and to develop more of the positive qualities of the sign, capitalising on the skills that have already been developed in using the energies of the sign in the past. When the Sun conjuncts the North Node, there is an urgent need to develop the positive qualities of that sign in which they are placed.

Aspects to the Nodes
Planets which conjunct the South Node are continually pulled back into old patterns and may be the source of powerful sub-personalities or dissociated complexes operating from deep within the subconscious. It is as though a facet of a previous personality had been transported whole and unchanged from another incarnation and located deep within the instinctual functioning of the present personality. From its firmly entrenched position it makes forays into consciousness, disrupting and sabotaging attempts by the developing Self to express itself more constructively through the North Node or occasionally offering a tantalising glimpse of a buried skill or asset. Saturn, for example, can indicate a very fearful, depend-

ent and depressive sub-personality, constantly inhibiting growth through its needs for safety, defensiveness and limits. There may also be a powerful inner critic or saboteur figure who wrecks any possibility of growth through its undermining internal comments and doubts, but occasionally great strength emerges in times of need. Mars may indicate an angry sub-personality who lashes out from time to time, or a courageous one which surfaces in extreme crisis only to disappear from view again when things calm down.

Mars conjunct the South Node may also be anger which is disowned and projected out into the world. A client with a first house Libra South Node-Mars conjunction was jilted by her fiance. During counselling she denied being angry about this and said she understood the cultural pressures which had led to his decision (Libra South Node bending over backwards to be 'fair' and adaptable) – he was of a different race and religion. As she said this, a very large angry wasp buzzed in through the window and circled around her head. It then got stuck in the double glazing and its loud buzzing punctuated her further denials of anger. When she went back to her bedroom, it had been invaded by a swarm of wild bees which were clearly demonstrating both her anger and her feeling of trapped helplessness within the situation.

South Node conjunctions need reworking so that the trapped energies can be released into consciousness and used constructively. That Saturn-South Node conjunction has reserves of inner strength, discipline and resilience – once the fear is released – which can be harnessed to the North Node to consolidate and structure its development. The Mars energy can be channelled into active growth, drawing on its assertiveness and courage to make changes aligned to the spiritual Will.

A client with Pluto-Mars-Moon conjunct the South Node in Cancer was regressed back to a former life in which he experienced being 'abandoned' by the death of his mother. He commented afterwards that for many years he had been aware of an 'angry child' sub-personality who needed constant reassurance. During the regression he was able to accept the child, incorporating it into his present being. After several years the powerful healing energies contained within the conjunction were released when he healed himself of cancer. He developed his ability further and became a successful healer, thereby satisfying and incorporating his Capricorn North Node.

An alcoholic had a Mercury-Neptune conjunction to his Libra South Node. He was seen as a sadhu in a past life, one who had totally withdrawn from everyday life into a permanent, drug-induced haze of disassociation and ecstasy. The escapist traits had been carried over into the present life. As a child he was two people: one bright and intelligent, the other sensitive and withdrawn. He was sent to a conventional boarding school where the emphasis was on academic achievement. He then 'chose' a highly pressured career (Aries North Node). Whenever the pressures of living became too much he escaped into his 'other self', at first into mental withdrawal, then into meditation, soft drugs and drink, finally into breakdown and benders.

As part of his recovery programme in Alcoholics Anonymous he was introduced to computers and was able to lose himself in fantasy games. Later he rediscovered his artistic talent and channelled his energies into painting bouts instead of alcoholic benders. However, he had not yet found the inner motivation to bring about an integration of the nodal axis which would have harnessed the positive, visionary qualities of Mercury-Neptune to the Aries North Node. He said that he could not face becoming that which he knew he could be. 'The alcoholic has many, many 'good reasons' for his drinking, and all of them are solidly based in Neptune. He drinks, finally, because he wants to drink, because he has to drink. And, finally, he must reach his own moment of truth, and want not to drink."[10] Ultimately, when Chiron conjoined his North Node, he was able to find this place within himself and to fulfil his enormous potential, becoming an expert in a highly innovative – and intuitive – branch of medicine.

Conjunctions to the North Node propel the incarnating soul forward into a new way of being, emphasis being placed on the planetary energies – which may be overwhelming as they manifest. A Pluto conjunction to the eighth house Leo North Node brought one client close to death on several occasions, each time bringing out her latent psychic abilities more forcefully. She found it extremely difficult to cope with her vivid psychic experiences and the pressure was such that she had to develop her ability as a medium as otherwise she 'would go mad'. As soon as she began to utilise the psychic energy the intensity of her experiences diminished and the power came under her control. Another client, with Uranus conjunct the North Node in twelfth house Libra, left England and went to live in an Israeli kibbutz 'to regain my heritage and, hopefully, to find a mate – English men are much too tame and ordinary for me'. She had, as a teenager, expressed her Uranian Node by distributing underground Jewish literature in Russia whilst masquerading as a tourist. She dismissed any hazard to herself with a shrug of the shoulders: 'It is something I have to do.'

Planets squaring the nodal axis indicate the potential for synthesis of the past and future, but the soul may experience pressure from both ends of the axis and may find this destructive, feeling literally torn in two. Uranus, for example, may offer a creative and humanitarian resolution of the nodal dilemma, or it may be disturbed and antisocial, acting out all the archaic energies inherent within the opposing forces. Trines and sextiles to the Nodes may help with the integration of the energies, but the soul will often vacillate back to the old ways.

A transit may be the trigger required to bring in a more harmonious functioning of planets and Nodes, particularly where the aspect is a close one, as the transiting energy can mediate in the natal conflict. At times, such triggers may, however, act as a brutal catalyst to resolve the seemingly unresolvable, literally propelling the soul into a new way of being through the inner dynamics of the irreconcilable opposites.

Resolution of the Nodal Dilemma

Engaging in a dialogue with the Nodes and planets aspecting and transiting the Nodes can result in an understanding of the underlying purpose, and indicate a way forward into synthesis. Attunement and alignment to the karmic purpose is a crucial stage of evolution, providing boundless energy for change. It can be achieved through fully understanding, integrating and living the nodal axis.

THE PRE-NATAL ECLIPSE

My attention was drawn to the karmic significance of pre-natal eclipses by Cornish astrologer Sue Bladon. She recommended *Spiritual Astrology*, by Jan Spiller and Karen McCoy, who had been researching the effect of eclipses on individual destiny. These eclipses are those that occur whilst we are in the womb, the ones immediately preceding our birth being the most important in their eyes. However, when I looked further into this, I found that the first eclipses, if they occur close to conception, may make such an impact that it is late in life before the lessons or gifts of the other pair make themselves felt. The solar eclipse is 'our responsibility to the collective whole', indicating our spiritual destiny and what we are here to teach. The lunar eclipse is our personal destiny, the qualities we need to integrate and the lessons we have to learn.

Pre-Birth Solar and Lunar Eclipse[11]

Aries	Solar	Teaching assertiveness, self-reliance and courage of convictions.
	Lunar	Learning to stand on own feet, develop confidence and defending own beliefs.
Taurus	Solar	Teaching prosperity consciousness and moral/spiritual values.
	Lunar	Learning to develop prosperity and using spiritual energies wisely.
Gemini	Solar	Teaching correct communication and open perception.
	Lunar	Learning how to communicate and be sociable.

Cancer	Solar	Teaching how to express emotions.
	Lunar	Learning emotional interaction.
Leo	Solar	Teaching how to accept love.
	Lunar	Learning how to accept love.
Virgo	Solar	Teaching use of analytical faculties.
	Lunar	Learning to get feet back on the ground, balancing material and spiritual worlds.
Libra	Solar	Teaching balance and harmony, especially in relationships.
	Lunar	Learning to be fair in all areas of life, and balance between giving and taking.
Scorpio	Solar	Teaching about personal responsibility and integrity.
	Lunar	Learning to realign principles and values. Working with boundaries.
Sagittarius	Solar	Teaching the common thread in all philosophies.
	Lunar	Breaking free from prejudice and finding the common thread.

Capricorn	Solar	Teaching the value of a good reputation and correct relationship to society.
	Lunar	Learning how to fit into society and maintain integrity in the outside world.
Aquarius	Solar	Teaching the lesson of dispassionate detachment and equality.
	Lunar	Learning detachment and release from possessiveness.
Pisces	Solar	Teaching empathy and sensitivity.
	Lunar	Learning to 'Let go and let God'.

BRINGING THINGS TO A HEAD

People often ask what triggers karmic intent. Many factors are involved and much depends on the urgency felt by the incarnating soul. At times a transit will give things a kickstart but at others there appears to be nothing happening in the chart. Much more subtle influences such as progressions or the effect of an eclipse are at work. No two people will respond to an astrological event in the same way *because their past experience is different.* Certain principles hold good, but within that there is individual difference. Some people respond inwardly, others outwardly through external events.

I am also asked which is the stronger factor: the Sun or the North Node. Both have to be integrated. Someone will undertake the task of their North Node in a way which reflects the energies of their sun-sign. Understanding factors such as cardinal, fixed and mutable, positive and negative, the elements and transits is undoubtedly helpful. An Aries North Node, for instance, will drag a watery or airy Sun into what may be. However, a fixed sign like Taurus or Scorpio can resist such pressure for an inordinate amount of time and may need a powerful transit to propel it into action. A watery Moon can duck and dive as it evades pressure to change – and then finds it has happened anyway. As you gain more experience you will learn instinctively to weigh up the strength of the different factors. But the best way to understand the working out of karmic intent is to study charts and correlate them with people's experiences. You can then project the results forward. Hindsight is a wonderful tool to work with. It wasn't until I had the opportunity to closely study forty years of one man's life that I recognised the role of the progressed Moon and the eclipse cycle in bringing out underlying karma and karmic potential, stimulating question that the soul must answer. It was sometime later that I saw the effect the progressed Sun could have.

Eclipses

Approximately twice a year there is an eclipse of the Sun followed fourteen days later by an eclipse of the Moon. Eclipses occur at the New and Full Moons. Due to the way eclipses are distributed around the heavens, some people will never personally feel the powerful effects they can have when transiting charts. In another chart however, the eclipses regularly trigger major karmic experiences. In studying the effect of eclipses, I was able to gain an understanding of how the 'light of consciousness' (the Sun or ego) is blotted out by the process so that the subconscious and collective forces (the Moon) are able to surface and be resolved; and conversely how the instinctual behaviours of the Moon are eclipsed so that new energies arise. Karmically this is a productive time when we can rid ourselves of ingrained attitudes, let go of the past and move forward into our future. But if we have been trying to suppress parts of our life then this can be an explosive time when things burst through. The house in which the eclipse occurs is also significant, as is any planet it aspects, or if it falls on the midpoint of two planets. If transits are taking some time to move, an eclipse will bring out the energies inherent in the natal aspects to the transited planet.

When the eclipse (or the New Moon) touches a planet,

it gives rise to questions connected to the energy of that planet*. It has the same effect on a point like the Ascendant or I.C. The I.C., for instance, represents our inner self, our foundations and our home. An eclipse at this point strips away the armour we have lived behind for years. The question asked here would be 'How might I reach my core, the essence of who I am?'. On the M.C. it would be 'What am I like out there in the world, where everyone can see me?'. If an eclipse touches Pluto it brings life and death issues to the fore and makes us question what we can eliminate from our lives, then how we can regenerate ourselves from the experience. Uranus looks at where liberation is needed, and combined with an eclipse, can act as a catalyst. Saturn looks at responsibilities that have to be taken on, and, as Lord of Karma, stimulates karmic issues; Neptune prompts us to ask how we may atone for the past, and live up to our ideals for the future., and so on according to the nature of the planet. An eclipse on the Sun always challenges us to shine our brightest.

Eclipses also have the effect of speeding up the integration of the natal Sun and Moon, and the North and South Nodes. When an eclipse stimulates the North Node, it makes us question what we need to do or learn in order to fulfil our potential. If a South Node in Leo is affected by an eclipse, for example, then it is time to move out of the personal, individual 'specialness' of Leo – and the emotional games that sign can play – and into contact with the wider arena of humanity and collective responsibility.

Surprisingly, perhaps, the primary influence of an eclipse is felt in the six months preceding the actual eclipse, foreshadowing the future. Although if it contacts a planet that influence will be felt for the following six months. So, although an eclipse may not be an immediately apparent indicator when trying to understand shifting patterns, it is extremely significant. The usual orb allowed is 2^0, but I found that $3\text{-}4^0$ contact could have a strong effect, especially if several planets are being triggered, and the influence then gradually wanes as the orb widens.

---

*   *See Tracy Marks* The Astrology of Self-Discovery.

I had first become aware of eclipses when a client had an eclipse conjunct her Sun (and transiting Chiron squaring her natal Moon-Saturn opposition). Her father had died just after her birth and her mother had been told by her father's mother to have nothing more to do with the family. On the day of the eclipse, a private investigator knocked on her maternal grandmother's door and said that he had been hired by the family to find the granddaughter, now a young woman. In the eclipse of the Moon (the mother), the solar principle (the father) had been released. Contact was not made for another fortnight however, on the day the eclipse fell on her Ascendant. Through the contact with her father's family, she was able to more fully know who she was and bring to the surface the trauma their early rejection had created.

The Progressed Moon

The progression of the Moon around the chart indicates new ways in which the instinctual energy and its karmic lessons, can be expresses and balanced. It is much more subtle than the effect of a transit, a slowly unfolding process that leads to greater purpose. It tends to attract people and situations that mirror the energy of the sign or house through which the Moon is passing and the lessons that are being learnt from that energy. By secondary progression the Moon spends approximately two and a half years in each sign – although the Moon fluctuates considerably in its motion. Obviously, when using Placidus house cusps, the amount of time the progressed Moon spends in each house varies, but by tracking it back it is possible to identify the area of life in which the Moon was most strongly felt and relate this to the sign and house position. It can also be projected into the future to see which areas of karma will be triggered next.

For example, someone born with the Moon in Cancer will deeply crave nurturing and yet may fear that he or she will not receive the validation and support they need – there being an expectation of 'smother-mothering' that leaves little room for individuality. The progressed Moon moving into Leo helps the child find confidence and a sense of being special, although this may not occur on the first progression. For this child, it is when the Moon progresses over the Ascendant and into the first house that the self has the opportunity to blossom. Moving into Virgo the child learns to be of service, and may be offered an understanding of the soul's dis-ease, and in Libra it is brought face to face with relationship issues. When the Moon progresses into Scorpio, control and mastery issues are brought to the fore and the 'shadow' may have to be faced. This is often a time when the soul has to retreat within, taking a trip into the depths. Painful or traumatic karma may surface and need releasing, but once the soul has made this trip, a greater strength is revealed and it knows it will survive no matter what.

In Sagittarius there is the urge to explore the world and to find meaning. Philosophical issues arise as the soul makes sense of its world. Capricorn offers an opportunity to master inner discipline and to gain personal authority, ready for the move into Aquarius, where the child moves away from parental influence and out into the wider world. With the progressed Moon moving through Pisces, it is outgrown emotions and illusions that have to be released so that new spiritual insights can manifest. In Aries, the awareness of being an individual is complete and issues may well arise that challenge just how centred the soul is, whilst in Taurus issues arise that test the security and values the soul has developed. As the Moon progresses through Gemini the soul has to communicate with the world outside. Intellectual curiosity is stimulated, the mind is active, and social encounters will figure strongly as the soul shares what has been learnt. By the time the progressed Moon moves into Cancer again the soul should be feeling more confident and secure, capable of nurturing and supporting itself without having to rely on external props.

The progressed Sun takes a much longer time to move through a sign but can also have the effect of bringing karmic issues related to that sign to the fore. It will also trigger karmic intent when it contacts a natal conjunction or difficult aspect – and can provide an opportunity to release the karmic potential held within an aspect, as we will see in the case history that follows.

Susie's Story
Susie is a very sensitive and aware astrologer friend of mine. I asked her for her story because it is typical of how karmic purpose can burst through uncontrollably and yet not be understood – simply because, at the time, the soul does not comprehend the underlying purpose. In Susie's case, understanding was not helped by having the Ascendant progressed into Scorpio conjunct Neptune at the time of maximum upheaval – much like having a layer of skin missing whilst laying in cotton wool soaked in a corrosive substance! Her Cancer-Sun shell was no protection against the overwhelming forces that rose up to engulf her. Her defences had to be cracked to allow her potential to surface. With hindsight, and the aid of astrology, the unfolding potential became much clearer.

Susie's natal chart (Fig 13), shows an emotional and hypersensitive Cancer Sun heightened by its square to the Nodal axis, with Jupiter and Neptune conjunct the Libra North Node and Mars the Aries South Node; and a placement at the top of a Finger of Fate with Saturn and Chiron (reflecting a wounded sense of self and lack of confidence that was passed down through the family). She has a reversed nodal placement, with her Libra North Node in the first house, and her Aries South Node in the seventh. Part of the challenge in developing herself is to work through her relationships with other people, leaving behind the selfish isolation of the Aries South Node. She says that her memory of the past is of trying to do something courageous (Mars in Aries) like being in the French Resistance during the Second World War, but somehow being blamed when things went wrong. In addition she has a powerful Moon-Pluto conjunction at the beginning of Virgo. This is a psychic chart with deeply ingrained mothering issues and great healing potential. A potential that was to emerge with great force. We can see the contradictions of her tenth house Cancer Sun in her description of herself as a child:

> I was a strange mixture as a child - wanting attention and the opportunity to 'shine', but crumbling into uncertainty when the spotlight did shine on me. I felt I deserved the attention that others got at school, but whenever my chance came I fluffed it [a Mercury-Saturn pattern]. For example - getting the part of

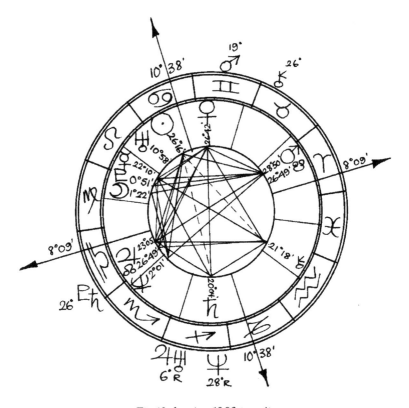

Fig 13 showing 1983 transits

Wendy in Peter Pan at primary school then forgetting my lines so I was replaced; messing up the pattern in the maypole dancing so the teachers had to untangle the mess in front of the parents; being promoted to the top group in Latin then failing miserably to translate a simple paragraph in front of the whole class [progressed Sun in Leo desperately wanting to shine but hampered by the Finger of Fate to the natal Sun]. Then as I grew older it turned into blushing furiously when my turn came to speak out, thus losing the credibility I so wanted in front of my peers and superiors [Uranus in Leo quintile Jupiter]. My body frequently let me down too. From as long ago as I can remember I suffered from severe lower back pain. [This would appear to be karmic and could relate to an old wound or blocked sexual energy/base chakra, the ruler of the sixth house, Neptune opposes Mars in Aries]. I had to give up gymnastics and horse riding because of back pain. I would have tremendous energy for a project then collapse with near exhaustion immediately after [South Node-Mars in Aries]. My memory also seemed to be unreliable and I landed in hot water more than once at work for forgetting to give people important messages [Mercury opposite Chiron and trine Saturn could well indicate an old communication problem or brain injury carried forward into the present life].

I felt I should have been much more capable at school, but resented having to cover the same boring ground that so many other students had covered [classic Saturn-Mercury]. I was one of only three girls not to go on to university from my school, which was mainly because I couldn't find a subject that interested me enough and provided the stimulation of learning something really new.

My cousin died of cancer in March 1983, and I remember being at the funeral with a searing backache. I wasn't close to my uncle but I remembered my mum telling me that he had given her healing for backache, so I asked if he would help me too. The healing experience was wonderful - all the usual warmth, light, peace and sense of well-being that is well documented these days. When he had finished I remember thinking, 'Now this I can do!'. I very shyly asked him if I could heal, and he said he had been waiting a long time for me to ask. He told me I would know when the time was right and to trust my intuition.

In June that year I was on a residential course with some people from work, one of whom was complaining about his back pain, the result of a car accident. We had all had a few drinks in the evening and this gave me the courage to ask him if I could help. We went to a quiet room and I just did as my uncle had done to me. As soon as I touched him my hands were on fire, and it felt as though I was up to my elbows in hot water. My whole body was hot and sweating as the healing energy literally poured out of me into him. We were both pretty shocked by the experience, but fortunately he was protected from the full heat that I experienced. The next morning at breakfast, my colleague announced in front of everyone present that this was the first night he had slept through without pain for 5 years and that I had a magical gift.

When we look at the transits and the progressed chart for June 1983 it is hardly surprising that Susie's healing talent should have burst out so strongly. There was a solar eclipse conjunct transiting Mars opposing her natal Saturn, the Lord of Karma.

Transiting Pluto and Saturn were conjunct her first house North Node with transiting Chiron inconjunct to it. In her progressed chart (Fig 13a) Jupiter and the North Node were conjunct the Ascendant, whilst the Sun and Uranus opposed Chiron. It was time for her to shine. However, with progressed Neptune close to the Ascendant in the first house, things were far from clear:

> Suddenly everyone was interested in me, which was very un-
> welcome as I was struggling to understand what had happened,
> especially as my hands were blistered and peeling from the heat
> that had come through them. I called my uncle from the course
> and he told me to wash my hands in cold water and imagine
> the coolness and calmness spreading through my body. This
> helped me physically, but inwardly I was in shock. Here was
> something that really did set me apart from other people (at that
> time there were very few healers around) and for the first time
> made me feel I had something unique to give. I also wondered
> how on earth I was supposed to get on with my life now this had
> happened. Back at work, the word had spread (in spite of me
> asking my colleague to be discreet) and before I knew it peo-
> ple were coming to be treated in the lunch hour. Every day a
> queue of people would form outside the nearby office, and I was
> too unsure of myself to tell them I needed some time and help
> to understand all this, and to please go away. My mother was
> also very excited and thought I should give freely of my time
> to those that needed it [a typical Moon-Pluto mother reaction,
> she was expecting her daughter to live out her own unfulfilled
> life, and although interested in such matters, her mother did not
> practise healing]. Thinking back, no-one in my family was es-
> pecially good at setting boundaries, either for themselves or
> others [first house Neptune].
>
> Soon after I started healing I realised I was tuning into peo-
> ple's lives. I could usually tell what was on their minds, and what
> was troubling them [Moon conjunct Pluto, wide Pluto-Mercury
> conjunction and Neptune quintile Mercury]. I could see all the
> characters in their lives drawn around, and who was influenc-
> ing them – the games they were playing with themselves and
> others. This gave me comfort as I realised that the things I had
> always worried about before, like fitting in with groups [Pluto
> in the eleventh house] and having lots of friends – important
> in your twenties – weren't as important as I had thought and
> that now I would have the chance to make friends more along
> the lines of my new interests. Now I was different but could

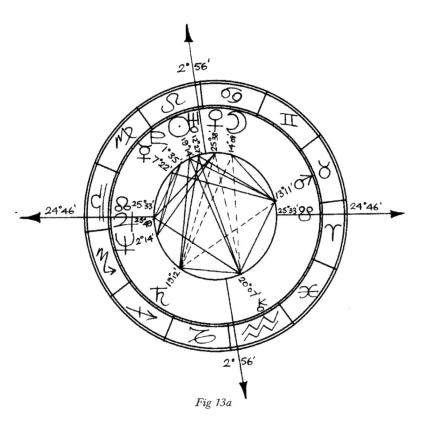

Fig 13a

rejoice in my difference from others – so of course I went completely over the top and wanted to heal the world [a common
delusion with Jupiter conjunct the North Node]. As a result of
this and the unrelenting pressure from my 'patients' I soon burnt
out.

I was also trying to answer where the healing energy came
from, and was failing miserably. My uncle was supportive but
very eccentric, so I couldn't relate personally to or repeat the
things he was telling me. I started to read voraciously [progressed
Moon in the ninth house] and swept through each book, thinking,
'I know this, what next?' Bear in mind that this was long before
the plethora of healing and self-help books that are around today. Reiki was unheard of, shiatsu was distinctly dodgy, and
acupuncture was regarded with great suspicion by most people. By the time I married in October 1986 I had decided to hang
up my healing 'hat' and concentrate on inner development. How
could I help others when I had led such a limited life myself?

This led to a big row with my mother who thought I had no right to withhold what she called my 'gift'. [Progressed Moon now in Virgo reflecting being told by mother to offer service.] By this time I was beginning to suspect that anybody could heal, and I wanted to play at being just like everyone else for a while.

Unsurprisingly, when Susie married it was on another eclipse This time the solar eclipse was at 10^0 Libra, close to her natal Ascendant and the lunar eclipse was on her Aries South Node-Mars conjunction. Blotting out the solar light brought her ego back into balance and threw her inward to look at her self presenting her with the question: 'Who am I?' As it was in Libra, it also asked her to look at the kind of relationships she would like to make rather than blindly following the patterns of selfish relationships from the past (the Aries South Node). She needed a relationship in which she could fully express who she was and of course within two years of her marriage her progressed Moon moved into Libra and then onto her North Node, bringing that question to a head. The eclipsed full Moon on the South Node gave her a new way to use Mars and her assertive energies. By transit, Uranus was moving up to her natal Saturn-Venus opposition. The ingrained pattern of Susie feeling undeserving of love was about to be challenged and transformed, as was her ability to love unconditionally (the Neptune-Venus-Chiron and Saturn kite).

Shortly after my marriage, and in pursuit of understanding myself, I started private yoga classes with a yoga teacher who was also a Bramacharyan (a Hindu monk). Her calm reassurance and unquestioning friendship gave me the space to explore what was going on. The yoga classes would often turn into spontaneous healing sessions. My mother was diagnosed with breast cancer in 1987 and, because of the healing ability, I felt totally and utterly responsible for her welfare (Moon-Pluto symbiosis and the progressed Moon in Virgo, plus the innate guilt of the natal Mars-Neptune opposition). Pent-up emotions poured out at these sessions, and my teacher helped me to understand that I could not be responsible for either my mother's illness or her ability to survive it.

In 1993 my progressed Sun moved towards my Moon-Pluto conjunction (which is sextile Jupiter-North Node-Neptune). My mother was losing her battle with cancer [progressed Moon in Sagittarius moving towards natal Saturn], and at the end of 1992 we had discovered my father had lung cancer. We knew that my mother was holding on until my second child was born, and my father was waiting for her because he didn't want to leave her alone. Much like a row of dominoes, all that was needed was the push to start the whole lot rolling. This came in February 1993 when our second son was born. Eleven days after his birth my mother died, then three weeks after that my father had a massive heart attack and also died. The drama of those weeks was to take many years to surface but I remember feeling troubled that I had such a close contact with 'the other side' now. As a child I had always been scared of ghosts and spooky stories, which my mum found most amusing as she was fascinated by the whole area of the paranormal. It was also her early interest in astrology that prompted me to take classes. Shortly after my father died I woke up to find my mother leaning over my baby son's cot, just smiling at him. I was absolutely terrified. On the psychic level I felt wide open, and was convinced that bad stuff could come through as well as the good. I went to see a medium, who found little of any help, but did say that my parents were very distressed at upsetting me and that in future they would come to me in dreams.

Susie's experience under the progressed Sun triggering her Moon-Pluto conjunction is classic for this contact (Fig 13b). At some time or another, anyone with this combination has to take a trip down into the underworld into the Lord of Death's abode*. It quite literally feels like being dismembered – and indeed it is the classic shaman's initiation. This powerful combination has enormous psychic ability and healing power but it also has an intimate acquaintance with trauma and death preceding transformation. Transiting Saturn at this time was exactly conjunct natal Chiron, activating all the wounds around relationships that her Chiron-Venus carries, progressed Neptune was conjunct the progressed Ascendant and natal and progressed Uranus on the progressed M.C. The protective defences her sensitive soul had built up were not so much dismantled as blown away. It would take some time to emerge from the Neptunian fog that engulfed her, but having her pro-

---

*   *See* The Hades Moon

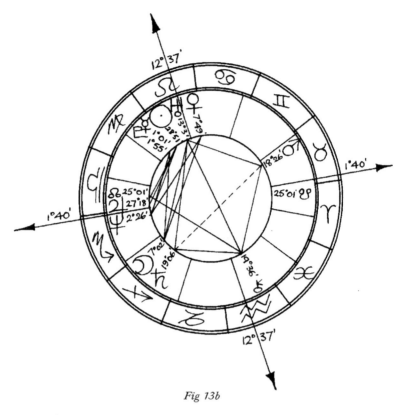

Fig 13b

gressed Mercury also on the natal Pluto-Moon conjunction did hold out hope of eventually understanding was what being brought to the surface. The progressed Uranus acted as a catalyst for change:

> That same year we moved to the South Coast. We had always wanted to live near the sea and now we were free to go. A new life, new friends, new me. Except for the emotions. The progressed Sun moved across the Moon-Pluto contact and I was distraught with grief and shock at what had happened in just one year. With the help of counselling, a wonderful husband and friends, I pulled through and regained some sanity. Something had changed so deeply within me that I knew I had to head in a new direction.
>
> In May 1995 1 went to an astrology workshop, and again felt 'I know this!' [progressed Moon moving into Gemini regaining old knowledge]. I drank in every word the teacher said and

couldn't wait for the proper course to start in September. As a direct result of this we started our own business in May 1996 [eclipses in March that year had once again triggered her Ascendant and South Node). I was over-excited, and we were both working far too hard - no time off, no time with the children, no holidays. I felt I had tapped into a special energy and was hooked on it. My intuition was running wild, and on the psychic level I was racing along. The right contacts naturally materialised, opportunities opened up, and we often seemed to be in the right place at the right time. Among other things we started to publish books which meant I was working even harder. The adrenaline of doing something new was pulling me along, but eventually my body decided enough was enough.

In May 1999, as Mars retrograded back over my Jupiter-North Node-Neptune conjunction, (thus activating the sextile to my Moon-Pluto conjunction), Jupiter transited my Mars-South Node conjunction and my temperature soared. The pain was unbelievable. It started at the base of my spine and hips, where I relived all the pain of the contractions of childbirth [an eclipse in February had been on her natal Uranus in Leo, associated with sudden back pain and this together with the contact to Moon-Pluto released the memories of old births]. Pain killers wore off long before their appointed time, and I resorted to pacing up and down to try to take my mind off the pain - just longing for the time to pass so I could take some more tablets. Everything I had learned in previous years seemed to be failing me. I wasn't able to meditate, visualise healing light, or give myself healing, and my high temperature refused to go. My one visit to the doctor was hopeless as he didn't have the remotest idea what was wrong with me except that I was obviously very ill.

I remember laying in bed one night feeling so low that I just prayed to be taken away from it all and given a break. I guess I was hallucinating, but all at once I was transported to what seemed like a comet. I could sense other souls along with me, and I felt that we were all ill - this seemed like a daytrip away from our troubles. I could feel a cool breeze on my face and I had a panoramic view of the universe in all its glory. I felt part of something so magnificent and vast it was overwhelming. I also felt protected, loved and not the least bit frightened [transiting Neptune had not long opposed her natal Sun opening the way for this kind of transcendental experience as did the progressed Moon moving through Pisces]. I must have drifted into sleep after this, and woke later feeling strangely different. Even as I write this, the power of the vision is as strong as it was then.

Susie was in the throws of her Uranus opposition. Uranus had made its first pass and was retrograding back (reaching exact opposition in September and then again in November-December before moving off). Her higher chakras were awakening. It was time to move beyond the emotions and into the mental body. This is the time when we can direct the kundalini life-force from its home in the base chakra up the spine to meet the 'mind-force' and open new levels of creation. In Susie's case, it was propelled both by Mars and by a lunar eclipse close to her natal Chiron opposition to Mercury and the Moon-Pluto conjunction (the eclipse working to bring these together through their mid-point). The lunar eclipse in early August was on her natal Chiron and, bearing in mind the effect of eclipses prior to their occurrence, was opening the way for healing:

> The intense heat and pain moved up my spine, until eventually it left through the top of my head. I had been aware almost from the beginning that this wasn't just about being ill. I knew my body well enough to realise it was going through a violent kind of kundalini awakening and I just had to go with it. Some of me rejoiced at the new awareness it was bringing, but on another level I was desperate for the pain to stop. Mars continued to aggravate the conjunction in my first house until well into July, but with the help of a medical herbalist (who is also an astrologer) I struggled back to the point where I could work a little and take part in family life again.

> Looking back in the context of astrology, I can see how different I am now from the 'me' of June 1983, when Pluto made its final pass over my North Node and the transiting North Node and Mars were conjunct my natal Venus in Gemini in the ninth house. The Sun's progression towards my Moon-Pluto conjunction in 1993 very forcibly moved me onto the path that I am now following, and the see-saw effect of the Mars-Jupiter opposition simply broke through my remaining resistance. Being so ill means you have to let others in to help, something I had never found very easy. Moon-Pluto doesn't give up its control without a fight.

When Moon-Pluto is transformed however, and harnessed to the power of the North-Node, a remarkable individual emerges. I think it unlikely that Susie will be content to remain in the background for much longer. Her karmic purpose means she has to go out to meet the world, something she already does in marketing the books but this is unlikely to be sufficient to fulfil the promise of that nodal axis and its powerful contacts. With Jupiter opposite Mars, whatever she can imagine can come into being and such powerful healing ability needs a stronger expression than talking to people at a bookstall. The solar eclipse in early July 2000 on her Midheaven reassesses the impact she makes on the world and what she strives for. This is repeated in the second eclipse at the end of July, opposite her Sun, which underlines the conflict between the Cancerian need to retreat into a stable homelife, and the Sun's highly visible position in the tenth house. At the same time, transiting Uranus is heading for natal Chiron (although retrograde motion means that it will take a year or so to reach an exact conjunction). She is likely to be propelled into yet more change. The more willingly she goes, the better the outcome.

PATTERNS OF THE PAST

6

The Wound of the Soul

Your pain is the breaking of the shell that encloses
your understanding.

Khalil Gibran, The Prophet

Chiron is a cosmic messenger who communicates the need to
change our world and heal our wounds. It is a seemingly minor body, however, its influence is not limited by its size, as it
indicates both the presence of a wound from the past – which
can be very large indeed – and the means to heal that wound.
It may also show an area of vulnerability where the soul can
be wounded in the present life – almost always because the
susceptibility was created in another life. Although this is not
intended to be a comprehensive coverage (readers are referred to Melanie Reinhart's book[1]), there are several karmic
factors which I have noted time and time again in connection
with Chiron. It must, however be borne in mind that the
placement of, and aspects to, Chiron can also link with other
issues not covered here.

Chiron's elliptical orbit enables us to reach out beyond
the purely personal and bring into that awareness all that separates and wounds us, creating suffering. It enables us also to
bring into consciousness all the higher transformational energies represented by the outer planets. As the fusion between
the animal nature and the spiritual essence, between the conscious and unconscious, Chiron is the path to evolution.
Chiron represents the integration of the animal, instinctual
side of man with the higher spiritual energies: without which
man, or woman, cannot be whole. This planet brings together
the warrior and the healer; suffering and transcendence. The
wounded healer becomes whole again.

Origins

Chiron was discovered by the astronomer Charles Kowal on 1 November 1977. It had been photographed as far back as 1895 but not recognised as anything of importance. It is a small body positioned between Saturn and Uranus, although its orbit is so erratic that it actually passes between Saturn and Jupiter at times. A truly maverick planet, it is something of a puzzle to scientists. It had been designated an asteroid and a 'planetoid', but astrologers treat it as a planet in the same way as the Sun and Moon. The latest astronomical theory is that it is a comet which has become trapped in our solar system and it has been designated as one of 16 objects officially classified as Centaurs. In a letter to The Mountain Astrologer (April 2000), Melanie Reinhart points out that this has considerably expanded Chiron's sphere of influence.

In her research, Melanie found that Rudolf Steiner had said that comets have the function of taking collective psychic debris created by human suffering down through the ages (in other words, karma) out of the solar system. This suffering is the result of soul separation and ignorance of our divine roots. We have to look at where suffering, a Chiron concept, takes place and what its causes are. Much of this suffering is created by separation, and fragmentation, not accepting ourselves as part of the whole. It is created out of ignorance and greed. Healing comes when we are able to integrate all the many disparate energies within the individual and humanity; to create a fusion of opposites and paradoxes and resolve dilemmas. To become whole. Melanie feels that by becoming trapped, Chiron is saying 'Deal with it yourself'. By taking responsibility, you become a co-creator with God. In other words, it is the planet of integration and fusion of the human with the divine. Since Chiron's discovery, the transition to the new astrological Age of Aquarius has accelerated and the planet is prominent in the charts of 'New Age' healers and prophets.

The Wounded Healer

Chiron is 'the wounded healer' in Greek mythology and astrologers have resonated to this meaning, although the planet is much more than this as will become apparent. Briefly,

Chiron's story is that he was a centaur (half man, half horse) who was rejected at birth by his mother and fostered by the gods. His father, a god, was Saturn, his grandfather, Uranus. He became a great teacher and healer, and was given the gift of immortality. Paradoxically, he taught healing and warfare, just one of many apparent contradictions associated with this planet, so he is the spiritual warrior. Chiron was wounded but, because he was immortal, he could not die; he is the Shaman. The gift became a curse and he was in constant agony. Eventually he gave up his immortality and took on someone else's burden, becoming a positive scapegoat. He died and was given a place in the heavens by the gods. In some sources, Chiron's wound was in 'the thigh', which is often a euphemism for castration and loss of procreative power. Chiron's natal position may indicate where physical generative power has to be sacrificed in order to achieve a 'higher' level of creative energy − a transmutation of power.

Chiron's placement in the chart shows the repeating pattern of our inner distress, where we are stuck. This planet has an intimate connection with the suffering that we, and all humankind, feel as a result of unresolved fear, guilt and ignorance. This in turn, forms part of the karmic wound. Chiron shows us where we have to embrace our own wounds and where we have to give up suffering and allow ourselves to be healed. It is the point where we may have to make a sacrifice in order to be free from our pain.

For many people, giving up pain is in itself a painful process. Fear of what will take its place is a powerful block, and here the warrior nature of Chiron can be helpful as it gives the courage to risk all for the sake of the healing to come. Having healed our own wounds, we have the potential to heal those of others. Healing is not simply a question of 'making it better'. It is about assimilating the lessons embodied in our suffering, integrating the self-knowledge that results, and finding a way to resolve fear, pain and ignorance. Chiron is also a point where we can become a scapegoat to clear the collective suffering of humankind, or where we can sacrifice our separateness for the sake of others. Such a sacrifice or scapegoating may be a conscious choice or an unconscious acting out of Chiron's urges. This is the point where we must die to the past, go through our initiation and find our true self.

Chiron is a planet of fusion, integration and transformation, opening the way for new energies to flow. Such resolution may include 'acceptance of the things we cannot change, the courage to change the things we can change, and the wisdom to know the difference'.

Healing

Chiron is manifested in complementary medicine with its gentle, non-invasive approach to healing disease (which should more properly be written dis-ease); in the therapies that explore the holistic nature of humankind and its higher potential. These are the energies that have been liberated by Chiron's recognition.

The rise (or more properly re-discovery) of shamanism in the western world is intimately connected to the need for growth personified by Chiron. The shaman links the unseen forces, the spiritual realms, with the physical level and acts as a go-between. He or she has usually been wounded in some way, and had to find inner healing. Having been through many levels of initiation, and died to the old self, the powers of the spirit are activated. Then, the way is opened to act as healer for the tribe. Chironic energies initiate us through pain and suffering, pointing the way to where we can set ourselves free. It also points to where we may have suffered soul loss in the past and now need to retrieve and reintegrate lost parts of the Self.

The Cosmic Messenger

Chiron is the messenger through which the archetypal energies of the planets pour down to earth, so it is likely that anyone with several Chiron aspects is a channel for the archetypes and spiritual energies – and the chaos!

This planet shows where the veil between our own individual consciousness and that of the collective consciousness of humankind is permeable. Amongst their other functions, the planets symbolise archetypal energies and these energies pour through planets which contact Chiron. Archetypes are 'blueprints' for universal truths which always exist and express themselves in a particular way through all cultures and ages. The Greek gods, for instance, are archetypes, as are the planets named after them, acting as a funnel for all the other planetary archetypes to earth themselves.

We can also look at Chiron in terms of where a sacrifice has to be made. It is where we must sacrifice our individuality for the good of the whole, or where we may become a sacrifice on behalf of the collective. However, once the sacrifice has been made, we have to move on into the light of the healing process. We have to give up wounding ourselves and others, and we have to let go of our suffering: a difficult process for some people. So many people endlessly recreate the sacrifice (what a Christian friend of mine refers to as 'being stuck at the foot of the Cross rather than moving through into the joy of the resurrected self'). Chiron shows where we must give up this need to suffer, where we must move into contact with our higher self and allow its purpose to work out in our life. This may still entail being a scapegoat but it is a choice to use sacrifice in a constructive manner with a positive outcome in mind.

Expulsion into Separateness

The mythological Chiron was the product of an illicit union between Saturn and Philyra, daughter of Oceanus, the primeval deep. Caught in flagrante delicto by his wife, Saturn changed into a stallion and galloped off. When Philyra gave birth it was to what she perceived as a monster: half man, half beast. She prayed to the gods to have her child taken away, and was answered; Chiron was raised by Apollo and the other gods. Wounded by one of his pupils with poison from the Hydra, he underwent a long period of agony until he was able to give up his immortality by taking on the burden of Prometheus, he who had stolen fire from the gods. Chiron descended into the underworld but was then elevated to a place in the heavens by the gods. This is the classic shaman's journey.

As Howard Sasportas pointed out[2], Chiron's first wound was rejection by his mother, equating with the expulsion from the womb into separateness and new life. He then became a maker of heroes and it was one of those heroes, Hercules, who wounded him. Chiron was therefore wounded by his own creation.

In karmic work the placement of Chiron not only shows where the incarnating soul is traumatised but also indicates where it is attached to suffering and must release from the old pain. The reward is to be elevated, but letting go cannot be contingent upon reward. The soul must make a conscious, informed choice as Chiron did, freely relinquishing its hold on the world it has known and, where necessary, choosing to go through death of the old self in order that something greater may emerge.

CHIRON THROUGH THE SIGNS AND HOUSES

Chiron's position, by sign and house shows where we can give up our karmic suffering and move towards integration; it is the key to our future.

Chiron in Aries or the First House

Wound: The soul has a deep wound in the sense of self or the ego. Lessons include the overcoming of obstacles and dealing with aggressiveness and self-assertion; the taking of initiative and developing self-confidence. The early environment may be traumatic or healing.

Healing: Becoming centred in one's Self.

The soul with Chiron in Aries (or Chiron conjunct the Sun), incarnates with a deep wound. It has been through soul or ego-shattering experiences in past lives, or may go through this prior to a transformation in the present life. It must now heal its sense of Self, reconnecting to its own eternal, indestructible essence. A client with Chiron in Scorpio in the first house 'remembered' having been tortured and brainwashed in a previous life until he lost all sense of identity and 'babbled like an idiot'. He had died under that torture without regaining his shattered sense of who he was. In his present life he had encountered a series of traumatic events and mental breakdowns, following which he was painstakingly rebuilding himself.

Chiron in Taurus or the Second House

Wound: The wound centres around the physical body and values, security and resources. Incarnating fully may prove difficult.

Healing: Integrating body and soul and finding inner security bring about healing.

Chiron in Taurus or the second or sixth house brings back an old knowledge of healing and the possibility of release from suffering. Elisabeth Kubler-Ross, who was drawn to her work with dying patients by the experience of 'cleaning up' after the Nazi death camps, had Chiron in the second house, an old resource coming forward.

Christine Hartley, who was trained in past-life recall and esoteric work (over many incarnations), had Chiron in Scorpio on the cusp of the second and third houses. Her Jupiter in the twelfth house indicated links with ancient Egypt and the role of priestess and her Virgo Ascendant that she had incarnated with the intention of being of service to humanity. Although her Chiron pointed to resources carried over from previous lives to help in the present incarnation, and to a need to communicate her knowledge through teaching, the placement of Chiron in Scorpio indicated that she herself had some deep wounds connected with previous incarnations. During a past-life 'far seeing' she and two colleagues encountered a life in ancient Egypt. Christine described what happened:

> A. was instructed to take the lead and develop the story. She began by picturing the Nile with a dying moon shining on the land but leaving the river in darkness. Downstream was being propelled a boat or barge with about four or possibly six men plying the sweeps. On the barge was a sarcophagus and seated behind it were herself and F.P.D. wrapped in cloaks ... During this period I was completely out of the picture and found it almost impossible even to follow the scenes ...
>
> The boat went on up the Nile to a temple which was described as looming very large and black against the night sky. There was a hidden water entrance to it, through a sort of backwater be-

tween banks of undergrowth, terminating in an, arched and locked door. It was as they described the boat coming to this point that I woke up, fully conscious. It was horrible. I was in the sarcophagus and the blackness and the sensation of fear were terrible. Dimly I heard F.P.D. give a password at the door and it swung back and I knew that we were in a great hall filled with water and that I was still shut in on the barge. I could hardly control the agony that filled my mind. They took the lid off the coffin and then an inner shell and there I lay, with the blessed light on my face, my body bound round with grave clothes and no strength left in me. I was still dizzy from the drug I had been given to make me simulate death.[3]

This particular experience explained the life-long claustrophobia which Christine had suffered (Pluto on MC) and helped her to live with it. It was never, however, completely cured. When I knew her some thirty to forty years after her regression to the past she still could not bear to be in a confined space or to have the door to a room closed. Even in the depths of winter a window had to be open when she travelled by car and she would choose a bus or cab in preference to the Underground. She was not afraid of death and gave doctors at the local hospital strict instructions that she was not to be revived if she was brought in 'dead'. She was nevertheless extremely anxious that her coffin should not be nailed down until it was certain that she was definitely deceased. Her memory of that old experience was too vivid – the Chiron trauma is deep. Christine also had a horror of horses, but she did overcome that after she had seen herself killed under the hooves of a stampeding horse and, at the age of eighty-three, was extremely proud of herself when we managed to walk through a field of horses.

Her work in the present life involved writing, lecturing and teaching. She not only delved into past lives in order to heal people but also, on the occult level, battled during the Second World War with what she described as 'the powers of darkness' in order that mankind could survive. She felt called upon (Virgo Ascendant offering service) to confront personal, collective and archetypal injuries and release humanity from its suffering and pain through the resources of Chiron.

Chiron in Gemini or the Third House

Wound: There is a difficulty with communication, but nevertheless a need to speak out on contentious issues. Lessons may include overcoming these obstacles. Wounds may come through wounding words – one's own or others. There may well be a wounded sibling.

Healing: Comes through speaking one's truth.

Chiron in Gemini or the third house can experience a wound in its ability to communicate. Christine Hartley's book was in a sense before its time. During her life it did not sell well and the publisher consistently refused to republish, although Christine felt that it contained knowledge which was part of her karmic task to pass on to others. After her death there was a resurgence of interest in karmic matters and the book was reissued in paperback. Melanie Reinhart says that people with Chiron in the third house may need to undergo humbling experiences to counter high-flown ideals and mental sophistication, and she points out that this placement needs to learn through mistakes and that the mistakes are often outlandish! A comment that Christine and myself (we share the placement) would agree with.

As the third house is also the house of siblings, the karmic wound may involve a confrontation with or through a sibling, or with a wounded sibling. The Cancerian epileptic mentioned elsewhere has Chiron conjunct his sister's fourth house Moon. The latter was instinctively deeply aware of his and their parents' pain despite a conspiracy of silence. Her Chiron is in the third house (Virgo), indicating both being wounded by, and having, a wounded sibling. Her mother had always wanted a son and shortly after her brother's birth, at which she experienced a sense of abandonment and considerable rejection, she developed a psychosomatic, life-threatening illness (Virgo Chiron) which was virtually ignored by her mother. Her brother later took over the function of 'identified patient' and released the family stress through his 'dis-ease'. However, she had to live with the deep, dark secret of his illness which was never mentioned by the rest of the family and friends. The only healing possible was to bring this out into the open – an option that was firmly resisted by the family who refused to discuss it. She took herself into therapy, believing that when one person in the family is healed, the others ultimately have to change. Eventually her brother found the courage to confront his own position in the family and the 'dis-ease' healed.

Chiron in Cancer or the Fourth House

Wound: Here Chiron indicates a deeply traumatised or painful home environment or someone who is 'not at home when they are home' (Melanie Reinhart). There may well be a wounded, or wounding, parent and deep emotional scars are likely to be carried forward. Lessons centre around letting go, and finding an inner home.

Healing: Comes through developing emotional detachment and learning to nurture oneself.

In the fourth house or Cancer, Chiron indicates a karmic wound located deep within the home environment, and this placement, together with Chiron-Moon aspects can signify deep pain around being parented. A sister and brother who both had Chiron in the fourth grew up from a young age 'knowing', in the way that children do, that their father had cancer. It was always denied, however, and they were never helped to come to terms with the prospect of his death. He died, leaving behind a deep fear of pain and feelings just as they were entering adolescence, later confirmed through regression as an inbuilt expectation of both siblings. The son became a doctor who felt that he had' 'failed' whenever someone died. His attitude to death was different from that of Elisabeth Kubler-Ross (Chiron in Taurus in the second house, indicating an old resource brought back to help in the present life). She understood from a very deep level that death is 'the final stage of growth' in this incarnation, and as such a creative and life-enhancing activity. Much later, the son was able to confront his deeply buried grief, first through a cycle of deaths of a beloved cat (who kept reincarnating) and then by attending two moving and powerful deaths of friends. He became a much better doctor as a result, helping his patients to die with dignity and much less pain and suffering where appropriate.

Chiron in Leo or the Fifth House

Wound: With Chiron in Leo there may be a wound in (and overcompensation for) a sense of or need for specialness. The soul wants to be seen as unique and powerful, but may find difficulty manifesting this. Creativity and self-expression may have been firmly squashed in the past or the soul may be carrying karma from old love affairs or 'a bleeding heart' and needs to learn healing and self-reliance.

Healing: Resolving the head-heart paradox, living from the heart and becoming soul-empowered heals the Leonine wound. Expressing creativity resolves fifth house pain.

Leo is connected with the child, as is the fifth house. Childhood may be damaging or a healing of old woundedness. Leo is a creative, extrovert sign, and this is the child who needs to shine. A woman with Chiron conjunct Pluto in Leo in the tenth house described her childhood experience:

> As an only child I always was special to my parents and felt very secure in that relationship. Until, at four years old, a mother and two girls – evacuees from London – came to live with my parents. I was quite precocious and the mother seemed to want to put me in my place. The experience that I saw in regression was when this woman said to me: "You're not special, my children are as important as you." This was particularly in their relationship to my father as their father was still in London and I very much felt my nose pushed out. Many years later, when I looked at this in an NLP workshop, it was described as an "hypnotic command". Its effect was that, deep down, I had internalised that message and it conflicted with my sense of myself. I changed the script and saw a different picture.
>
> I remember little about my early years. One of the few things that comes back from my childhood is from before I was 11. My teacher was the local drama society leader and we each had to do a small piece for the form. I wrote and performed something called King Rat. I stood on the high teacher's chair and said my piece. Afterwards she said to me that I should take it further. Later I joined the local amateur dramatic society but by then I

had had all the showman knocked out of me by my boarding school – Little Miss Show-off was definitely not encouraged. I used to do backstage work. Also being at a boarding school brought up a feeling of not wanting to be different from the children in the village. I wanted to be accepted.

An aspiring and extremely talented young artist with Chiron in the fifth house, who appeared strangely reluctant to paint, regressed back to a time when all her paintings were destroyed by a jealous, sadistic, teacher – who was also her lover in that, and the present life. That recognition freed up her talent.

Chiron in Virgo or the Sixth House

Wound: The soul has a deep impulse towards healing and service but finds it difficult to manifest these. The wound is a sense of not being good enough and the weapon a highly developed self-critical faculty that can also criticise others. The body may carry a karmic wound injury to the throat, chest or nervous system.

Healing: Altruistic, dispassionate service to others heals this wound, as does a concerted effort to be less self-critical.

Chiron in the sixth house or Virgo may bring a need to be healed as a catalyst for its own healing power to emerge. I have repeatedly observed the Sun conjunct or opposed Chiron in the charts of healers, and also in the eighth house – a house which can also be linked with how resources are shared with other people, including sexuality issues. There is a fundamental loss of identity, a need to heal the deep split between the ego and the Self which arose in past lives and is reiterated in the present-life childhood. Once this wound is healed, an integration is achieved which is then passed on as healing for others.

Chiron in Libra or the Seventh House

Wound: Difficulties here are experienced in or through partners (with whom there may well have been contact in the past). The pattern may be of sacrificing one's own needs to those of a another. The need is to become whole and self-sufficient within partnerships.

Healing: Creating an inner relationship with one's Self and a creative compromise between one's own needs and those of another.

The wound for Chiron in Libra or the seventh house, and for Venus conjunct Chiron, is in the area of relationships. A client with Chiron conjunct the North Node in the seventh asked: 'Why do I keep attracting such unsuitable men into my life since my husband's death?' The solution to her problem lay in giving up the suffering attached to unsuitable relationships, a karmic pattern, and focusing instead on dealing with the pain of her husband's death. (I have noted a close correlation between Chiron-Venus aspects and women whose husbands die or disappear at an early age.)

An elderly client had Venus conjunct Chiron in Aquarius in the twelfth house, trine Pluto and sextile Saturn. She had in the past been working on changing the obsessive, manipulative quality of the Venus-Pluto relationship pattern, and her painful difficulties around being loved and loving: Venus-Chiron sextile Saturn brought back these feelings as well as a deep pain around relationships. Hers was, historically, a prominent, tragic family. Her relationships had a peculiarly fated quality to them. She married late, at the beginning of the Second World War, and after only a year or so her husband was reported missing. It was almost two years before his death was confirmed – after many stories from escaped prisoners saying that they had seen him alive. Some years later her son and heir went missing from a sailboat in the Caribbean; he has not been seen or heard of since, and is presumed dead. She has a fourth house Neptune square twelfth house Sun-Mercury, representing confusion and misinformation, and with a Sun-Mercury quintile to Pluto and the Moon quintile Saturn she had to confront death and loss head-on, the quintile being an aspect of destiny.

The pattern is released and healing achieved by having the courage to move on in your relationships with others and never give up hope.

Chiron in Scorpio or the Eighth House

Wound: The wound may well be in use, or abuse, of sexual energy. It will certainly involve power and mastery. There is a need to experience the birth-death-rebirth cycle and to heal any wounds in levels of consciousness. Especially when placed in the eighth house, Chiron can indicate a loss or near death experience from which healing and integration grow.

Healing: Recognition and integration of the rejected parts of the self heals this wound.

The eighth house Chiron or Chiron in Scorpio experiences a significant life change after a death. This is usually connected to having experienced a particularly difficult or formative transition to the spiritual realms in a past life. It can also indicate an old ability to communicate with the 'abode of spirits', which is carried over into the present life. In five instances mothers with this placement became mediums following the death of their daughters. In each case the daughter 'knew' that she was going to die and she is now helping communication from the other side. And in each case the mother felt that she herself had undertaken this role before. In another 'disappearing husband' case a woman with this placement, having previously led a sheltered and protected life, was liberated by the declaration of her husband's death seven years after his disappearance.

Letting go, moving forward but taking all the insights gained from the experience and offering them to aid others heals this wound.

Chiron in Sagittarius or the Ninth House

Wound: The wound is through philosophy, beliefs, ethics and constraints on freedom. There may well be religious karma to overcome.

Healing: Reprogramming past beliefs heals old splits and paradoxes.

With Chiron in the ninth house or Sagittarius one would expect the wound to be in the area of religious beliefs and values.

One client regressed to a life during the English Reformation in which he had been a monk and, at the time of the dissolution of the monasteries, he had been turned out. He was involved in a similar experience in his present life – the turning out of elderly inmates from psychiatric hospitals into an inhospitable and unwelcoming 'community' – as he was an administrator involved in the reorganisation of psychiatric services. In that past life he was totally disorientated and incapable of fending for himself. His pain arose from the fact that his God, in whom he had placed all his trust and obedience, had seemingly abandoned him. In the present life he did all he could to mitigate the trauma for the hospital inmates who were being moved.

Healing for ninth house Chiron comes from developing spirituality and awareness of the eternal Self.

Chiron in Capricorn or the Tenth House

Wound: There is trauma connected with authority or public position in life which has been brought forward. The soul may carry a healing vocation. A parent may well have been wounded through interaction with the outside world.

Healing: Trusting in your instincts and building confidence in your own authority brings healing to this wound.

Capricorn and the tenth house have strong connections with authority figures and the soul may well have found itself in a position in a past life when it was either wounded by authority or was part of the wounding. Capricorn is also connected to fathering and I worked with one client, Ronald, who had Chiron in the last degree of Capricorn conjunct his Sun and Moon in Aquarius in the fourth house opposing Uranus-Jupiter in the tenth (the parental axis of the chart). Ronald's mother died when he was a teenager and his elder brother committed suicide a few years later. Ronald was never able to grieve or show emotion over either death. His father had always been a strange character (Uranus in the tenth): 'a really angry old bastard, not physically violent but a bad tempered, crotchety old crow.' From what Ronald told me, it sounded as though the father really needed psychiatric care. Ronald left as soon as possible to fend for himself and moved into a squat (so Aquarian). He was a loner, isolated and alienated from society. For many years he blamed himself for not getting on with his father, then in therapy he finally realised the effect that living with someone so unpredictable had had on him and he was able to express his anger at that. Eventually the father was taken into hospital and both Ronald and his sister asked that the machine keeping him alive should be switched off in accordance with a 'living will' document his father had signed previously. Taking back his power in this way released Ronald. In hypnotherapy he was able to 'change his script' and to release from some pretty traumatic past-life stuff that directly related to his expectations around parenting. In keeping with Chiron in Capricorn and placed in the fourth house, he learnt to parent himself.

The tenth and eleventh houses indicate interaction with the outside world, and Chiron in these houses incarnates with a wound linked to its experience with the external environment. In the tenth house the suffering may have been in the realm of 'business affairs'. A client with tenth house Chiron regressed to being the 'scapegoat' on whom a major financial disaster had been blamed. Not unnaturally, he was afraid that his own business would suffer.

Making your mark on the world is part of the tenth house. The woman with Chiron conjunct Pluto in Leo in the tenth house who was told as a small child that there was nothing special about her, was perceived by all her friends as an extremely powerful woman indeed. Someone who could 'Do anything she set her mind to'. But she did not recognise this in herself – despite knowing at an inner level that there was something special she had to do. In one-to-one work she was amazing, bringing about deep healing and soul integration, but in public it was a different story. She wanted to remain in the background. When she was present on my workshops her power made an enormous difference to the work that was done. I wanted her be a co-facilitator on these workshops, but she held back. I also wanted her to write a book on something she had discovered out of her own experience, but the response was 'Oh heck'. She could not take up a position of authority. As she said:

> On a very practical level and with things I have been trained in, such as upholstery and reflexology, I am happy to teach or to work with it. But things more esoteric which are not provable or could be interpreted as my vivid imagination – which was what I was told as a child – are different. I want to be involved and yet am worried it is my ego. If I haven't got any facts to prove what I am putting forward as my belief – when it's very 'I' centred – then I squirm, its pathetic. [Her body language graphically portrays this].
>
> Also there has always been a sense that I have something to do on a spiritual level but there is another little voice in there that is afraid that it is my ego and therefore I have problems speaking that except to special friends. But the strange thing is that many people I meet say "I see so much wisdom and power in you." I am uncomfortable with that and have problems accepting it. It is definitely a little voice like the inner critic that says: "Who do you think you are?" – something else I remember from childhood.
>
> In past life regression, when I tried to find the source, all I could see was somewhere around Mesopotamia about three thousand years ago. It had that a feeling that was rather like the Moslem religion but wasn't. They cut off the hand of the thief, the tongue of the liar, etc. My experience was I was stood in a desert place on a raised dais, in a robe and a tall hat, speaking to a crowd of people. I sense I was talking about a vision I had had when another religious faction came and took me away and gouged my eyes out. I was left there and withered up and died. [Again, graphic body language]. My confusion was why did they do this to me? I also feel that at some level I had gloried in it when I was on the stage and this took me down a peg or two – which was the experience I had as a child with the woman who told me I was not special. It ensured my ego did not become too inflated but it holds me back.
>
> There is an enormous fear of sounding big-headed. I can argue with you and say: "This is what I think" from a position of inner knowing and that's alright. But when confronted with a group or public situation, I cringe. I am so afraid people will think it's my ego talking.

I asked her partner how he perceived this:

She has existed for all of her life outside of society's norms and systems [Chiron in the tenth]. Managing to not have to do further education or to take a job in an office. She worked for herself. The tax man doesn't know she exists. She hates bureaucracy.

When she's asked to take the spotlight as an authoritative teacher, she goes into denial. Effectively saying that her viewpoint has no worth and apologising for being there. She becomes like a shy, cringing mouse. A typical example was when she asked by a workshop leader to elaborate a particular point from her own experience and spent ten minutes denying the value of her viewpoint before giving a very worthwhile teaching on the subject.

In her younger life she was always someone who became extrovert in a crowd, though not wanting to be responsible for anything. She was co-opted onto a committee as social secretary (Sun in Libra). Acting as an ideal supporter of a group leader but actually seeking to be in the limelight herself. For instance, when I first met her, her partner was the president of a canoeing club. She was an able and active networker seeking views and lobbying support for all issues, particularly related to keeping the group together. In this respect she took on an extrovert role to be centre of the group relating to all her peers and effectively leading the group as a whole – but not holding office. This was particularly relevant when she was canoeing. It was like the larger the group the stronger showing of the bold adventurous qualities she has. A competitive situation brought them out. The Libran sheepdog keeping the pack together turned into the leader of the pack.

I am quite convinced that she does have a task to do and that in time she will own and share her own special qualities with the waiting world. She can teach us all about Chironic soul integration and the use of Plutonian power. Watch this space!

Chiron in Aquarius or the Eleventh House

Wound: This is the outcast or scapegoat karma. The soul feels different and alien, an outsider looking in. In the past the soul has followed 'the different drum' and suffered for it. It will undoubtedly have experienced conflicts with authority.

Healing: Reconciling the needs of the individual with those of society heals the Aquarian wound.

Chiron in Aquarius or the eleventh house can so easily feel the outsider. This is where Chiron's rejection is most poignantly felt. In the past, the Aquarian ability to see what humanity needs, and the natural urge to rebel, may well have created separation from the group. Revolution is not always welcomed, even when the change would be for the better and so Chiron is made to suffer for trying to change the world.

In the eleventh house Chiron may have experienced betrayal by a friend or the group with which the soul was associated with and carry deep scars from this experience. A man with eleventh house Chiron experienced considerable pain in a previous incarnation in which he had, initially been 'blackballed' by his club during the days of British India, and then had been drummed out of his regiment as a result of his taking up the case of one of the local people. His disgrace had been engineered by those who, opposing his stand, had taken action 'for the honour of the regiment'. He, not unnaturally, reincarnated with severe difficulties in trusting a group.

Chiron in Pisces or the Twelfth House

Wound: This is the victim or martyr from the past. The soul participates in collective karma. Boundary issues arise, there is confusion in differentiating between 'me' and 'them'. A deeply traumatising past life is indicated by twelfth house Chiron which may need therapy to heal and integrate.

Healing: Recognising the divinity within oneself and integrating this into everyday life will help heal the division.

The roots of the Chiron twelfth house or Pisces pain are very deep and very old indeed, and they can be difficult to trace. They may include a close identification with the collective, ancestral and individual suffering of humanity and a need to work towards healing the splits that recur throughout time, as is shown in the following example which has a symbolic twelfth house Chiron in the sunrise chart.

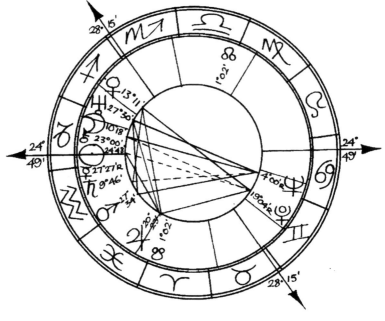

Fig 14

Omm Sety

One of the most interesting and detailed manifestations of karma is contained in the life of the extraordinary English lady Dorothy Eady (Fig. 14), known for most of her life as Omm Sety, who had the Sun conjunct Chiron and Mercury. When she was three she fell downstairs and was to all appearances dead. Sometime later, however, she recovered, but from that time on she wanted to go 'home'. 'Home' turned out to be Egypt three thousand years earlier. In her teens she began to receive visitations from the Pharaoh Sety I, with whom she had a love affair in that previous life. Then she had been a young priestess of the temple of Isis, and as such sacred, virgin and untouchable. When her pregnancy had been discovered by the priests, they had questioned her at length. She had not revealed the name of her seducer, whom she loved more than anything and who was not immune, even as Pharaoh, to punishment for his offence against the goddess. In the end the young priestess had committed suicide in order to protect her lover. For his part in the affair Sety had been condemned by the gods to wander in darkness until he found her again. He had searched unceasingly for three thousand years – this synchronistically being the time span allotted by the Egyptian Book of the Dead for a soul to transmigrate from species to species until it is able once again to take human form. Sety could well then have expected the soul who became Dorothy Eady not to take human form again until the twentieth century. In the course of his search Sety explored most of the solar system and other planes of being until this was forbidden by the gods.

Omm Sety was a very determined soul (Uranus sextile Mars has a strong Will) who knew that she just had to return to Egypt. She married, and was divorced from, an Egyptian, and lived and worked in Egypt for the rest of her life. She revealed an uncanny knowledge of how things had been in ancient Egypt and an amazing ability to read previously indecipherable hieroglyphic inscriptions.

Omm Sety began an incredible, secret, sexual (Mars trine Neptune) affair with the 'dead' Pharaoh who manifested to her physically in the present life, but the sexual side of the relationship came to an end when she moved back to her temple at Abydos and became once more consecrated to Isis (the Mars-Neptune aspect works on attuning to the spiritual purpose and Will). She displayed a remarkable knowledge of the temple, pinpointing among many other things the site of the old, previously unknown, temple garden in which she used to meet the Pharaoh in her other life. She adhered to the old religion, kept the festivals and made votive offerings to the gods. She also became an expert in Egyptian magic and healing, curing many ailments with water from the Osirion (a sacred well) and local herbs, and could inflict an effective curse on anyone who upset her. Although His Majesty, as she called Sety in her diaries, continued to visit her frequently, and she him in the 'astral' realms, in order to reverse the karmic sentence laid on him they had to remain celibate for the rest of her earthly life while she fulfilled the reneged vow of temple service. In time she passed on to Amenti (the Otherworld), where it is to be hoped she was reunited with her Pharaoh.

Omm Sety had Chiron conjunct Sun-Mercury in Capricorn, that most down-to-earth of signs. Many people have wondered whether the early fall had in fact damaged her brain in some way which either gave her delusions or enabled the past life to break through. Her biographer, Jonathan Cott, discussed this question with psychologist Dr. Michael Gruber:

> I think it would have been an extreme loss to have seen her simply as someone who was hallucinating or who was out of touch or split off - it would have been a diminution of her being ...
>
> The adventure she acts out is not only her own. She is not selfish. We have to remember that Omm Sety had an uncanny sense of Abydos, so she wasn't acting out just a personal myth ... that's the interesting thing to me. The way she seems to have processed the light that entered her after her fall afforded her an intuitive or imaginative glimpse of knowledge that, after all, was only available to initiates during an entirely different period of history. This seems to me to somehow 'speak' beyond a personal mania or just an acting out of a personal myth.
>
> To accuse Omm Sety of 'mythomania' or 'schizophrenia' is to analyse away her experience. Her experience, as we know it, yielded a meaningful life. If our criterion of health or sanity has to do with whether one can live in a creative, compassionate, and disciplined way, then Omm Sety surely did that ...
>
> It is important to remember that Sety first appears to Dorothy Eady as a mummy. Both of them have to go through a kind of purification and rebirth process so that Sety can appear as a man, and so that Dorothy Eady will not be simply victimised or ravished, as she was at fourteen. For Omm Sety and Sety are involved in the process of remembrance that's also atonement for what they had transgressed together during a previous lifetime and, on her part, an atonement for her own sense of not being at one with the 'masculine', energetic form that is called 'Sety' (The Chiron conjunction in Capricorn indicates a fundamental split in her sense of self). It is this sense of at-one-merit that is connected to the notion of the 'heavenly marriage' of Isis and Osiris ...
>
> Whatever the inspiration or even 'otherworldly' origin of Omm Sety's vision, it's important to reassert that she found a way to make that vision meaningful, creative, and of this world. She was able to be faithful to her love at the same time that she loved the world she was living in. Her life had meaning to it, it

embodied values ... that is what I think important - rather than whether she was sane or insane, or whether her vision was real or unreal. For those questions may reveal more of the questioners' insecurity about their own sense of reality.[4]

Omm Sety was extremely psychic and had many out of body experiences – her Capricorn Moon opposes Neptune with the orb widening as the day progresses (there is no time of birth available). As she had been a priestess this would have been an old skill and the orb does not need to be a close one. She has Venus opposing Pluto, an aspect which frequently means that the soul experiences the death of a lover as a way of changing old, obsessive, ways of relating. Omm Sety appears to have turned this around so that her relationship was with someone who was 'dead' but with whom she was nevertheless working out an old karmic pattern. Her North Node is in Libra and her karmic purpose worked itself out through this most unlikely relationship with a 'dead' Pharaoh, which is also indicated in the Grand Cross of the Nodes squaring the Moon opposition to Neptune. Neptune has an ability to see beyond the physical plane and can carry on a relationship with a discarnate spirit (as happens in channelling for example).

Neptune-Moon can idealise, or idolise, a relationship or a person. Omm Sety appears to have done this in both lives as, in her eyes, her Pharaoh could do no wrong. It also has the potential to sacrifice itself for the beloved as she did when she committed suicide rather than reveal his name to the priests. She also has Jupiter in Pisces forming a T-square with the Venus opposition to Pluto, a link to the Egyptian priestess who, although chosen to represent Isis at the Mysteries, sacrificed all for love.

The chart also has a wide Moon inconjunct Pluto, indicating that she had an old karma around mothering. In her incarnation as the priestess Bentreshyt, Omm Sety had been abandoned at the temple following the death of her mother. Her father, a soldier, had been unable to look after her and she was brought up by the priests – her Capricorn Moon had experienced a religious figure as a surrogate parent and when she herself was about to become a mother she was judged by that 'parent' for breaking her religious vow. She has Saturn sextile Venus, indicating an old feeling of being unlovable and certainly in her English incarnation she was distant from her parents as she believed they were not her real family: they in turn found it extremely difficult to understand this stranger who was suddenly in their midst. The difficulty around mothering re-emerged in the present life, her son was taken to another country by her husband, who considered her a most unsuitable mother. She never saw her son again - in this life. As Dr. Gruber points out, Omm Sety worked on the issues of healing and mothering (both connected with the Moon-Pluto inconjunct) in the present life, specifically through the area of childbirth:

> She ministered to the people in the village where she lived - even if her healing techniques were unorthodox and came from some personal interpretation of certain ancient magical texts (though she also used natural medicines and herbs). In addition, she helped women reinstate faith around the crucial cultural issue for women in Egypt - childbearing. She was able to help in a compassionate way that allowed them to fulfil what they considered to be their proper role.[5]

Omm Sety used spells, incantations and offerings to Isis to cure childlessness and impotence and was usually present at village births as a kind of talisman – although she recorded in her diary that she doubted that she was of any real use during the physical process of birth.

The life of this unique woman depicts the creative balancing out of an ancient pattern and, as Dr. Gruber pointed out, it does not matter whether the facts of that previous life were true. What matters is that Omm Sety was enabled by her belief in that life to fulfil her destiny in this life by making a substantial contribution on many levels, including knowledge about ancient Egypt which could not have been obtained from any other source.

CHIRON IN ASPECT

Planets which conjunct or aspect Chiron can take on karmic pain in varying degrees according to the nature of the planet, the house placement and the aspect. Chiron in transit to a planet can a similar effect, especially when the planet being transited is part of a bigger aspect pattern.

Chiron in Aspect to the Sun (or Chiron in Leo)

When Chiron aspects the Sun there is a fundamental wound in the person's sense of identity and ability to make an impact 'out there' on the world. Melanie Reinhart has pointed out that this aspect can indicate that a person shines and yet does not recognise it because there is an estrangement from the inner self. (See for example the woman with Chiron conjunct Pluto in Leo in the section on tenth house Leo.) It may also indicate the adored child, made to feel incredibly special at home but rejected by the outside world. Indeed, all too often the person will meet what he or she sees as problems 'out there' and not even begin to recognise that there is an inner wound or a negative pattern operating.

Part of the Chironic initiation experience is about being in touch with Self, the eternal part of one's being that can never be taken away. With this sense of solid ground within, you are safe and unshakeable no matter what happens externally. For some people the price paid for this is often too much to bear; it means being different from some of those whose approval we crave, and that is too threatening. Lacking a sense of their own Self, these people use others as a crutch or a whipping boy.

People without inner security or a calm centre often suffer from a high level of anxiety, and a deep desire to please. Their lack of faith in themselves means they are unable to reach out with love and trust to others; it is the self-blame that expects, and unconsciously elicits, punishment for perceived guilt. If this is the case, there can be a paranoia which demands retaliation in advance of anticipated wrongs. It lashes out and rails against the world, from anger born of helplessness. These people often try to appear special by projecting an over-inflated ego, but in reality this just serves to antagonise others; the very act of being 'ordinary', letting go sufficiently to allow the true Self to come forward will enable us to feel special and be able to reach out to others.

An authentic sense of Self is based on an inner self-worth and value. It is often confused with self-confidence but this is not necessarily the same as a sense of Self. The Self does not suffer from fear, doubt or inadequacy; it is infinite and in harmony, complete in itself. It does not strive to be, it merely is. It has Self-confidence rather than the ego-confidence which may mask deep anxieties and yet be projected as self-confidence. Indeed, self-confidence may actually get in the way of developing a sense of Self as it may lead to a situation of 'I know the answers: I am right, you are wrong'. This is usually based more on confidence in one's beliefs and attitudes, which must be right and therefore anyone who disagrees is wrong, than in the inner rightness of Self.

Chiron-Sun aspects can also indicate a difficulty in dealing with the masculine principle – usually projected into a difficult 'father' relationship. As Melanie Reinhart says: 'it is a question of coming face to face with the controlling, destructive and autocratic side of the masculine principle'. Only by recognising this as an inner 'shadow' quality, embracing and integrating it, can the deep split of Sun-Chiron aspects be healed – in both sexes.

Chiron-Moon (or Chiron in Cancer)
Here the wound is in the emotions: deep hurts from the past are strongly repressed and defended against. There may also be pain around mothering and being mothered and in handling the feminine principle – a wound which, in men, is usually projected on to the mother or other significant woman.

Going public
I have found that Chiron can conceal personal pain which simply has to become public knowledge in order for it to heal. It is as though the person whose Chiron is being affected has to do the healing on a wider scale. It is a moment of catharsis. Other people resonate with the event – as in the huge public outpouring of grief when Diana, Princess of Wales died. They feel 'this is my experience, I know what this is like'. The degree of how public it becomes varies from friends and family

to a whole nation, and maybe more. The archetypal memories which pass down through Chiron affect everyone. By going public with the experience, the collective is able to let go of the pain. This was especially relevant for a client of mine who seemed to be strongly attuned to the collective. His chart centred around Chiron, which formed part of a Grand Cross. I am including his story because I have had several clients who shared this experience and it throws valuable light on the experience of Crucifixion, another Chironic archetype.

This client had Moon conjunct Uranus in Cancer. Tracy Marks says that people with the Moon in Cancer feel the whole cycle of the Moon psychologically. They are more aware of internal oscillations created by the cycle of the luminaries. This client certainly reacted to the Moon and its eclipses very strongly. He became part of an eternal triangle, having an affair with his healing partner during which they practised tantric sex as a means of healing the earth. (A not uncommon practice according to my postbag!). A child was born as a result. Not unnaturally, the client's wife was devastated and the healing partnership ended. The healing partner then went to the press with the story. Saturn in opposition to Venus and square the Moon, and Chiron opposite the Moon and square Venus have a history of great pain and betrayal around relationships and can inflict great hurt.

At this time the client was undergoing a solar eclipse to his Moon-Uranus conjunction, which acts as a catharsis. He had to relive old emotional pain so that he could be freed from it. He said at the time that he was emotionally drained, there was nothing left: 'I feel as though I've been emptied out'. Earlier in the year we had looked at a similar pattern that went way back in time and worked at removing a sensation of dread and a 'lump' he had carried in his stomach. The regression appeared to be an emotional purging. At the time I did not know about the pregnancy but it was later apparent just how much guilt had been present and how it linked into the past. The eclipse triggered a Grand cross in his chart, which involved the Moon, Uranus Neptune and Chiron. Tracy Marks says that 'eclipses also have to do with our capacity to transcend our most deeply rooted and disturbing inner conflicts'. It is a time of 'direct confrontation with our own demons and angels, or indirectly in projected form through confrontation with others'. Conjunct the Moon, we also have to look at our patterns of accepting and revealing our inner emotional needs. This was certainly true for my client, who was confronting all his emotional pain, with aeons of illusions, delusions and betrayals coming together in an extremely public experience. The most painful thing for him, and the most difficult to understand was the reason for his healing partner's public confession. He had been sure that the physical contact between them reflected a union of spiritual energies that could only benefit the planet. Of course, we don't know how much his own powers of self-deception were distorting his view of reality – he was strongly Neptunian. In her perception, however, she was the one who was betrayed. She had believed he would leave his wife, breaking the eternal triangle (a common misconception).

In *Border Crossing: a Psychological Perspective on Carlos Castaneda's Path of Knowledge*, author Donald Williams pinpoints a shamanistic state all too familiar to this client and many others:

> 'Thus he balances the joy of a man about to find his life with the sadness of a man rendered lonely, foolish and perhaps even fearsome by his vision. Both the sadness and joy are genuine'

In this way Chiron reveals the paradox at the heart of the reconciliation of opposites. This planet is the key to the fusion of the instincts with the spirit, of the human nature with the divine, and of fate and free will.

When something is hidden, there is always the dread that it will be revealed. When I heard about the pregnancy, I suggested that the client make his own statement to the press, or at the very least to his family and friends. Going public would have taken the heat out of the situation, and the press may not have found it particularly interesting. It certainly wouldn't have been hyped to the extent it was, and some people may even have been sympathetic to his situation. In the event, he did not do this, so we must ask whether it was all this woman or was she co-operating with his karma. Most appropriately, while all this was going on Mars was opposing natal Neptune. As Robert Hand points out: 'During this time you may have to face the unpleasant consequences of past actions that you would rather avoid ... you have to bury your ego for a while and take a good look at your past actions, face them and take whatever action is necessary'. He opted to forgive himself as well as her. It looked as though he had finally moved out of the pain and bitterness and that the healing of the Chironic wound could proceed.

Chiron-Mercury (or Chiron in an Air Sign or Virgo)

Mercury aspecting Chiron can indicate an old wound connected with communication or related to how the intellect has been used in the past. I have seen this aspect in a child born with a cleft palate (in that case retributive karma) and in someone who regressed to a life in which his tongue was cut out as punishment for informing.

A client consulted me because of her lack of confidence. After the reading she told me that she often had to speak to small groups of people but when she opened her mouth, nothing came out. She had Chiron in Gemini in the eleventh house, opposing Mercury. The first past life which I picked up on was described as follows:

> I had a very strong impression of a nun in a silent order, and when I say silent I really mean this as all the prayer times were silent and there wasn't even any chanting to relieve the total silence. I don't feel you used your voice for many, many years. You also seem to be totally alone, you slept in single cells and didn't even have the companionship of the other nuns. There is also this feeling coming forward of being so unworthy, a sense of sinfulness and being inadequate in the Lord's eyes. As though you wanted to be perfect spiritually and yet felt that you failed so often, when really it was the standards that were so impossibly high no human being could ever reach them. Also because there was no companionship with the other nuns, and no shared worship in the sense that each joined with the others - prayers were communal but silent, individual - there was no shared spiritual dimension to give you strength. In fact the spiritual dimension seems to be the most devastating and most lacking

of all, as though the real purpose behind the convent's existence had been forgotten...

The other life which I'm picking up strongly was diametrically opposed to this. This is probably Tudor times but I have the sense of you being 'Mistress' to someone quite exalted. You look very pretty but there wasn't much in the way of brains there, in fact there's an almost childlike innocence with this despite the obviously sexual side of the relationship. You seem to have lived for pretty clothes, jewellery. And this very besotted male seems to have supplied them in great abundance and shown you off whenever possible - but as a 'possession' not a partner. There is the impression of 'smile and show everyone how ravishing you are, but don't dare open your mouth'. Although at the time this did not upset you at all, I'm sure that later when you were reviewing the life it left an inhibition and a feeling of being stupid which is no longer appropriate for you but which has lingered beneath the surface.

Her feedback, made as notes at the time of listening to the taped reading, is enlightening as to how experiences are carried over into the present incarnation:

I was pulled into this world (breech) to the sound of swearing and screaming as my mother lashed out at the doctor for hurting her so badly as he hauled me out.

When I was born I was unable to cry at all. Apparently I made all the motions of crying but it wasn't until I was six months old that any sound came out. Then I let the world know of my existence, but my mother couldn't bear the sound of babies crying and as soon as I was fed in the morning she would put me in the pram and push me way down the bottom of the garden behind the woodshed and leave me there until it was time to be fed again (could this be the reason for my occasional resorting to comfort eating in times of stress?).

At one year old I had a head-on collision with my older brother and I remained concussed for two days. When my mother finally managed to wake me up I went into convulsions and in her panic she rolled me up in a blanket and laid me out on the garden path whilst she fetched a neighbour to help her. I had two fits in all and she was told that a third could be fatal and therefore she was not to be left alone with me as she was well into her next pregnancy. So the neighbour took to looking after me until I eventually was out of any further danger (what a start in life). [She has the Moon bi-quintile Pluto on the Ascendant, an aspect of 'fate' related to mothering and being mothered, and a close brush with death in her 'past']. Being the oldest girl it was always my task to look after the latest baby in the family and I loved every minute of it. They were my own real-life dolls ... When I was eight years old a baby died as it was premature. I can still feel the terrible disappointment and bewilderment that I felt when I saw my little newborn sister, who weighed 2 lb, lying in her coffin ready to be taken away to be buried. Up to that time I had always thought that only our farm animals and birds and cats and dogs died and got buried.

When I am with others I can talk reasonably freely one to one until I sense their gaze intent upon me. Then I feel stripped naked, vulnerable and go to pieces.

There seems to be a strong tie in between the nun incarnation and my silent entry into this life. I still have a need to have a quiet time at each end of the day in which to relax, pray and meditate. I feel quite cheated if my husband comes to bed at the same time as me, and equally if he is in a chatty mood first thing in the morning.

Healing for this aspect is found a little at a time. For an experience such as the one above, Past Life Therapy* might be needed to 'reframe the past', flower essences such as the Australian Bush essence 'Confidessence' can aid the development of confidence when speaking in public.

Chiron-Venus

With this aspect the soul has experienced considerable pain and trauma in past relationships, and carries the internal message – and karmic expectation that love hurts. The soul tends to be drawn into relationships that will reinforce the belief, being let down or hurt by partners. Previous relationships may have been so traumatising that the soul holds back from risking another sexual encounter. In some cases the soul has idealistic or romantic expectations to such a degree that no partner could possibly live up to them. This soul needs to experience the nurturing and sharing of a true relationship as healing for the past. Injuries such as a broken heart may need

---

*   See *Principles of Past Life Therapy*

to be repaired, or a part of the soul – or the heart retrieved from the place where it took refuge from the pain.

Chiron-Mars

The pain of Chiron in aspect to Mars stems from violence, or misused Will or assertion energy, and it can involve a violation of trust in the past. This aspect can, for example, fit in with the priest/healer who commits an act of violence or blasphemy; it can also indicate karma resulting from having taken part in 'Holy Wars' or crusades, or indicate membership of one of the military orders of monks, such as the Knights Templar or Knights of St. John. Unfortunately, despite the vows of obedience, poverty and chastity, many of the sieges carried out by the Crusader Knights led to the sacking and pillaging of towns and the slaughter of the populace. This aspect could also delineate a soul who has been the victim of a war or other violent confrontation in a prior life. The root cause can be indicated by the sign in which Chiron is placed and other aspects in the chart.

A client travelled many thousands of miles to attend a workshop in order to explore her compulsion and repulsion around becoming a healer. Her chart had Chiron exactly conjunct the South Node in Gemini, very widely opposing Mars in the ninth, and exactly squaring Neptune in the seventh. In a regression she went back to being a doctor in a prisoner-of-war camp who was forced to carry out surgery which (s)he felt was totally unethical. Eventually (s)he was shot for refusing to co-operate further. At the 'between life' stage she said that she was coming back to atone for all the blood that had been wrongly spilt. During the regression she kept trying to wipe off the blood which covered her arms and when the regression was completed she had to shower in order to symbolically cleanse herself. This particular experience may well have connected to ancestral karma as Chiron was in the fourth house.

Pluto-Chiron-Mars

A client (Fig. 15) with Pluto widely opposing a Mars-Chiron conjunction in Aquarius, Venus-Moon in Pisces inconjunct

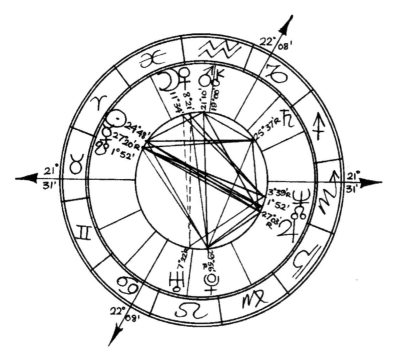

Fig 15

Uranus, and Sun-Mercury-South Node opposing Jupiter-North Node-Neptune had power and assertion issues and was plagued with psychic visions:

> As a qualified nurse I have become rather more than surprised at the many occasions I have witnessed and actually 'seen' a presence on the ward.
>
> I have the same kind of experience at home and since the age of nine years old several of my friends have been somewhat unnerved by 'the strange goings-on' when they are with me.
>
> A close friend of mine bought a very old house and moved with his family. I had never seen the house but I sensed very strongly that the children were in danger when playing in the garden. So much so that I felt quite sick and faint. To cut a long story short, we unearthed a deep cesspit which had been over-looked by the surveyor. My fiance has witnessed various things, he says I occasionally hold conversations with him when I seem to belong to a past era. He feels I have a magnetic hold over him.

This was a instance of uncontrolled psychic abilities being 'contaminated' by emotional and psychiatric difficulties both from this life and from the past. It was suggested to her that she should undergo therapy for these problems and at the same time attend classes which would teach her how to control her psychic abilities. A relevant past life which came up was one in which she had:

> ... used her powers unwisely in order to ensnare a man she was attracted to, and in so doing attracted the attention of the witch-finders. She seemed to have been totally at the mercy of her emotions and to have lost all the training and common sense which she had before this man came along. She had been a 'white Witch', using her powers wisely up to that point and doing a lot of good. There was a sense of being involved in the worship of the 'great mother' a very old tradition dating from before Christianity which was handed on from mother to daughter to keep it 'pure'. She went against this tradition in order to 'get her man' and it all rebounded on her and ended in her death. There was a lot of resentment coming forward, with frustration and anger (Pluto opposing Chiron-Mars) that she did not get what she wanted. There was deep emotional trauma because afterwards the depth of her emotion and the lengths she was prepared to go to get this man really surprised and frightened her - there was a picture of her in a cell locked up awaiting 'trial' and suddenly clearly seeing what had been going on as though she had been a different person while in the grip of this emotion.

Although I had been asked to look at the older interaction with her fiance, this was one occasion when I felt that it was inappropriate as they needed to learn to relate to the here and now, to have a relationship based on love rather than on obsession and compulsion, on freedom and acceptance of each other as individuals rather than one trying to mould the other by and to her Will. (There were a total of eight inconjuncts in the synastry between the charts, her Pluto opposition to Chiron-Mars squared his Mercury and her Neptune-North Node opposed his Sun).

Scapegoat or Redeemer: Chiron-Neptune

Planets do not cause events, they represent the inner energies which are activated, but Neptune more than most does correlate with breakdown and inner illumination. Neptune is a planet representing extremes: enlightened spirituality versus the greatest escape and disintegration, truth and beauty or illusion and deception; exceptional clarity compounded by the deepest confusion, or isolation. Neptune dissolves, it brings illumination – if you are ready! With Neptune, all rational thought is suspended and it feels like you are being taken over at an unconscious level. Operating during a Neptune transit is like walking in a fog or being hypnotised. When the transit is finally over, it feels like someone has snapped their fingers and you are back in the conscious world again. Add Chiron into the mix whether by aspect or transit, and the effect is quadrupled.

Neptune, with its openness to what is all around on extremely subtle levels, tends to act like a psychic sponge, indiscriminately soaking up whatever is in the atmosphere. It is also involved in clearing collective karma. This clearing of collective karma is rather like acting as a psychic vacuum cleaner. Some people have the ability to draw in energies out of the collective pool and transform them either by their own actions or by passing them through their bodies. However, it is an act that can be performed on the conscious or unconscious level. Performed unconsciously, this can be an extremely self-destructive act. When it is performed with due awareness, it is a positive experience: 'redemptive karma', in other words someone will deliberately take on a huge chunk of karma and play out a role such as the scapegoat in order to take these energies out of the collective pool and, in so doing, 'redeem' humankind: the Jesus story is a classic example. We can also look on it as an example of the microcosm, one person, acting out what is needed for the macrocosm, the whole, because everything an individual does affects the whole.

Neptune is also involved in the scapegoat experience, as is Chiron. Chiron took on the burden of mortality from Prometheus and, as a result, was able to die and be elevated to a position in the heavens. Neptune represents guilt, and guilt unconsciously seeks punishment – hence the scapegoat. Closely linked to this 'scapegoat experience' is the Neptunian, Chironic 'emotional crucifixion'. One of the founders of modern psychology, C.G. Jung described crucifixion:

> This condition of the crucifixion, then, is a symbolic expression for the state of extreme conflict, where one simply has to give up, where one no longer knows, where one almost loses one's mind. Out of that condition grows the thing which is really fought for.... We would say it was the birth of the self.[6]

It is therefore part of the burning away of the old self. The time when we have to surrender (Neptune) to the inevitability of our transformation (Chiron) from what we have been to what we might be. It is a time when all our inherent conflicts and imbalances become apparent – an unbearable explosion that forces release upon us. In the depths of crucifixion, at the 'My God why has thou forsaken me' moment, we reach out to something other and find that it is within us all the time: our true self.

The role of the scapegoat is to be a focus for carrying away other people's negative energy (also linked to Chiron in Capricorn), but it is possible to be a passive scapegoat, a Neptunian victim, who simply absorbs all this energy and feels helpless to do anything about it. Used constructively it can be a positive scapegoat that takes the energy and transforms it and many people are incarnating with this ability today.

An Alien in a Strange Land – Chiron and Alienation

I find an interesting parallel between Chiron and the many people now in incarnation who feel that they do not originate from earth. They believe they are 'star children' who have become trapped within the solar system and feel that their task is to raise the vibrations of Earth sufficiently for the barrier – sometimes known as a vortex - to be released. A client whose Chiron forms part of a prominent karmic Grand Cross, was told in a channelling that some souls, himself included, have the ability to communicate outside this 'vortex' to the other levels of creation who are trying to aid the evolution of the Earth. We can see Chiron as a cosmic messenger from outside our solar system who brings these healing energies in and, through an eccentric orbit moving from Uranus past Saturn to Jupiter, infuses the inner planets so that the energies are accessible to our conscious selves.

More and more people who consult me are convinced they are 'star children' and it makes sense to me that evolved beings should be trying to help the earth out in this difficult time. Some beings seem to be able to come without getting caught up in the earth's vibrations, but for many it is experienced as 'a trap' which results in many lives here. Such people do not feel at home on earth, they long to return to the other realms. One of the reasons, I believe, for the drug and meditation explosion in the 1960's and shamanism in the late 1990's is that people were seeking a return to the oneness symbolised by Neptune. I get many people asking for readings who feel that they have come for a specific reason and they need to recover the memory in order that they can bear to stay on earth.

Geoff Boltwood, a powerful healer and channeller, told one of my clients that, at the time of Atlantis, a vortex was created that cut off the earth from the rest of the cosmos and trapped many souls. This vortex also cut off communication with 'the divine mind' except through those souls who were able to embody it because of their unique energy frequencies. Geoff says that energy changes are taking place to release this vortex and free the souls, allowing access to the divine mind once again.

This explanation accords with the experiences of clients during regressions to other lives, many of whom speak of the energy changes and of the new types of vibrational healing that are needed now. It appears to me that many of the people who were involved in the Atlantean upheaval are on earth again to try to prevent the calamity repeating itself. Also, many people have 'technological karma' from Atlantis which they have to work out and this has been the first opportunity to do so since the destruction of Atlantis. Although I do not think we can equate the two kinds of technology, the ethical issues raised by the use of that technology are however the same.

We have to think here for a moment about the nature of time. To me it is not a linear, chronological sequence stretching back and forward endlessly. It is more like a spiral, through which we can move upwards or downwards as required. Therefore, to say it is 'the first opportunity', does not mean that people have been waiting around for however many thousand years it took.

The Wound Emerges

Chiron's wound often emerges in childhood, together with any other issues related to it. For example, a man with a natal Saturn inconjunct to the Sun (which was trine Chiron) carried over lack of self confidence from several lives and found public speaking excruciatingly difficult (Chiron squared Mercury). He told me that when he was young he was in the school play He took the part of a tree and Prince Charming was supposed to come along and cut the tree down but did not pass remotely near enough. The small boy remained frozen, standing 'while the audience fell about at the sight of this silly sod still stood there with his arms in the air'. This story rang many bells with me - after all he was speaking to someone who had gone on stage in a fairy dress hut who had forgotten to remove her harem costume trousers first! The burst of laughter shattered what fragile confidence I had and kept me off the stage and kept my mouth shut for many years. We shared a third house Chiron placement and Chiron was active by transit when the incident occurred. Chiron in the third has an old pattern of being deeply wounded by words in the past in our case, being laugher reinforced the old pain. I had heard the comedian John Cleese (Chiron in Cancer in the eleventh house trine Mercury in the third house) tell a very similar story day or two earlier. In his case, he decided to become a clown, using the incident somewhat more positively by making people laugh to cover his own sense of inadequacy.

I pondered long and hard about such seemingly small incidents that shape a life, In my own case, public speaking, no matter how small the group, was agony for many years despite my Leo Ascendant. I queried why shame and humiliation should be considered a fitting preparation for public appearances. I was told that, on one level, at least we would always know that we would not die of shame no matter how dire the embarrassment. Lack of confidence can also have its positive side in that it makes you question, 'Is this right?', and 'I really meant to do this?', before you put your head in the lion's mouth.

On another level however, it was part of a total breakdown in our sense of self. This is the sense of self which relates to the ego, the small self, the 'me' which develops during an incarnation and which can be carried over in a personal way to the next incarnation. A disintegration and dissolving of the small self, and the personality traits associated with it, is necessary to break deeply ingrained traits such as egotism or self-abasement, self-importance or self-negation, arrogance or fawning humility, always thinking you are right or never believing in yourself, etc. It is not related to the Higher Self which is the eternal part of our being Nevertheless, the purpose of the breakdown of the small self is to allow the Higher Self to make its presence felt, to show us that we are all eternal beings who are learning and growing. We all need to develop a strong and constructive sense of self, what many people call the ego, as without this we have no inner resources to meet life's challenges. We cannot surrender that 'ego' and achieve divine wholeness unless we have fully developed our individual self first, so a strong ego is a necessary step in reaching the Higher Self. Chiron helps us to break away from outdated behaviour and to integrate new aspects of the Self.

On yet another level, incidents like this also have to do with the development of 'sub-personalities', seemingly separate parts of one's self signified by the planets, such as a saboteur (Saturn or Neptune) or scapegoat (Neptune or Churn) or a showman (Jupiter) who emerge at the most inconvenient moments and trip us up. These figures make themselves known throughout our lives, but they have their roots in the past. When Chiron aspects these planets, natally or by transit, it is an opportunity to get to know them, find out if they have any positive value and if not, to leave them behind.

CHIRON IN TRANSIT TO CHIRON

When Chiron transits itself, especially on the squares and oppositions, it tends to both provoke a crisis of meaning and
bring out the wound for healing. It is also a period when we
begin to move into another dimension, expanding consciousness.

Chiron's transits to itself are erratic and do not follow a
set pattern due to elliptical orbit. The major hard aspects are
vital turning points and karmic lessons, and the pattern may
re-emerge with each hard aspect. The first Chiron square
can take place any time between the ages of 5 and 23. This is
the time when the karmic wound emerges and focuses. Often
traumatic, it frequently correlates with physical 'dis-ease'
reflecting the wound. The first square separates from what
comforts most, and the soul feels lost, homeless. 'Chiron crisis
is designed to get one to recognise that the soul exists in that
body ...... the first realisation often comes that the soul is imprisoned in the body' (Philip Sedgewick).

The earlier the square occurs, the sooner the soul is
opened to higher consciousness. At the opposition, there is a
possibility of healing or re-focusing. At the last square, the lesson is reiterated. The Chiron Return is an opportunity to clear
the wound and unfinished business once and for all and is often accompanied by a 'Life Review'. This is Decision Time.
The soul experiences a major life crisis leading to greater
awareness and fulfilment of life purpose. The return is an 'opportunity to achieve freedom from the Saturnian past, and
freedom from anxiety about the Uranian future.' (Zane
Stein). It offers: 'A true mastery of self and integration of all the
phases that have led up to this time.' (Barbara Hand Clow).
Chiron transits to the other planets bring out the woundedness
but are an opportunity to integrate that energy fully. Transiting
houses, Chiron stimulates that particular area of life.

The Chiron Square
The Chiron square is often a time of profound spiritual crisis
and a triggering of past life memories or experiences can take
place. It is when the karmic wound emerges. My own experience shows just how life threatening the square can be. For

me, it came when I was five. I developed bronchial pneumonia. When I regressed to this time, it was clear that I had never fully committed myself to incarnation. Age five was difficult for me emotionally and a brief separation from my beloved grandmother was the final straw – I wanted to go 'home' (definitely not earth). Eventually I was reunited with my grandmother, and decided to stay around, but I don't think I was really committed to being here until the opposition of Chiron to itself took place when I was 24. I had a near-death-experience in childbirth (which set me on my path-way) and relived a previous death in childbirth. The guides who were with me told me I had a choice, I could repeat the experience or I could get on and learn the lessons I had come for and take up my karmic purpose. Realising that I would have to go through it all again if I died, I chose to stay. On the next Chiron square, which coincided with my spiritual awakening, I had a car crash that, to quote an ambulance man, 'should have been fatal' but I was untouched. I suffered deep depression for some weeks, however, which I finally realised was because I was angry at still being alive. In coming to terms with that fact, I found my spiritual purpose.

SOUL EVOLUTION

I feel it is important that we should not see past lives as 'fact'. We should see them as telling us the story of our soul's evolution, with all the lessons we have had to learn set out in these archetypal experiences. For me, the only reason for looking at past lives is to see how they can help us to understand our present situation, to teach us how we can grow in accordance with our soul's purpose. If we use reincarnation in this way, it does not matter whether it is absolute fact or not, it is true for us on the inner levels. I believe we have to keep an open mind – on everything. When we believe we have found all the answers, 'life' has a habit of reminding us that we can never remain static. Things are continuously changing and we are evolving all the time, this is what astrology is all about!

So often Chiron is involved in the modern shaman's initiation, and as previously discussed, it shows where we must take a shamanic test. Shaman are 'chosen' to form the link between their community and the spiritual forces. They are the healers and seers and are marked out when young, often by an illness or traumatic experience. In tribal societies their development is carefully guided by the elders as they go through the different levels of initiatory experience. In our modern society, however, we have lost touch with this link. Nevertheless, many people today are developing as shamans. Initiations have several well-defined stages, there is often a testing, some kind of ordeal, in which the initiate is alone and has to battle with his psychological demons. S/he usually experiences 'death', often in a dramatic and graphic breakdown of the physical self and the persona attached to it. A woman who was extremely ill with a heart condition describes this moment:

> I was going through a process of letting go of everything in this life because of my health issues: my work, my leisure pursuits, my relationship, everything. All of which are my perception of how things are. There is nothing left. It brings me to standing in the now, in the present and this actually is who I am now.
>
> But as I turn into the other direction to the future I see a bridge and a being standing waiting for me on the bridge to guide me over. It was wonderful. Then I began to cry as I realise I can't go yet and I have to stay in the now. I have to wait on this side of the bridge to help others over. I cannot go myself. I have a task to do.

And indeed she did not die. She was undergoing a transit of Pluto and Chiron to her natal Chiron and Pluto. Piece by piece she began to deal with the causes of her dis-ease and to heal herself. Having let go of everything, a new life emerged.

Some people have to undergo a public initiation in order to see more fully the pitfalls of the path, and also the possibilities. They have to experience facing the past, and all their emotional patterns, so that they can be 'burned off' and transmuted. In the process of finding healing for themselves, they may well discover their own healing ability. Facing up to their part in the process and wresting with their psychological demons is a necessary part of the move towards the shamanic level of consciousness – without it they cannot fully move forward, no matter how much they may think otherwise. The soul's evolution is held back.

In the old days, and in so-called 'primitive' societies today, candidates for spiritual initiation were carefully chosen and prepared: the natural 'defence mechanisms' were lowered as the chakras were systematically opened, and the inflow of spiritual energies contained. Nowadays, it is happening without guidance, sometimes to a mind blown open by drugs or uncontrolled psychic experiences, as the energy changes activate the chakras in receptive souls regardless of readiness. The explosion of interest in shamanistic and native teachings shows just how much this old knowledge appeals to the primal core of humankind. Undergoing initiation within a group, under an experienced leader, the effect is explained and contained, and the spiritual experience is grounded into everyday life. Alone, everything happens so fast there are no controls. But the Chironic rewards are great for the soul who successfully undergoes shamanic initiation.

Karmic Dis-ease

I am ill because of wounds to the soul, to the deep emotional self

Attributed to D.H. Lawrence

The incarnating soul carries over burdens and baggage from past lives which are mapped out in the natal chart and may manifest physically as illness or handicap, or as emotional difficulties and problems in handling the daily business of living.

THE KARMA OF HEALTH

The body can be regarded as the 'last stop' for karma. The etheric body holds the imprint at death of old injuries, illnesses or attitudes and incorporates them into the 'blueprint' from which the current-life body takes shape: it is a kind of organising field.

Chronic health problems or handicaps frequently reflect an underlying karmic basis. The incarnating soul may choose to undergo a particular experience to reverse previous patterns of bodily abuse, misuse or neglect, or to offset emotional imbalances and chronically ingrained attitudes. When this is the case disease should more properly be written 'dis-ease', as it signifies a basic disharmony creating lack of ease between the different levels of being. Conversely, the soul may need to go through the experience to develop qualities such as courage, fortitude and acceptance. The experience may also be an unselfish act to facilitate the growth of another soul as well as its own, as in the case of the disabled child whose parents grow through caring for him or her. Karmic astrology can identify the old pattern underpinning illness or handicap and indicate how best to respond to it.

Retributive and organic karma are carried in the sixth house and the signs describe how the energy of a planet in this house has been used, or abused, in the past, and how it will manifest in the present incarnation. In fixed signs the karma has developed over many lifetimes, whereas in cardinal or mutable signs it is the result of a dominant 'recent' past life or it is in the making. Planetary aspects may also indicate the karma involved.

In his past-life work psychiatrist Arthur Guirdham found that specific parts of the body were often subjected to repeated patterns of injury, and this phenomenon has been confirmed again and again in regression work and by the researches of Professor Ian Stevenson.

In a spontaneous regression to a Roman incarnation, I uncovered a life in which my chest had been opened up by a sword wound. This experience was confirmed, as far as these things ever can be, by a friend who, when massaging my feet, 'saw' leather armour torn open over a gaping chest wound. The friend 'remembered' being a servant at that time and using massage and herbs to heal the wounds of war. Another friend, who also had past-life recall, suddenly said: 'We were Roman soldiers together and you were wounded in the chest. You were also stabbed in the chest way back before that in Egypt.' Another life involved my being burnt at the stake and choking to death on the smoke. In my current life my karmic chest weakness had manifested when I was a child as bronchial pneumonia, which had scarred the lungs and trachea and caused an on-going 'dis-ease'. This weakness is linked in the chart to an overemphasis on the Air and Fire elements and a lack of Earth planets (Chiron in Virgo being the only Earth) and to Capricorn on the cusp of the sixth house. Saturn, the ruler of Capricorn, is in Gemini, and conjuncts Mars, indicating an old wound and constriction on breathing. The comment was made that I only breathed into my head and was unconnected to the earth – something I had been endeavouring to overcome for fifteen years. Some karmic lessons can take a long time to absorb, and the step between the head cognitively understanding and the heart then putting the understanding into practice can be a long one.

Some ten years after I first wrote this piece – and was coerced into attributing it to 'a woman' instead of myself – I once again contracted pneumonia and – yet again – almost died. (I have had three near death experiences, all linked to transiting Chiron aspects to natal Chiron or other significant planets.) Transiting Pluto had briefly moved into Sagittarius and was heading towards my Sun, until it retreated back to Scorpio and my stay in hospital was enlivened by a succession of astrologers ringing to say wasn't it marvellous how graphically I was living out my Pluto transit! In hospital, I retrieved two further significant memories in regard to my chest. In the first I had gone with a group of priests to repair and reconstitute the sacred defences of a tomb that had been raided by robbers. Unknowingly, we stepped into the remnants of a 'gas trap'. It was not enough to kill us, but it was rather like having been part of a First World War mustard gas attack. My chest was never the same again.

I had always 'known' that I had been walled up in a tomb but had not had the details. Now, suddenly, the information came. I, along with a young assistant, was sealed into the tomb to help the soul of the dead person make a significant but difficult transition through 'the other world'. I had the task of, in deepest meditation, leaving my body and accompanying him as far as was allowed. My assistant was supposed to aid this process, and watch over me. However, he became very agitated when he was unable to rouse me after some considerable time, and there wasn't any sign of anyone coming to release us. He began to chip away at the plaster round the door, raising an enormous cloud of dust. The air was becoming thin, which I was experiencing myself in the current life as panic from oxygen depletion. Back there in Egypt, my soul was so far from my body, I didn't feel any of the physical symptoms. But in Dorset, my body struggled for breath and I would wake panting in panic and reach for my flower essences and the oxygen mask. In that other life, I died choking on the dust and my assistant with me. When I realised the carry-over, I was able to do some healing and the panics subsided. Later I went back and reframed it completely.

However, two positive things came from that experience. The first was that I had rediscovered an ability to accompany a soul through death. Which was fortunate as, with Pluto moving close to my Sun again, I was shortly called on to accompany first Mac as he died of cancer and then a dear friend, Justin Carson, as he made a conscious choice not to have any more toxic treatment. Knowing Justin had been both a joy and a privilege, and being present with him for ten days as his powerful mind worked to let go of his ailing body was an experience that took me to levels of consciousness I had not been aware of previously. (Transiting Chiron was on my natal Sun, transiting Pluto and the Moon on my Mercury and the North Node on my Jupiter.)

The second gift came when Chiron was on my Sun and Pluto on my Merury-Uranus opposition. My chest problems were diagnosed via a computerised radionic box (Mercury-Uranus!) to stem from an ancestral miasm of renal tuberculosis which had been passed through the family. At the same time, I met Josephine Miller who prescribed a tuberculosis nosode for T.B. that had passed down the family. This was an example of 'right timing' as the first homoeopathic remedy I had been given twenty years previously had been a tuberculosis nosode. It had helped but not cured. My partner, Dr Robert Jacobs, had saved my life when the pneumonia struck, using new German homoeopathic antibiotics, but he had not been able to clear the root-cause – sometimes partners are too close. Jo's objectivity enabled her to diagnose and treat several acquired toxins from my present life as well. My breathing became better than it had been for the whole of my life thus far. Transiting Neptune had been moving through my sixth house for the whole of the experience, bringing to the surface the hidden ancestral pattern and the factors from my own 'past' that were required for healing.

In the course of the Pluto to the Sun transit I finally birthed a book that had been thirteen years in the writing. *The Hades Moon* was about Pluto in aspect to the Moon. It was intended to be completed when Pluto conjuncted my Scorpio Moon but I needed the light of the Sun to bring the book to fruition – and the insights that my own karmic dis-ease afforded me.

The ME Disease

The 'fixed' nature of past-life patterns is shown in the chart of a client (fig. 16) who had suffered with ME for the past fifteen years, following glandular fever as a student, and yet who had the potential to be fully healthy; his Sun-Mars conjunction in Taurus in the sixth house had tremendous drive, endurance and energy available. Although he appeared to want to become well, he was constantly sabotaged in his attempts by an unconscious need to stay weak and helpless (Neptune inconjunct Sun-Mars, and Sun-Mars square Pluto and trine Saturn). Both Saturn and Neptune can take the role of saboteur: Saturn out of ingrained fear and Neptune because of old illusions and lack of clarity. His karmic pattern is one of abuse of the body as, for example, when he was a monk and fasted and scourged himself constantly to escape from the 'evils of the flesh', and in another life when he over-indulged his appetites. In the present life he could not digest his food and his weight was down to seven stone. His Saturn in Virgo indicated chronic

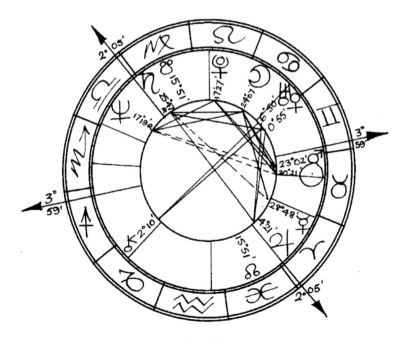

Fig 16

fear and worry affecting the digestive system. He spoke of a 'permanent, problem of disorientation, (Neptune), hearing a voice, seeing a body and yet not being part of it'. With his Sun in Taurus in the sixth house and his Saturn in Virgo, one of his karmic lessons was to become aware of the psychosomatic component of disease. He must recognise how the mind, emotions, and underlying beliefs, affected the physical body and how inner disharmony will manifest as illness. He also had to learn how to be at one with a physical body and how to integrate the four levels of being – physical-emotional-mental-spiritual – into himself.

There are old power and anger issues in the Pluto squares, and he also needed to deal with the Will (Saturn trine Mars); it is only when he truly recognises on the inner level that it lies within his power to become well and accepts his own responsibility (Saturn) in this process; that a change can take place. He is strongly defensive of his feelings, having been subjected to the emotional chaos of an unstable mother (tenth house Neptune square Moon in Cancer) in addition to past-life problems. His chart lacks Air with only Neptune in Libra, but his intellectual function is overdeveloped. Talking and rationalising (Virgo South Node) are his defences against feeling, and he used to take refuge from the body in prolonged meditation (Neptune) until he recognised and closed that escape route.

A chronic over-breather, hyperventilating through anxiety, he did not use his breath to ground and nourish himself. His condition was linked to the lack of control over the Air element function, and to the old grief and disharmony embodied in Neptune inconjunct Sun-Mars.

Working with the body through bio-energetics was one of the most successful therapies of the many he tried. And yet he 'lacked the energy to carry through the exercises' as the ME made him physically weak. With the Sun-Mars conjunction in Earth and three planets and the Ascendant in Fire, he could, if he persevered, actually build up his stamina and reserves of energy through exercise, and release the physical blockages which have built up within his body as a manifestation of his old dis-ease.

Karmically he lacked positive experience in relationships, and relating in general was a source of great difficulty for him (Chiron opposing Venus-Uranus in the seventh house). The wound of Chiron in this case was opposing the uncommitted, unpredictable Venus-Uranus style of relating in the house of relationships. The T-square of Venus to the Saturn opposition to Jupiter indicated an old inability to perceive himself as loveable, and the tendency to go to extremes within a relationship. The sexual area in particular gave him problems. Although he felt mentally aroused, he had too little physical energy or drive to carry it through. Saturn-Mars aspects frequently indicate sexual problems such as a lack of sex drive and fear of one's potency. My first astrology teacher, Robert Tully always drew Mars afflicted by Saturn with a drooping arrow: he described it as 'brewer's droop without the need for alcohol'. Under the Neptune, Saturn and Uranus transits of his Chiron this client experienced the birth, life and death of his first ever 'proper' 'relationship. The break-up of the relationship afforded him an opportunity to finally face his feelings and deal with his pain and grief. A breakthrough seemed likely in his disease and distress as the planets – the representatives of his inner energy – forced a resolution and a new way of being by the very nature of their heavyweight combination. However, it was not to be. Despite his strenuous efforts to overcome the dis-ease, the ME continued. Some bodily karma can be tenacious in the extreme.

One of my clients, a forensic psychiatrist, thinks that ME is well named. It often attacks chronic over-achievers and workaholics. As she says, 'This dis-ease caused me to focus on ME for the first time in many lives. I simply had to deal with the issues, and look at what I really wanted out of life'. The result was a radical reorganisation of her lifestyle and a blossoming of her spiritual beliefs.

Changing the Pattern

I have long believed that many, although not all, dis-eases can be dealt with by healing the etheric blueprint, or by intervening before it becomes an ingrained pattern, just as deeply fixed illness can be aided by past life therapy or emotional release work.

An example of bodily karma-in-the-making which was reversed is illustrated by the brother of a client who was interested in alternative therapies. The brother had Pluto in Virgo in the sixth and all the symptoms of multiple sclerosis, but the tests proved negative – Pluto can indicate an illness which is extremely difficult to diagnose or attach to a cause. He was due for more tests and my client persuaded him to work with his strong Jupiter through the power of creative imaging. His symptoms cleared and he became well again.

PLANETS IN THE SIXTH HOUSE

The energies manifested by planets in the sixth house are particularly relevant to the karma of physical health. They also indicate the type of energies available for working on the body and how they may be used. These energies may manifest negatively as disease, ultimately leading to physical or mental illness; positively as old wisdom and skills; or as a sanguine attitude which can in turn be used to overcome disease. Aspects from other planets, and the sign on the cusp of the sixth house will affect how the karma manifests. The placement of, and aspects to, the ruler of the sixth house should also be taken into account.

The Sun

The Sun in the sixth house (especially with Taurus on the cusp), or difficult aspects to the Sun when it is the ruler of the sixth, indicates that particular attention should be paid to the body in the present life as it may have been misused or abused in a past life. The need is to refine the gross physical material to a higher level of functioning. Planets aspecting the Sun will illustrate the old pattern. For example, Jupiter aspects show that the body is now reaping the effects of over-indulgence or impracticality in the past; Saturn aspects indicate the results of previous over-disciplining or rigid repression of the body; and Pluto may indicate the results of past compulsions or cruelty. The Sun is also linked to the heart and to old emotional patterns such as impatience, arrogance and pride. In the present life the soul is then offered the opportunity to change these energies into love, kindness and compassion.

The use of energy is particularly important for the Sun in the sixth house as this placement can be a power-house resource to call upon in times of need, or may produce an unconscious leakage of energy. In a Fire sign energy can easily burn itself out if the incarnating soul fails to pay attention to the body's need for sufficient rest and recharging. However, with this placement it may also have learnt to handle stress well in the past and thus have a seemingly inexhaustible fund of energy to draw upon. The Earth Sun in the sixth may well have a pattern of putting all its energy into work, particularly of the physical type, and ignoring the need for relaxation and play, or of having over-indulged in the so-called 'finer things of life' in the past. Ultimately the imbalance will result in physical or mental dis-ease. The Water/sixth house Sun imbalance is often expressed through an excess of emotional energy, which literally drains the body. Women are particularly familiar with the 'washed out' feeling which follows a crying session, but men can experience this through inner tears. Similarly intense fatigue accompanies an angry outburst which has been 'buried'. A similar reaction can occur from the Air sixth house Sun, which can cause mental benders – bouts of excessive mental activity - resulting in total exhaustion even though nothing has actually been achieved. Nevertheless, once these are seen as old patterns repeating themselves, a more constructive use of energy can be made.

The Moon

The Moon, or Cancer, in the sixth house, or difficult aspects to the Moon, may relate to disease passed on through the mother. They are particularly significant for women and can indicate the possibility of a reproductive system malfunction stemming from old problems with sexuality, menstruation or pregnancy. They may point to a hereditary disease which is genetically passed via the mother, or there can be a pattern of ancestral attitude carried over from the past. If the great-grandmother, grandmother and mother have all seen menstruation and childbirth as a painful curse, it is likely that the daughter will inherit this belief and manifest it physically. If Mars and

Pluto are in aspect to the Moon, then pent-up rage or frustration from the past can have a physical manifestation as painful cramps, fibroids, etc. Where old resentment or guilt has gone forward, it may present itself as a cancer 'eating away inside'.

It should be borne in mind that the guilt and repressed emotion behind disease are not necessarily from a past incarnation. They can just be from 'the past' – although the potential for the disease may well have been laid down in past lives through failure to learn the lesson of a continuing pattern. A woman with the sixth house Moon in mutable Gemini, square Neptune, lost her husband and son within a short time of each other (Moon sextile seventh house Chiron, a wound around relationships). She then became involved with a man she described as 'almost psychotic', but whom she could not leave because she believed that she could cure him by loving him (Neptune square Moon is prone to this type of delusion). She became pregnant and was diagnosed as having Idiopathic Thrombocytopenic Purpura, 'my immune system had gone haywire'.

Idiopathic means of unknown cause or origin (Neptune squares the Moon, obscuring the emotional cause of the disease) and the blood and immune systems are involved in the illness (Mars inconjunct Moon, Mars opposition Saturn-Uranus). My doctor-partner has pointed out that this is an auto-immune disease, a tendency which can run in families so that she could have inherited it (Moon aspects). It is also more usually a disease of childhood, which may indicate that the stress she was under reduced her to being a child again:

> I was producing antibodies against the platelets in my blood. I began to miscarry the baby and had to go on to massive doses of steroids to stay alive. I feel very strongly that the disease was the result of the terrible strain of living with this man, but also the fact that when my husband died the pain of grief was so terrible I kept running away from it. The same pattern occurred with my son's death.

However, she continued to live with this violent man until eventually her deceased husband told her, through a medium, that she must not stay with him as he was destroying her. She subsequently refused to go on with orthodox medical treatment, which consisted of steroids and the removal of her spleen – in Taoist medicine the spleen is linked to the negative emotion of worry, as is Virgo, the sign also indicating psychosomatic illness and the body/mind link. There was considerable danger of a spontaneous haemorrhage and she was particularly frightened of having a stroke and being helpless. She specifically requested information in her reading on what she should be learning from the present life as she felt that was what she should be concentrating on although she had virtually answered her own question already. I suggested to her that she should work with a therapist through her grief and pain and tackle the guilt which her sexual relationship had brought out. In that way she could perhaps connect to why she had 'punished' herself by attracting this violent, psychopathic man into her life, and gain insight into the resulting illness.

Another side of the Moon energy presented problems to a young girl who consulted me. She had Pluto-Uranus-Moon in Virgo in the sixth opposing Saturn-Chiron in Pisces and had never known her biological father. Her mother had married another man before she was born and the latter had a strong sense of owing the child a debt from a previous lifetime. The girl was extremely psychic (Pluto-Uranus-Moon indicates an old ability carried forward) and was having difficulty handling the strong energies which were emerging as minor poltergeist activity and spontaneous past-life recall. The hormonal changes linked to menstruation, pregnancy and menopause can, in susceptible women, bring about the onset of psychic experiences. Her problems were focused physically as dysmenorrhea following a late onset of the menses – the effect of the Saturn-Chiron opposition to the sixth house planets and a carry-over from her mother's emotional trauma at the time of her pregnancy and childbirth. She 'saw' herself in many lives as the priestess of the ancient Mysteries, sometimes involved in sexual rites, at other times in sacrifice, and using her psychic powers as an oracle. She said that she had grown to hate the men who 'used' her and had been glad to see them sacrificed – her sixth house planets were sextile Neptune in

Scorpio in the seventh. She was aware of having been killed as a witch, and was frightened of her psychic powers as these had been the direct cause of that earlier death. Her breakthrough came when she began to use her creative energy in the present life in a different way. She wrote and illustrated a children's book which was snapped up by a publisher, and her physical and psychic problems disappeared.

Mars

Mars in the sixth house, or difficult aspects to Mars, particularly when it is the ruler of the sixth or twelfth house, indicates inner feelings of long-term anger and frustration which will eventually manifest physically. The body's defence mechanism may then attack itself, producing problems such as Aids, ME, arthritis, Parkinson's disease, cancer and ulcers. The liver, although ruled by Jupiter, is the organ related to anger in the Taoist system, and is susceptible to diseases resulting from internalised anger, blocked rage (particularly when there are aspects from Saturn), and over-indulgence (when Mars is in Sagittarius or Taurus, or has aspects to Jupiter). Too much rich fatty food may then trigger liver dysfunction or heart trouble, depending on the sign in which Mars is located. Alcoholism usually produces cirrhosis of the liver, and alcoholics tend to be very angry people although this is frequently repressed unless 'under the influence'.

Aspects of Mars to the Sun, Jupiter, Uranus and Neptune are common in the charts of alcoholics. (When working in alcohol counselling, I looked at the sunrise charts of 169 clients, 168 had close Neptune Mars aspects. The other client had Neptune in Scorpio and Mars in Pisces.) Guilt from the past, linked to Neptune-Mars, is also an underlying feature of both alcoholism and repressed rage, and can produce the symptom of throat or digestive-tract cancers (especially when Mercury is in the twelfth house or adversely aspected). It is as though on an inner level the alcoholic, or cancer sufferer, bitterly regrets the angry things that may have been said in the past, whenever that was. On the other hand the 'victim' may have suffered in silence while 'it made my gorge rise' or 'the bile of bitterness was hard to swallow', or gulped down emotions whenever they threatened to surface. It may take several life-times before the physical symptom of this inner 'swallowing' of the emotions manifests.

Old injuries also come forward with the sixth house Mars or Mars as the ruler of the sixth, and 'retributive' karma may result from injuries inflicted on another person. I have rarely seen a chart in which an illness, injury, or disability appeared to be a direct consequence of 'an eye for an eye' in the sense of a man who had put out the eyes of another in the past being born blind in the present life – probably because people requesting readings tend to have evolved some way along the spiritual pathway. However, Edgar Cayce did once warn one man who was deaf in this life never again to close his ears to cries for help and I have seen examples of this type of 'attitudinal' karma returning as a physical handicap. I have also seen a man with a mutable sixth house Mars become deaf, literally shutting himself off, because he did not want to communicate with others following the death of his wife – an example of karma-in-the-making.

There can be a link between old injuries and attitudinal karma. A Taurean woman with Mars in Capricorn in the sixth burnt with a very slow fuse as she had been taught as a child that it was wrong to show anger. However, when she finally 'blew' she took her anger out on her daughter (with whom she lived) by beating her across the upper back. She had a long-standing back problem centred on this area herself and felt constant fatigue linked to blocked anger. When regressed, she went back to a life on board ship as a sailor in which she had been pinned down by a spar falling across her upper back. Paralysed as a result, she had spent many years nursing her resentment and anger, taking them out on her daughter through angry words. Her daughter, however, would simply walk away and refuse to listen. In the present life the mother was connecting to that old resentment whenever she felt angry with her daughter. Following the regression her back problem was cured and she became more able to express her anger as and when appropriate. This allowed the fatigue problem to clear.

A blind musician who attended one of my workshops was asked by a participant, in a rather arch way, what he thought of karma. He gently replied that he thought the question told him rather a lot about the questioner's beliefs. He did not feel that his blindness was a punishment but rather something which he had chosen to experience for his own growth. He had learnt to see with inner vision and had developed his other senses and his music to compensate. He did not feel deprived in any way and his blindness was certainly not a handicap – he had travelled from Ireland to London, entirely unaided, in order to attend the workshop. As a traditional Indian saying goes:

> Who is blind?
> The man that cannot see another world.
> Who is dumb?
> The man that cannot say a kind word at the right time.
> Who is poor?
> The man plagued with too strong desires.
> Who is rich?
> The man whose heart is contented.

Jupiter

Jupiter in the sixth or twelfth house, or difficult aspects to Jupiter, can reflect a past misuse of the appetites, particularly sensuality (aspects to Venus-Mars), or over-indulgence (frequently linked to Taurus and, surprisingly perhaps, to Capricorn). They can be linked to food allergies or compulsive-eating disorders, especially when attached to the Water element or Saturn aspects in which case there may be an old compensatory pattern of starvation/overeating. Sixth house Jupiter may indicate a past-life death where the fear is 'there won't be enough for me'. Past Life therapist Roger Woolger says he frequently finds that alcoholics regress to being injured on board ship or after a battle. They watch the rum bottle being passed around (it was used for anaesthetic) worrying all the time that it will run out and their pain will not be dulled.

Reason enough to be born with an insatiable urge for alcohol, but one that is easily cured with regression therapy. Jupiter can also be linked to liver dysfunction or disease as a result of old, inappropriate, eating patterns. If Jupiter is in an Earth sign, then there may be an old blockage around the body image which needs to be adjusted as otherwise it can manifest as anorexia, etc., particularly if aspects to Saturn or Neptune are involved). Also, if Jupiter is in an Air sign then the body image may be perceived totally differently from what it really is. Neptune aspects add to such confusion, which may also be a consequence of previous 'religious' lifetimes during which the body was kept clothed all the time and never seen. Jupiter, particularly when in the Water element, may indulge in comfort eating in order to quell emotional unease, or to stave off old memories of deprivation. Jupiter transits may trigger off these old patterns so that the weight fluctuates in accordance with the season and sign in which Jupiter is located. Jupiter transiting Taurus, for example, will tend to manifest as weight going on to the body, adding substance; transiting Gemini it will roll off again, only to return as Cancer seeks comfort in food.

A woman with Jupiter in Gemini in the sixth, squaring Neptune in Virgo in the ninth, had a long-standing weight problem which fluctuated between too fat and too thin. During an imaging session it became clear that her body image was totally distorted. She was regressed back to a harsh life in a convent during which she had always been on the verge of starvation. She was never allowed to be naked, even the cold bath which all in the convent were subjected to was taken in a coarse linen shift. Her hair had been cut off and her feet were all deformed with chilblains and arthritis. Her present-life mother appeared in the regression as the Mistress of Novices who was responsible for cutting off her hair. In the present life her mother had hacked off her waist-length blonde hair in a rage when she had started seeing a boy at the age of fifteen. Her 'beautiful feet' were now this woman's pride and joy, the only part of her body which she considered acceptable, and she always pampered them with expensive shoes, even though the rest of her clothes came from Oxfam. In order to change her body image she had to visualise stripping off her nun's clothing, burning it, and discovering the body underneath. She then imaged putting on luxurious, silky underwear and attractive outer garments. This was followed by several massage treatments in which she learnt to take pleasure in her body again. And her weight stabilised.

On the positive side Jupiter is a powerful tool to use in healing: through creative visualisation old disharmonies can be balanced out, the body image adjusted to a realistic one, and the body encouraged to fight off the invasion of 'aliens' such as viruses, against which conventional medicine has, so far, not found an effective defence but which homoeopathy can easily deal with using the principle of giving in a minute substance dose, something which would if taken in excess (Jupiter) cause the condition.

Saturn

Saturn or Capricorn in the sixth house, or difficult aspects to Saturn, can indicate a rigidity carried over from the past which leads to immobility. Its root cause may be found in inflexible attitudes or behaviour, or deep suppression of anger. It may be linked to fear or paralysis of the Will which, having prevented the soul from making progress in the past, is now manifesting physically. On the other hand, the disability may have been taken on in order to learn patience, self-control and acceptance. It may also be linked to the incarnating soul's refusal in the past to take responsibility for its own health, or a shirking of its duty to care for another. This placement indicates a need to explore the mind-body link and to understand psychosomatic and chronic illness. The lesson may be learnt through caring for, or nursing, the chronically sick, or may be encountered in one's own body. Past-life attitudes such as having 'a chip on the shoulder', or 'refusing to bow down to anyone', or looking down on those weaker than oneself, may manifest physically as scoliosis, etc. Saturn in this house may also point to the potential for a career in osteopathy, chiropractic, physiotherapy, etc., which deal with the underlying structure of the body.

Uranus

Uranus in, or as the ruler of, the sixth can be linked to an old disruption of the vibrational pattern of the body, an inner disease and misalignment carried over from life to life which may go all the way back to Atlantis and the "high-tech' medicine practised there. It can manifest as a mis-firing of neurons in the nervous system or disturbances in brain chemistry.

A client with Huntington's chorea – a hereditary disease passed on through the mother – had Venus conjunct Uranus in Taurus in the sixth house, inconjunct Mars and trine the Moon. It is typically Uranian in that Huntington's chorea symptoms strike suddenly, usually in middle age. From that stage on the progress of the disintegration into senility and of the physical loss of control can be rapid and irreversible. The chorea related back to torture in a previous life that had left its mark in the etheric body. The soul was then attracted to a body with the genetic prospensity for a dis-ease that mimicked the effect of the torture.

On the positive side, sixth house Uranus signifies a deep understanding of the subtle effect of vibration in realigning dis-ease and restoring harmony, and it can lead into many related fields of healing.

Neptune

Neptune or Pisces in the sixth house is wide open to outside influence. It acts like a 'psychic sponge' soaking up everything around it, including other people's dis-eases and environmental stresses. It points to a high susceptibility to reaction to ingested substances such as food or drugs, which can cause allergies and illness, or to emotions and vibrations given off by other people. It also indicates a need to learn to use the aura as a barrier to external influences, and to control substances which are taken into the body. An organic detoxifying diet and homoeopathic, rather than allopathic, medicine are essential as otherwise minute traces of 'alien' chemicals can result in biochemical imbalances and disturbances. A lack of trace elements and essential nutrients can lead to similar problems. The glands of the body, the endocrine system, are liable to inefficient functioning due to the non-synchronisation of the physical and 'etheric' bodies. Such disharmony may stem from past-life abuse of alcohol or drugs (aspects to Mars or Pisces), mental states (aspects to Mercury or Virgo), occult practices (aspects to Pluto or Scorpio), or spiritual initiations which 'failed' (aspects to Uranus and Chiron or Aquarius or Pisces). The process is always from the etheric body into the physical, the imbalance exists on the higher level before it reaches the lower. It may manifest in a subtle way as neurological disorders such as multiple sclerosis, motor neurone disease, etc., or through dis-eases with a biochemical basis such as adrenal failure or over-activity, parathyroid malfunction, early kidney or liver failure, etc., depending on the planetary aspects.

Cellist Jacqueline du. Pré (Fig. 17), who died at a young age from the effects of multiple sclerosis, had sixth house Jupiter in Virgo and Neptune conjunct Chiron in Libra. Her illness, which appears to have been rooted in an old disregard for, or over-indulgence of, the body, was subtle and resulted from an old wound to the soul. (At the time I wrote the following piece, little was known about her private life although a biography had just been published when the book was edited. The editor took out much of what I had written about the family so this is now lost. Subsequent revelations have confirmed much of what the astrology shows.)

There is an indication in her chart of a previous contact with both parents. The Moon's placement in the third house shows that her mother may well have been her sibling in a prior life, and the Sun in the tenth that her father may well have been her father in a former life. Jacqueline's mother was a powerful influence on her present life (fourth house Pluto and Cancer Moon-North Node) and she nurtured the development of her early talent. However, from the chart it would appear that Jacqueline was a child valued for what she achieved rather than for herself (Moon very widely conjunct Saturn, and Saturn inconjunct the Sun), and her consequent sense of unworthiness may have driven her on in her need to succeed (tenth house Sun-Midheaven in Capricorn). On the other hand, these aspects also indicate that she was capable of great self-discipline and of dedication to her music. When no longer able to perform, she utilised her previous life ability to teach and communicate her skills through her Master classes

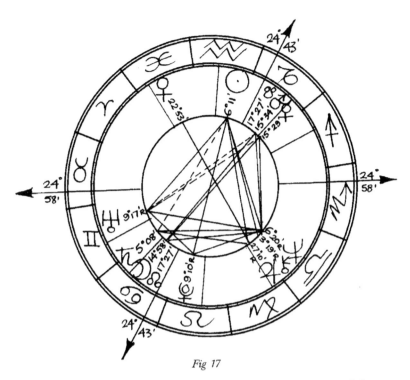

Fig 17

(Saturn, the teacher nurturing the talent of others, widely opposing Mercury, the sixth house ruler, and Capricorn South
Node). An over-developed Saturnian self-discipline may have
compensated for a lack of confidence and a feeling of being
unlovable, as well as for a previous lack of discipline (Jupiter).
Her present-life need was to love, nurture and accept herself
(Moon-North Node in Cancer), and to be valued by others for
who she truly was (the aspects to Saturn), and part of her karmic task (Pluto opposing the Sun) was to reclaim the power
she had projected on to her father, or other powerful males,
and own it for herself. She could have achieved this through
her work and, in spite of having become physically powerless,
as a result of her illness.

Cancer is a very emotional, instinctual sign, but Saturn
acted to separate her from the emotions, whilst the square of
the Moon to the Jupiter opposition to Venus in Pisces urged
her to expand and lose herself in her emotional experience –
which she did through the discipline of her music. It was pos-

sible that only by returning to the childlike, dependent states symbolised by her illness (Moon in Cancer widely opposing Capricorn South Node-Mercury) and to an apparent helplessness, that she could resolve her conflict and be reconnected to the source of the strength of her inner Self. It seems that somewhere in childhood (an echo of the older Saturnian pattern), within the limitations and restrictions of her hours of practice, her ability to be a totally spontaneous child was lost and her feelings pushed into the background, thereby trapping her in that child and its demands. This was reinforced by her conversion – which I psychically saw as a return to the Jewish faith, with its authoritarian, judgmental 'Father-God' symbol (Capricorn South Node). This religion was at odds with the needs of her Aquarian Sun and with the T-square which indicated that her religion should be a reflection of the spiritual quality of universal love, not something imposed from outside herself.

Karmically, she needed to transcend the expectations of others and the limitations of her conditioning (Sun inconjunct Saturn, and Moon conjunct the Cancer North Node) to find her inner freedom, which is the freedom to be her Self. Thus her illness can be looked upon as her Self engineering time for meeting herself face to face. A great deal in her chart points to the expression of the collective vision (Aquarius and the Kite) and to her needing time to look inwards in order to find all the areas that were left unexpressed in her great creative outpouring, thereby nurturing and integrating herself through the reconciliation of the Cancer-Capricorn and Aquarius-Leo axes. The sixth house Jupiter-Neptune-Chiron conjunction forms part of a Kite configuration (with tenth house Sun in Aquarius and first house Uranus in Gemini and the Sun opposing Pluto in the fourth), indicating a susceptibility to vibration and dis-ease as well as a subtle disruption of the biochemical and neurone functioning.

Conflict is repeated throughout her chart and her past lives together with a lack of balance and disharmony between the different facets of her life and her Self which was reflected in her disease. Having on the one hand to express the immense creativity of her Kite and the all-encompassing vision related to it, she also needed to come to terms with the everyday needs of her body and their emotional expression on the physical level (Taurus Ascendant, the T-square, and Virgo on the sixth house cusp). But, more particularly, she had to learn the effect the emotions and environment have on the body and health (Virgo). It would appear from the chart that, always racing to express her creative side, she was so caught up in the impetus of her first house Uranian energies that she was too impatient with the slow plodding Taurus Ascendant – except where it gave her the discipline to practise – and its need to learn about the physical senses and the material world. This frenetic effect is exaggerated by her lack of Fire; the little Fire there is would have a tendency to burn itself out very quickly and be unable to regenerate energy.

It could be said that her illness developed to anchor and focus her on the body (Taurus is connected to roots and can be so fixed and slow-acting that it results in immobility despite enduring for so long). She needed to surrender to Neptune and Chiron, to go with the flow, secure in the knowledge that everything was exactly as it should be for the stage she had reached, and for the life lessons she had come to learn. This need to surrender was, however, different from a passive acceptance of fate because it contained within itself the dynamic seeds of action - a readiness, through Uranus, to do whatever was necessary to bring about changes, so that rather than trying to force and mould her life to a rigid pattern, as an Aquarian she needed to attune herself to her own life-plan and the music of her own soul.

The pain of her situation had value in that it was genuinely and uniquely hers to experience and share in a direct and courageous way. Nevertheless, with that sixth house Jupiter-Chiron-Neptune and the Sun opposition to Pluto, she had to let go of past ambitions and compulsions in order to explore the present. She also needed acceptance from everyone she was intimately connected with, including herself, of her karmic need to be the way she was. To see this as an opportunity to explore ways of getting in touch with the energies she had ignored or overlooked in the past; not to sigh for what might have been, but to see the value in what is. In that way, she could be supported and share her new perceptions, the thoughts and feelings which she so badly needed to express. But at the same time, she needed to take responsibility for that expression, so that she would be able to control and direct what she allowed to be. Not cushioned from its harshness nor shut off from its pain, but following the impetus towards self-knowledge and growth with a willing heart.

Pluto

Pluto indicates a deep-seated illness, with roots way back in the distant past, usually defying diagnosis in the initial stages, and this type of illness brings the soul face to face with the possibility of death. As with Neptune, it may be related to food or drug allergies – particularly the side-effects of drugs taken perhaps many years previously – or to repressed emotions. The reproductive system can be affected, in men or women, and an overbearing, possessive mother or a past life in which this was a feature may be a contributory factor.

This placement is also linked to past-life compulsions and obsessions. It featured in the chart of a woman who believed that a breast tumour she had was 'the manifestation of her dead lover within her breast'. She had for many years been obsessed by an eighteenth-century poet with whom she believed she had a deeply unhappy, compulsive love affair in a past life. She would not allow surgery on her tumour as this would have meant separation from her love again - he had committed suicide in the past life. Strangely enough, the tumour did not seem to be life-threatening, presumably being benign, as she lived for at least ten years like that and may well still be alive today.

Pluto or Scorpio in the sixth house also has the potential to heal, particularly through therapies which involve exploring depths of the psyche and dealing with the subtle energies which govern health. For example, Flower Remedies may be used to gently ease out old emotional disorder, or homoeopathy to bring the soul back into balance and reach the subtle imbalances which lie at the root of Plutonian dis-ease.

SEXUAL MALFUNCTIONING

Karmic factors related to bodily malfunctions in the sexual areas, are indicated by aspects of the outer planets to Venus and Mars, Saturn or Uranus in the eighth house, or a strong placement of Pluto. Pluto has difficulty in letting go, in opening itself up to another person, and the soul with a strong Pluto placement may experience sexual difficulties linked into old power, manipulation or abuse issues whereby it fears that the sexual partner will, in its most vulnerable moment, have some control over it. In women this can result in difficulty in relaxing enough to achieve orgasm. Strong Pluto aspects – particularly to Mars – can also indicate the masochist who is pre-programmed to find pleasure in pain. In men these difficulties may be expressed as a preference for masturbation, which may include the use of a female in order to achieve orgasm but not to share feelings; the sadist who receives his pleasure by inflicting pain; or the man who uses his sexual power achieve mastery and blames his partner for his own inability to commune on a deep emotional level. In both sexes Plutonian difficulties in attuning and opening to another can lead to promiscuity as the person seeks fulfilment through a series of partners instead of looking within for the release which would heal the difficulty. Developing trust is a prerequisite to transforming the problem.

Saturn in aspect to Mars expressing itself as impotence in men has already been touched upon. Part of its root cause may be an old vow of celibacy that has not been rescinded or other restraints on sexual expression – also seen in Saturn in the eighth house. Women with Saturn-Mars aspects may be anorgasmic, as their inability to reach orgasm may be due to repressed anger, although I have seen this linked to a past life in a chastity belt – at other times the belt was symbolic or attitudinal. Saturn-Venus contacts can also be frigid or non-orgasmic because in its heart of hearts the soul with this aspect believes itself to be unlovable, or sinful, and is therefore incapable of responding. In her book on Saturn, Liz Greene explores the links of Saturn-Venus aspects and prostitution, prostitution not only meaning the selling of one's body to a stranger. As she points out, many wives 'prostitute' themselves to their husbands in return for the housekeeping money. However, a past life may well include prostitution or repressed sexuality as a contributory factor to the present-life sexual difficulty. Healing comes from accepting the body and sexuality as sacred.

Premature ejaculation can be linked to Uranus aspects to Mars or the Sun, or to Aries energy, particularly in the eighth house, and it may be linked to a past-life persona who was always in a hurry, rushing here there and everywhere and never taking time to finish anything. It may also connect to guilty or 'sinful' encounters during which it was felt, usually for religious or moral reasons, that what was happening was 'wrong', and therefore something to be got over with as quickly as possible. It may also relate to 'stolen' sexual experiences where discovery may have been imminent, often a feature of teenage sex in the present life. One man regressed to 'screwing the maid in the linen cupboard at every opportunity but we had to watch out for the old girl (wife/housekeeper?) coming so it had to be quick; on one occasion she caught me with my trousers down and gave me hell and sacked the poor girl'. In the present life his sexual experiences had started with furtive fumbles in his bedroom, on which his mother may have walked in at any point. It immediately triggered off the past-life reaction.

I have only ever met one person who admitted to being a nymphomaniac; she happened to also be a dipsomaniac. She had Neptune conjunct Mars and Venus and always swore that her condition was the direct result of having been 'unwillingly locked up in a convent with a load of bloody women' in a past life!

Sexual difficulties connected with violence or cruelty may arise from past-life causes when linked to Pluto-Mars aspects, and/or to abuse as a child in the present or a past life. In the 1987 Cleveland child sex-abuse case, 197 children were taken into care in a six-week period following allegations of parental abuse. Dr Marietta Higgs, one of the doctors involved, has Mars trine Pluto, Scorpio Sun conjunct the South Node, and

Pluto sextile Neptune-Mercury. Although the initial investigation into her allegations of abuse exonerated the parents, she did perform a valuable service to the community at large by bringing to public attention the whole question of child abuse and the way it is handled by society (her Saturn is sextile Uranus). It could be that her Pluto-Mars and Scorpio energy was tuned into abuse as it would appear to be an issue which she had been working on in former lives. However, her Neptune conjunction to Mercury appears to have obscured the issue and she arrived at a conclusion which may not have been warranted by the physical evidence – and may well have been influenced by her own far-past experience of abuse. The continuing demands for re-investigation into the whole affair nicely illustrated the effect of Neptune creating confusion in this Plutonian can of worms, as has the way social workers have taken up the idea of Satanic abuse – as though projecting all the 'badness' out there onto a devil instead of seeing abuse as something that needs healing as the abuser has so often been the abused.

One of the interesting manifestations of Pluto moving into Sagittarius and bringing things previously hidden out into the light of day has been the court cases in England against abusers from children's homes. In many cases men now in their forties and fifties had tried all their lives to be heard. Finally, their abusers are being brought to justice and the scarred lives can be healed.

The abuse may of course be from a previous life, not the current one. Men and women may have to deal with the repercussions of rape or sexual maltreatment (often indicated by planets in Scorpio or the eighth house as well as Pluto-Mars or Venus contacts). A man with a Pluto-Mars contact remembered dozens of incarnations, all of them as a man. He said that he 'just loved incarnating back into a physical body'. When regressed back to being a woman in ancient Greece, he relived a mass rape, after which he had sworn that he would never return again as a woman. In the present life he had been 'interfered with' by a man within the family as a young child, and had difficulty in achieving a normal sexual relationship with a woman as he inwardly craved and fantasised violence but rejected his fantasies as 'abnormal'. Healing came when he was able to forgive those who had abused him in that dim and distant past that was, paradoxically, so close to the present.

A surprising number of people with Pluto-Mars aspects have come to expect violence and need the adrenaline rush which fear and violence present to them. It is a powerful addiction that can be hard to break. A friend took in a girl who had a violent husband. In the middle of the night she was shaking and begging to be hit as only violence could end her withdrawal symptoms. She went back to her husband the next day.

GENDER DIFFICULTIES

Difficulties with sexual identity or gender problems often relate directly back to past-life experiences. A soul that has had many incarnations as a man, for example, may decide that it needs to learn about the feminine perspective and therefore incarnate into a woman's body. However, if masculine traits carried over from the past are strong, then adapting to being a woman will not be easy: there may be a powerful animus energy linked to the past 'male experience' – which requires to be integrated into the new personality. Furthermore, the incarnating soul may well retreat back for several incarnations into taking the masculine role, either as a dominating woman within a heterosexual relationship or within a lesbian relationship, until it becomes comfortable with the receptive, passive feminine energies. Similarly, a woman who incarnates into a male body might then become the highly sensitive 'bitchy', anima-possessed, feminine male who so often appears in stereotyped portrayals of homosexual men, but who is based nonetheless on a real person, and can also be linked with over-identification with the mother and the Moon energies.

Some charts have a strong imbalance of positive and negative energies, or the Sun, Moon, Venus or Mars in the 'opposite' quality to that it is attuned to (Mars in Pisces or Venus in Aries, for example), which indicates that the soul is trying to change sexual role and overcome a past pattern, but which can manifest as a blockage in present-life functioning as 'male' or 'female'. Although feminists would probably argue that such stereotyped roles have to change, we are not looking here at the roles within society, we are examining how the energy functions within the person. Both male and female need to learn how to manifest their negative 'feminine' energy in a sensitive, nurturing, caring way. Conversely, both sexes need to express their positive, outgoing 'masculine' energy, particularly when the opposite energy has been expressed throughout many incarnations. This is a stage on the road to integration of both types of energy within one soul, leading to wholeness. However, integration can be a difficult lesson to learn as the soul continually falls back into the old pattern, aided and abetted by cultural expectations and role models.

One woman had nine planets in negative signs and yet looked like a, not very good, female impersonator. She was dominating, aggressive, and totally 'unfeminine': nails bitten down to the quick, hard skin, short hair and stocky body. She had married late in life and never adapted to the role of housewife – many women with her kind of personality prefer not to marry, finding their fulfilment in the 'masculine' business world, as she had until her marriage. Inwardly, however, she felt that she needed to work on her softer, more receptive qualities. She became a reflexologist, but used her positive energy (Sun-Mars conjunction in Pisces) to 'force' a physical healing, flooding the patient's system with toxins which resulted in an overwhelming 'healing crisis'. Her work was at its best when she teamed up with a spiritual healer who worked on the non-physical levels, adjusting the imbalances on the etheric body. However, she was unable to take an equal position in this partnership, she simply had to dominate. One patient complained of being the yo-yo in the middle, bounced back and forth by the underlying conflict. Needless to say the partnership ceased and she returned to her solitary 'masculine' pathway.

This is the type of ferociously mannish woman to whom Emma Jung is referring when, in a discussion on the animus, she points out that there are those women in whom not only has the integration of the masculine principle failed to occur, but the animus has actively become predominant, resulting in an overly aggressive, non-feminine approach to life and loving which is set apart from the feelings. This is the virago or shrewish termagant we are warned against by the old morality plays. At her best, she may successfully fulfil a male role in society under the guise of escaping from the stereotyped female role. At her worst, she is destructive and inwardly sterile, because she has sought to replace men rather than to allow her feminine qualities to complement and be fertilised by the male energy within herself which is represented by the animus.

As Emma Jung points out, women need to resist the unconscious invasion by the animus in order to maintain their creative, feminine power. When the animus is successfully integrated, however, the soul who has incarnated into a female body can function on the highest level and in the fullest sense as 'woman', thereby fulfilling her destiny for the present incarnation.

The eternal Self appears to be non-sexual in its function and composition, integrating both masculine and feminine within its Being, but the portion which incarnates as the soul takes on, to a greater or lesser extent, the gender characteristics of the physical body into which it incarnates. It can be argued that the anima or animus is composed of all the qualities which the soul learnt whilst inhabiting the physical bodies of the opposite sex. The same argument can apply to the particular archetype to which the soul is attuned. If it has had considerable experience as, for example, the Puer who refuses to grow up (Mercury) then it will manifest those qualities when incarnating within the male physical body, or will be attracted to those qualities in a male if it has incarnated as a female. The man who has incarnated many times in the physical body of a woman and carries within himself the archetype of the 'devouring mother' (Moon aspects to Pluto) will attract such a mother to himself and carry this over into his marriage, choosing a partner who carries similar archetypal characteristics. He may think he needs, and is choosing, someone very different, but his burden from the past will manifest time and time again as confrontation with a dominating woman until he resolves the conflict within himself and attunes to a different archetypal energy.

Aids

I have had two close friends die from Aids. Both of them brought about profound spiritual growth in me and the many people they touched by their example of how they lived. One was an astrologer and spiritual teacher. In a dream I had after his death, his soul had got so big his body simply could not contain it any longer. It left his body and, whilst a portion rose to another level, the soul burst into a shower of golden rain that fell on all of us who had worked with him. Each of us, together with his pupils, took a drop of his essence and incorporated it into our own work. He had been an extremely self-sufficient person. But when he developed Aids, he had to allow himself to be helped – a difficult lesson. As he said, it countered the arrogance he knew he had displayed in countless other lives. He also felt that his present condition arose out of many abuses of his body both in the past and in the present life (Taurus Moon). He had a powerful self-destruct button that was activated on many occasions – which was how he contracted Aids. He seemed to get pleasure out of risking everything (Mars in Scorpio) and pushing against the limits. However, right up to the end he refused to believe he was about to die. At the very last moment, he accepted the situation and set about having a positive death.

The other friend was also a spiritual teacher, somewhat less flamboyant but equally charismatic. His work was concerned with healing and he was a remarkable example of living what he taught: forgiveness, compassion, abundance and a positive attitude. He lived with full-blown Aids for seven years, recovering from two cancers in the process and touching many peoples lives. In his chart he had a Finger of Fate. Chiron at the point in Capricorn on the cusp of the fourth and fifth houses opposing Venus-Uranus-South Node-Mercury with inconjuncts to Pluto in Leo and the Sun in Gemini. He believed it was part of his task to educate the medical profession and would lecture to medical students on alternative approaches to Aids. Remarkably healthy most of the time, he embraced the idea of death as wholeheartedly as he lived.

When it was time to leave the planet (as transiting Saturn went over the eighth house cusp), he did so very positively. He saw all his relatives and friends to say goodbye, planned his funeral service and, a typical Gemini, told each person what they most needed to hear. His death gave everyone a great gift: a knowledge of immortality. So far as he was concerned, his time on earth was over and he was off on the next great adventure. Since his death he has been busy communicating to my partner new ways of healing Aids – and much else besides. It is difficult to mourn for someone who is still so vibrantly alive and, as he said the other day: 'I'm not dead. I just left my body behind.'

What I find interesting about the position now, at the start of the year 2000, and the situation when I wrote *The Karmic Journey* in the 1980s is that it is no longer the gay community who are most at risk. They have embraced the idea of safer sex and modified their behaviour and the numbers of Aids sufferers has held steady. The fastest growing group of HIV positive people in both the UK and USA is in women – and we hear nothing about this. Nor do we hear about the Aids epidemic sweeping Africa and parts of the Far East. The idea of retribution, heard quite strongly in the 1980s, has had to be modified. It is difficult to say that a woman who has contracted HIV from her male partner is in any way to blame. I have left the rest of this piece as I wrote it because I feel it is still relevant today.

With perfect synchronicity, as I was writing this section of *The Karmic Journey*, the charts of two men who had contracted Aids arrived on my desk, both having Sun in Leo with Chiron conjunct the Midheaven, and both having most of the planets 'squashed' into a small section of the chart, one 'extrovert' (top half of the chart) and one 'introvert' (bottom part of the chart). The chart (fig. 18) shown is an angry chart. Aries is on the cusp of the 'empty' sixth house. Mars, its ruler, being in Taurus in the seventh widely squaring the nodal axis. It is through the will, or assertive energy, that the karmic purpose will be resolved. It has the feel of a 'fated' chart. He has chosen to take

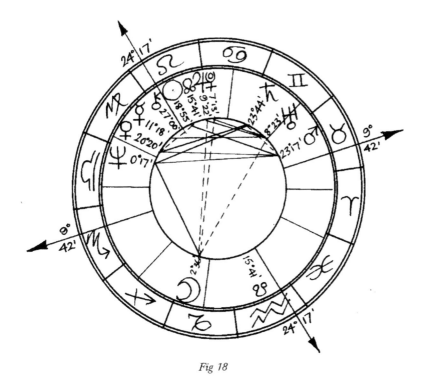

Fig 18

this path because he has to take this path for his own evolution: Mars is exactly quintile Pluto (an aspect of fate or destiny) and there is a Finger of Fate (Uranus inconjunct Moon, Moon inconjunct Pluto-Jupiter in Leo), indicating old emotional karma to be resolved. The Sun, North Node and Chiron are also in Leo, so that there is an emphasis on the heart energy and on empowering. With Mars trine Neptune in the eleventh, this man may not have faced his destiny in the past but he has been working on this issue. His Ascendant is Scorpio, indicating that he must penetrate the depths of the taboo areas of life and bring back insights to help in the evolution and survival of humankind.

Various theories have been put forward to account for the arrival of Aids, many of them judgmental and concerned with 'the visitation of a plague as retribution from On High for unnatural practices'. The 'practices' in question, however, appear to have existed since the beginning of time and to have been glorified by cultures such as the ancient Greeks and, in a non-physical way, by the Sufis. One only has to read the official (modern) Turkish Guidebook to the Shrine of the Sufi Mevlana Celaleddin Rumi to appreciate how different the approach was, and is, to brotherhood and love between men. Love and the Beloved were an inseparable spiritual reality for Rumi and the concept of love should not be limited to the English interpretation of this complex activity. Unfortunately, sources differ on Rumi's birth date so no chart is available. The following excerpts are quoted verbatim from the delightful prose. The first describes Rumi's meeting with his teacher, Shemseddin Tebrizi:

> He (Mevlana) was returning home from the Medrese, in the middle of the street two hands suddenly grasped the reins of the mule he was riding on. This man was a wandering dervish, and Mevlana not knowing who he was replied the questions of the Dervish without any ornamentation, sophistication and complexity. These straightforward and single-hearted answers got the Dervish excited and spurred stimulation in his soul. Getting off his mule Mevlana embraced the Dervish and they went home together. After that day the door of the soul of Mevlana was opened with the key of divine-love.

The story is a dramatic one: Shems disappeared, Mevlana was devastated; Shems reappeared, Mevlana was ecstatic, and the followers of Mevlana became jealous of the influence Shems had on him and had Shems murdered:

> Mevlana's lonesome bruised heart and confused mind never calmed then ... The absence of Shems influenced Mevlana deeply and was burnt by a flame of melancholy and trance, so that he was dragged into love's spell in an everlasting mystery. (However,) while he was living in a gloomy forlorn darkness without Shems, one day another Shems arose in his horizon ... Mevlana praised him so ... 'The Radiant Light of God among the human beings'. He also said that the set sun in the existence of Shems rose again in the being of Selahaddin ... Reverend Mevlana passed many happy days full of joy and love. [But then tragedy struck again and Selahaddin died.] Sometime after the

death of Selehaddin, Mevlana found another sun ... because he couldn't live any longer in his loneliness ... supposedly the spirit of Shems had resurrected in the Being of Husameddin.

Mevlana was married and had a family, and yet it was accepted that he needed the spiritual companionship and love of another man in order to achieve union with God. As Talat Sait, a Turkish commentator on the Dervishes, points out:

> This sequence of events was, in fact, a perfect mystic phenomenon. For Mevlana, Sems constituted the embodiment of God as well as the symbol of humanity. He in effect found God and became part of the Godhead. The disappearance of Sems had its correlative in God's abandoning mankind, in Sems absence Mevlana was to undertake an arduous mystical search ... (when Sems returned) symbolically Mevlaria had found God again, this time to merge his soul utterly and inseparably.[1]

As the spiritual teacher 'Jesus' pointed out in a channelling:

> Aids is a healing opportunity for all who have it and even for all in fear of having it. Aids is a blessing and spiritual opportunity for one to advance in his or her soul growth. It is not evil, bad or sinful to have Aids. This disease is a natural result of sexual guilt, fear and judgement. It is a form of self-punishment ... Aids is a way for individuals to learn self-love and love for family, friends and life. Aids is a planetary disease to open up compassion ...It is time that sex be seen as an expression of love and not just lust, power or pleasure ...Aids is a sexually transmitted opportunity to know one's self as a divine expression of God or love![2]

Other theories to account for Aids include one which says that, having incarnated into a minority group, the soul is not happy within the physical body and the body therefore 'turns against the soul' (which could well be linked to Mars and was certainly true of the friend of mine who had the strongest death wish of anyone I have ever encountered and yet managed to live most energetically). Yet another theory says that many souls, before their present incarnation, elected to 'sacrifice' themselves (Neptune), through Aids, to raise or to awaken the world's consciousness to a more moral standard, and to encourage the development of compassion instead of superiority. At the time of the changeover to the Aquarian Age casual sex may need to be abandoned in favour of the more committed and spiritually based relationships required by the New Age – relationships which would equate to those of Mevlana and his companions of the soul, and yet would incorporate the body, so that it would be a true merging on the physical, emotional, mental and spiritual levels. Certainly the level of tenderness and caring that can exist between partners who have Aids has a spiritual dimension, and I have met more than one Aids patient whose use of complementary therapies and herbs has opened the eyes of conventional doctors to possibilities that go beyond their drug-bound world.

To return to the Aids chart, Chiron is in the tenth house and it may indicate that the family of origin (Russian Jewish) did not fit into society, or that this client will not fit into the society to which his family 'belongs'. Either way there is a family wound which manifests through the soul's interaction with the outer world and which included the family disowning the fact that their son had Aids (In stark contrast to my second friend with fourth house Chiron whose Jewish family embraced and supported his situation with unconditional love). This wound, however, eventually opened the way to the family displaying love and compassion, after the unexpected death of his father, and facing in unity the prospect of death – another Aids client described his death as a 'gift' which he offered to his family in order that they may learn from it to be together and to love each other fully and openly.

Mars in the seventh house indicates old karma and pain coming from an aggressive relationship, particularly as Mars squares Chiron on the Midheaven. Mars trining the eleventh house Neptune indicates that the soul has been working on spiritualising the Will and forgiving itself, and possibly working towards some kind of reparation for past misdeeds. Neptune in the eleventh does indicate the potential for sacrificing himself for the good of the greater whole.

Uranus is on the cusp of the eighth house, square Venus. It is an ambiguous, ambivalent, unconventional energy which often indicates confusion around gender identity or sexual orientation. I have often found it to be bi-sexual rather than ho-mosexual, taking refuge in celibacy as a way of escaping from long-standing difficulties or trying both male and female rela-tionship with little fulfilment or commitment. For the subject of this chart, contracting Aids in the present life effectively cuts off indiscriminate, 'unsafe' sexual contacts if he exercises the responsibility towards others called for by his eighth house Saturn. Taking into account the Finger of Fate, this is an old emotional pattern which needs to be resolved. Mars quintile Pluto would seem again to indicate some kind of 'fate' or 'des-tiny' at work in the confrontation with death and the challenge of making this final stage of growth in the present incarnation, a creative one. Aids involves meeting this challenge, as does the eighth house Saturn, which also squares Neptune bringing in the need to resolve the mystic/pragmatist dilemma.

This chart therefore indicates that the incarnating soul has the potential, whilst working on its own karma, to aid the evolution of humankind. The level of unselfish, unconditional loving and caring which can exist in a relationship between partners with Aids, and their families, certainly fits into the Leo North Node need to work with the heart energy, and sat-isfy the ninth house Node need for a new way of Being. The Leo heart energy may well be involved in a resolution of the dis-ease. The Sun rules the thymus gland, situated close to the heart (Leo Sun) and a deficiency of thymus dependent T-cells is responsible for the body's vulnerability to invasion (Mars square Chiron) by foreign bodies such as bacteria, viruses, mutation of cells, etc. If the heart energy could be merged with the Mars energy and channelled into regenerating the thymus activity, the cells could be given new life and the aggressive energy required to fight off infection. Jupiter, and the power of the creative imagination, could be the tool used to fuse these energies and bring into being a balance and ease within the body.

The need to make death a 'creative choice' is outlined in the channelled teaching of 'Bartholomew' regarding Aids:

> Death can be a moment of absolute heroic wonder, beauty and clarity when experienced from an empowered position ...It is

empowering to say: 'I've got five, months to live - and I am going to live like a warrior. I am going to get my life in order ... to be powerfully alive to the end. That is a dynamic and aware way to die.[3]

PATTERNS OF 'DIS-EASE'

Some charts carry within them a pattern of fundamental dis-harmony and dis-ease. The chart shown here (Fig. 19) is that of an alcoholic manic-depressive woman who ended up in an institution suffering from total disintegration of the personality. There is an emphasis on inconjunct aspects, including three Fingers of Fate. This is the picture of a disunited soul. A line spoken by a psychiatric inpatient in a Radio 4 short story 'Survivors' seems to sum up the difficulty this woman had in relating and explain why she withdrew from the world: 'We come here to escape from love. They make love safe here. They make it manageable.'

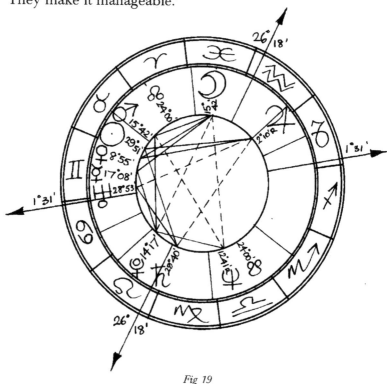

Fig 19

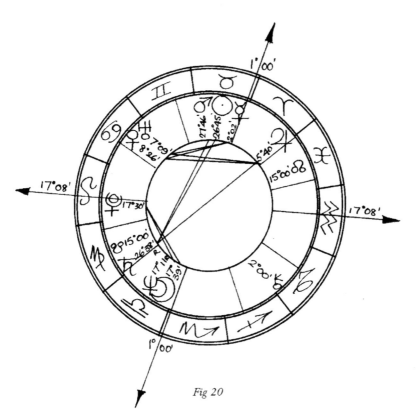

Fig 20

Split Charts

Another fundamental pattern of dis-ease is that of the 'split' chart where there are two, or more, distinct and separate parts to the chart; The pattern shown here (fig. 20) manifested as schizophrenia. As the person concerned, pointed out: 'I was hospitalised and given electric-shock treatment for what you get paid for.' He heard voices from the past 'persecuting' him. Pluto sextile Neptune-Moon represents old psychic abilities and delusory emotional states, and the 'split off' from the Uranus sextile Mercury energy represents the electric-shock treatment misused to 'treat' it. In this case it also linked back to torture inflicted on him in a past life. Such charts are indicative of old conflicts which manifest as separate personality styles or traits. Although they do not always result in schizophrenia, they do seem prone to manifest as deep depressive troughs and as 'splits' in the person who finds it hard to cope and switches between different modes of behaviour indicated by the 'split' planets. They may also manifest as a distinct sub-personality that appears in times of stress or crisis, sometimes constructively, sometimes not. Such deep 'splits' need to be healed on the soul level, and the energies integrated into the whole. Therapies such as Psychosynthesis, which integrates all the 'split off' parts and works with the sub-personalities, are particularly valuable in dealing with these charts as in the course of the therapy the underlying past-life trauma and 'splits' will often surface into consciousness. Shamanic soul retrieval can also help in bringing back parts of the soul that have fled from trauma and dis-ease, reintegrating the soul back to wholeness.

Dissociated Planets

Planets which are separate from the chart, having no aspects linking them into the rest of the chart, may also manifest a past-life block according to the planetary energy concerned. A client with an exact Mercury-Neptune conjunction dissociated from the rest of the chart suffered an overwhelming, and on-going, mental breakdown. In his imaging Mercury was a poor, weak little fellow who did not have the strength to stand up and was blotted out by an enormous, amorphous Neptune. In his past-life work he regressed back to a life in which his mind had been all-important, and he had ignored a call to spiritual work. He then went into a life in which the mind was totally subjugated to a 'spiritual' concept. Unfortunately his rational mind had kept rebelling against what it was being asked to believe in, and finally he had broken under the strain. He came into the present life with the energies in very tight as-pect, and was in the process of continuing the conflict. Gradually, through the use of imaging it was possible for him to negotiate a 'time-share' in order that Mercury could regain his strength, and he learnt to blend the two energies so that they could work in harmony. As past-life hypnotherapist Glen Williston points out:

> Illness is not always a simple past-life repression of some emo-
> tional pain that refuses to be subjugated any longer. Other
> reasons for disease that are related to past-life conditions [as-

trological indicators have been added for clarification] as well
as to the needs of the Greater Self include:

1. General lack of empathy for others in past lives, [or] bigotry.
[Difficult Saturn aspects, Saturn in aspect to Neptune. Saturn
in the ninth or Pisces, strong Earth or Water imbalance, emphasis
on fixed signs.]
2. Unwillingness to help others who are debilitated by disease
in a past life. [Twelfth or sixth house Neptune or Saturn, Air
imbalance.]
3. Unwillingness to develop creative potentialities that are struggling to be expressed. [Fifth house Saturn, Jupiter square Saturn,
Saturn in a Cardinal sign.]
4. Conflicting energies of many past selves that interfere with
present-self focus. [Sun and Moon and/or Venus and Mars in
conflicting signs, planets in hard aspect, strong twelfth house,
split or dissociate charts.]
5. A strongly negative past self trying to live again emotionally in this time frame (negativity is a breeding ground for illness).
[Planet, particularly Saturn or Pluto, conjunct the South Node
or the Moon. Moon in Capricorn in the sixth.]
6. A specific affliction or impairment from the past that is influencing the present self, a direct carryover. [This will be obvious
from the karmic houses and aspects, aspects to the South Node,
or from the first house.][4]

The Sins of Omission and Commission

Not all karmic burdens and blocks are physical or psychological in manifestation. Many involve the so-called 'cardinal sins'
and also the 'sins of omission' where the soul has refused to
face up to issues over many lifetimes; such 'sins' are ubiquitous
and universal and, as Richard Coates of the Findhorn Foundation pointed out in a lecture: 'If everyone openly admitted
their sins and fears, the biggest complaint would be lack of
originality.' These 'sins' can be indicated by both planetary
aspects and placement.

The Ninth House

The ninth house is the house of moral, ethical, philosophical
or religious attitudes or beliefs carried over from the past
which may be a burden or handicap when dealing with the

present life. Saturn can indicate a past attitude such as bigotry or a rigid adherence to a conventional, restrictive religion which tends to equate pleasure with sin. The soul has carried over a sense of being sinful and feels a need for 'punishment' or reparation. It may appear to have a vocation towards the Church in its present life, but may find it too constricting to its spiritual growth. A French client with this placement began his career as a minister of the French Protestant religion. He made a shift of awareness and ended it as an 'astrological counsellor offering structure and meaning to the perplexed'.

Pluto in this house may indicate coercion or experience of the fanatic; someone who forcibly inculcated his belief system into another person – either as victim or perpetrator. In the present life the incarnating soul may try to continue this pathway, or to become concerned with environmental issues, trying to transform the public conscience and heal the planet. Neptune in the ninth on the other hand, is the mystic, or the escapist, who now has to find a way of expressing his innate sense of the oneness of life.

The dual signs of Gemini, Sagittarius and Pisces, or Libra, in the ninth may indicate past 'sins' of hypocrisy, insincerity or being two-faced about beliefs coming forward from the past, particularly when there are, for example, difficult aspects of Mercury to Neptune or Saturn.

The First House
The first house planets, and especially Saturn, can also indicate burdens of unfulfilled obligation, or responsibility or fear, which have been carried over from past lives. The incarnating soul may not have taken up this burden in a past life, or the burden may be one that weighs very heavily because it is a continuation of a past experience. In either case a child with this placement is one who is old before its time: it often becomes younger as it gets older and the burden eases. Such a placement usually indicates a burden picked up at a young age in the present life within the family into which the soul incarnates. It can involve deep loneliness as in the case of the child of elderly parents, when the generation gap cannot be bridged, or there may be no other young children within the

family or social circle, so that the child is cut off from its own generation. Caring for a sick or aged parent, or younger children, or living in poverty are just three examples of how the Saturn burden can manifest. This burden often appears to be punitive and relentless, but it has its positive effects, as Stephen Arroyo points out: 'A remarkable inner strength can develop from Saturn's pressure, a strength that comes in part from knowing that we have done the required work, earned the results, and taken full responsibility for our own development.'[5]

Neptune

Neptune on one of the angles of the chart can bring back with it the burden of addiction or of being too open to 'possession' - undue influence from another soul whether living or dead, and not necessarily in physical proximity. This type of possession is often the result of having been trained in past lives to open up psychically and merge with another soul, or of having undergone a total mental breakdown. Having become unsure of its own boundaries the soul will not be able to put up any barrier to the 'take-over'. After a drug trip one client experienced what she termed a 'walk-in' from an alien being who needed a physical body to manifest through. Although she did retain partial consciousness, she acquiesced, if somewhat unwillingly, to this 'other being' using her faculties, as she felt he was all-knowing – a common Neptune delusion.

A case of 'possession' by a person living contemporaneously on earth was experienced by a girl who had Neptune right on the Midheaven. She had had old occult contact with the man, and was now in unwelcome telepathic contact with him across an ocean. He manipulated her to the extent of affecting physiological processes in her body. The lesson she had to learn was that no one has the right to take over the body of another person in this way, and she also had to strengthen her defences and bring her Will energy into being to ensure that the 'possession' ceased. Her position was weakened by an element imbalance within the chart involving an overemphasis on Water and a lack of Air, which left her vulnerable on the unconscious feeling level and lacking in objective perception. Shamanic soul retrieval can help in such cases, as 'possession' cannot occur when the soul is whole and integrated. Possession or undue influence (often indicated by Neptune, Saturn or Pluto interaspects to Mercury across charts) can only occur when there is soul loss.

THE ELEMENTS

As we have seen, the four elements of the chart each equate to a particular function of consciousness and describe the incarnating soul's previous pattern of experience with these functions, as well as the present-life attunement to these creative energies:

> Air signs are correlated with the mind's sensation, perception and expression, especially related to geometrical thought forms. Fire signs express the warming, radiating, energising life principle which can manifest as enthusiasm or love or as ego. Water signs symbolise the cooling, healing, soothing principle of sensitivity and feeling response. Earth signs reveal an attunement with the physical forms and a practical ability to utilise the material world.[6]

The element balance within the chart indicates areas for the incarnating soul to work on, or to overcome. Lack of an element may mean that it has been successfully developed in the past, or it may indicate that this is an important area to begin working on. When assessing this from the chart, it can be helpful to look at the balance of planets within the element houses. If, for example, there is a lack of Water and the fourth, eighth and twelfth houses are 'full', then there may be a need to become conscious of and develop, the Water function further. If there is a lack of planets in Water signs and these houses are 'empty' then it may be that the feeling function has been balanced out in the past.

Fire

An overemphasis on the Fire element represents the need to control impulsiveness and to cultivate the balancing qualities of receptivity and stillness. It can also be helpful to develop sensitivity and thinking with one's mind instead of one's mouth, in order to counteract a tendency to be hasty and tactless. A disciplined use of energy is called for as otherwise burnout can occur, although the Fire element usually has reserves of stamina available in a crisis. The habits of circulating energy around the body or 'cat-napping' can be useful ones to cultivate to counteract the tendency to scatter too much energy outwards.

Too much Fire can also indicate a fierce independence carried forward from the past and an inability to ask for help when required – the 'sin' of pride may have featured in a previous incarnation. It is important to balance this out by learning to accept assistance when it is appropriate. It may be more blessed to give than to receive but someone has to be on the receiving end in order for the blessing to flow, and becoming receptive is an important spiritual lesson. An old lady with a preponderance of Fire developed cataracts in both eyes and, although she had always refused any aid before, found that she simply could not manage alone. Once she had recognised and learnt the lesson from her situation, her cataracts were operated on and her sight returned. She commented that she had also learnt the invaluable quality of patience at long last – courtesy of the NHS which had kept her waiting so long.

Too little Fire can manifest as a lack of energy and initiative. This is frequently experienced as lethargy and is reflected in very passive past life experiences in which the soul was always under the control of another person, as in the elderly companion who was totally lost without her bossy employer to tell her what to do. Far from resenting the bossiness and control, she had welcomed it and had found the same type of relationship again with her husband in the present life. When the latter died, she was again lost, not even able to organise herself to shop for food without someone else suggesting it. Conversely, the incarnating soul may have a history of wasting energy and has come back depleted.

The lack of energy experienced by the low Fire chart can be counterbalanced by physical exercise, even if only a brisk walk. When the person feels least like exercising is when it will do the most good: that brisk walk will result in a rush of energy which can then be used to carry on with the task in hand. A daily exercise programme can be particularly beneficial in balancing out past lives in which either too much or too little energy was expended. Stephen Arroyo points out that the Fire-deficient body cannot digest heavy concentrated foods and that therefore diet is also an important factor in combating the lack of Fire.

When there is a fire imbalance, there may be a constant but unnoticed draining of vital energy when working with other people. It is as though the life force goes out to the other person. Then, one day, it becomes apparent there is nothing left; it is as though the plug has been pulled. Psychic protection techniques can prevent this type of burn-out*.

Air

The element of Air needs to combine disciplined thought processes with action. Too much Air can indicate an over attachment to ideas and the intellect, and too little connection with the feelings. The over-active mind of the Air element can be linked to past lives in which the emphasis was on being academic, or rational and analytical, at the expense of the emotions and senses. There can be a lack of understanding of anything beyond the facts, and a deep seated difficulty in trusting the intuition. A client with a strong Air-Fire chart, and a Mercury-Saturn opposition to Uranus (the intellect versus the intuition), spent years training as a homoeopath. He had an insatiable urge for more and more knowledge. His intuition and attunement to the 'Higher Mind' symbolised by Uranus would tell him within ten minutes which particular remedy a patient required. His intellect, aided by the mistrustful Mercury-Saturn conjunction, would then spend the next fifty minutes of the consultation justifying that choice. Once he learned to trust his intuition; using his long experience and knowledge to make fast, seemingly non-rational decisions, he became a much better homoeopath, and was able to see many more patients.

---

* See *The Art of Psychic Protection* and *Principles of Psychic Protection*

Part of the imbalance of the past-life pattern can stem from having been too detached, or too objective, lacking a connection to how both itself and others felt, and therefore cut off from those around it. Spicy foods can help to ground the Air element into awareness of the physical level of being, and sensitivity to the feelings of others can redress the balance.

Too little Air acts on feelings and emotions rather than rational and logical thought, and is incapable of an objective perspective. It lacks stamina and can experience great difficulty in understanding or co-operating with others as it is incapable of projecting itself into their shoes and seeing a different point of view. Such an incarnating soul has never lost the omnipotent feeling of babyhood, it still sees everyone else as an extension of its own being. Its past-life pattern may well have been one of not having to worry about what other people thought or felt as it had total control over their lives anyway. With an Air-deficient chart the soul must learn detachment without losing its connection to the feelings, and utilise the mind and spiritual awareness to connect to, and understand, the world in which it finds itself.

Water
An imbalance of Water points to an undue influence from the emotions and feelings. A chart with an overemphasis on Water is literally water-(emotion)-logged, reacting to any and every emotional stimulus in a completely instinctual way, and it is therefore untrustworthy. With such an imbalance, the soul needs to learn to plan ahead and move forward purposefully, to be in touch with, and then to detach itself from, the emotions so that it can formulate a response to situations instead of endlessly falling back into the old pattern of reaction. Stephen Arroyo describes this imbalance as 'cast adrift on the open sea in a small boat with no rudder, no sail, no air, and no compass easily influenced by any wind that blows ...'[7]

The past-life pattern is usually full of insecurity and excessive, uncontrolled emotions. A client with an extremely unbalanced chart, six planets in a large sixth house (Virgo cusp), six planets in Water, one in Fire and Earth, and two in Air, presented a charming facade of intelligent, unemotional competence – Leo Ascendant and Taurus MC which is seen by the world as efficient and practical – although he was not in fact in the least organised. He was involved with the New Age movement as the organiser for, and facilitator of, 'growth' groups of many different kinds (Mercury-Saturn-Neptune conjunction), and yet he presented the following problem:

> Periodic outbursts of alarming and intimidating physical violence [North Node-Mars square Neptune] towards my wife when mentally [Mercury-Saturn square Uranus] and emotionally frustrated and blocked [Venus trine Uranus]. Difficulties in channelling sexual energy [Mars in Capricorn square her Mars in Aries] within our relationship - sexual frustration. Challenge of creating and channelling prosperity and abundance in our lives despite history of negative attitudes and lack of material means.

Although his chart had many conjunctions, squares and sextiles, it lacked oppositions to act as a focus for the blocked energy contained within it. One of the squares was from the Scorpio Moon to Pluto – a seething mass of traumatic and very fixed emotions from the past forcibly clamped down. He found it difficult to understand, other than in a superficial intellectual way, that it was his own negative attitudes that were manifesting as a lack of material means. He found it even harder to understand that it was his own emotions, of which he was unaware except when they surfaced uncontrollably (Pisces on the cusp of the twelfth), that were the cause of the periodic outbursts. He could relate to the past-life patterns of himself as an emotional person, but not to the present-life picture. To make matters worse he was a 'crisis counsellor' and, with Neptune in the sixth, was soaking up his client's negative and violent emotional energies; he then unconsciously channelled them into the difficult Mars square between him and his wife. Mars was in the ninth house in each chart signifying a fundamental clash of beliefs and values between the two of them, as well as a clash of egos (his Mars conjunct her Sun square to Mars). When his inner perception of conflict became too much to bear and demanded expression, instead of verbalising the disharmony he exploded into violence.

Too little Water in the chart does not mean a lack of emotion or feelings, but it does indicate a person who has, particularly in a past life, been too successful at detaching from the emotions and is now out of touch with any motivation springing from that source. This was expressed to the extreme in the chart (Fig. 21) of a brain-damaged child with no Water, two Earth, three Fire and five Air planets, and an Air Ascendant. She appeared to lack hearing, although at times it was possible to attract her attention by sound, and her problem seemed primarily to be one of non-attention to the messages her senses were sending her. She lived in her head 'in her own little world' of too much Air; she did not speak and her sight was limited. She responded a little to touch and could at times be aware enough of another person to reach out to them, and yet she was totally disconnected from her emotions and cut off from the world or interaction with the environment (Cancer South Node conjunct MC). She never cried, never laughed,

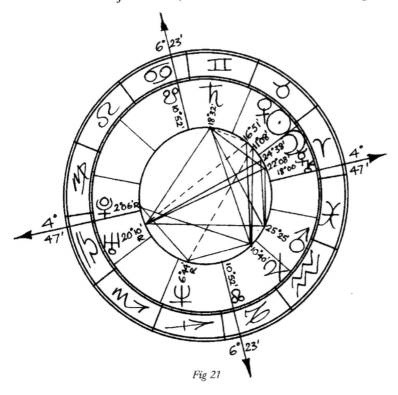

Fig 21

never appeared to vary in her blank, non-emotional response. Had it not been for the handicap, she would have been highly, and moodily, emotional (Uranus opposing Moon-Mercury-Chiron and inconjunct Venus). There was a lack of Will energy in her chart, a lethargy which I felt was more responsible for the lack of interaction than the actual brain damage, indicated by the 'lazy', erratic energy of her Grand Trine (fifth house Mars trine Saturn, trine Uranus). The energy was as intermittent and unpredictable as her responses. Ways of stimulating her, such as introducing her to shapes and textures to capitalise on her sense of touch, and the Metamorphic foot therapy – to which she responded extremely well – to help her incarnate more fully into her body were suggested. Hydrotherapy and swimming were advised to counteract the lack of Water and to help in the elimination of the toxins which were a result of a blood/fluid imbalance. Robert Tully (my first astrology teacher and a highly experienced medical astrologer) felt that a complete change of blood was indicated, but we did not feel at the time that the NHS would view this as a valid treatment! Had she consulted me nowadays, I would have suggested blood ozonisation therapy and a consultation with a dark-field microscope practitioner – the new spagyric and homoeopathic remedies now emerging from Germany have a profound effect, as my partner had found within his own holistic medical practice.

Looking psychically at her lives, I had a sense of her being a soul who had been hurt physically, emotionally and mentally, and who had chosen to come back into lives in which she could retreat from the world, although not without some regrets. She had set up a pattern of not using her outer senses and needed to learn to use her body without carrying over the emotional difficulties which lay in her past. Although it was unlikely that she would ever develop to the extent of being able to deal in this life with the underlying emotional trauma, she did grow considerably into her mental capacity. Her parents, both of whom had an over-emphasis on Air, grew through the experience of struggling to understand her uncommunicated needs. Through caring for her with very little response or reward, they also learnt how to extend unconditional love, perception, empathy and compassion to another soul. As a friend who nursed disabled children pointed out: 'You may look after such a child for ten years, your only reward being one smile at the end of that time. But it is worth it.'

Earth

Too much attachment to the physical senses and survival needs are indicated by an emphasis on the Earth element. An over-emphasis points to prior lives in which material things were all that mattered, or in which the soul may have lost everything, or may have lived in extreme poverty. The lesson behind such experiences is that the security of material possessions is illusory; the only lasting security is the inner one of spiritual attunement and growth. Therefore the Earthy chart needs, whilst retaining its grounding, to explore the spiritual dimension of life through meditation which will take it beyond the confines of the body.

Any imbalance of Earth, too much or too little, can lead to difficulties stemming from the retention of toxins – physical, mental or emotional – and there is a need for a periodic cleansing of all the levels as otherwise it will ultimately manifest as disease.

Too little Earth is related to the need to become grounded, to cope with the demands of the practical, physical environment, and to learn how to be at one with the body. Many un-Earthed people feel incarcerated within an alien lump of flesh, and this can lead to long-term illness and disease as the incarnating soul struggles to learn the lesson of at-oneness with the physical level. Yoga, Tai Chi, postural integration and similar physically based techniques or meditations can be extremely helpful in grounding the soul into the body', as can massage and body-based therapies.

A client (Fig. 22) with no Earth planets and five Water planets had experienced a traumatic life. Her husband had died just before the birth of her baby. As she had Chiron square Venus, Moon in Scorpio and Pluto conjunct Mercury-Venus, she had incarnated expecting to undergo this type of emotional trauma in order to change her pattern. She was the seventh known

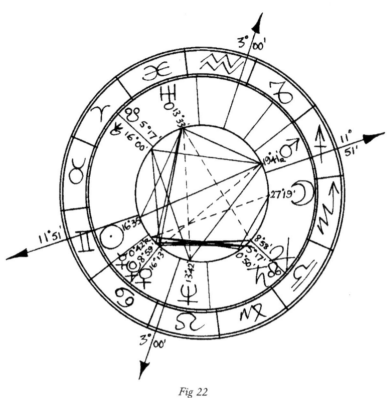

Fig 22

generation to carry an extremely rare, genetically transmitted disease (sixth house Moon). She had a Fire Grand Trine (Chiron-Neptune-Mars), indicating the potential to align the Will with the spiritual purpose in order to overcome her wound, and a Finger of Fate (Uranus at the point inconjunct Neptune and inconjunct Saturn-Jupiter-North Node - this was a transpersonal, collective karma she was dealing with). With a T-square from Uranus to Sun opposing Mars, she incarnated intending to take control and transform her previous-life pattern.

When she first contacted me she was totally paralysed from a rare, intractable, complex and defeating familial condition with no known cause, cure or name. She had a 'burning desire to end this misery'. The matriarchal family interaction was a tight one and it appeared that the same group had incarnated time after time, repeating the difficulty. Her Venus-Pluto contact and Scorpio Moon indicated an old pattern of emotional trauma and mothering karma, and the lack of Earth that she was not attuned to being comfortable within the physical body. She had been taught to view herself as a victim of the family curse from a very early age and was programmed to continue it unless she took control of her life. She was introduced to the 'carrot meditation' as a way of becoming comfortable within the physical body. The visualisation consists of imagining oneself to be a big, juicy, orange carrot, nurtured and cocooned by the warm earth with just the feathery tops waving above the ground. Although it can initially be an extremely uncomfortable meditation for the no-Earth chart, it does stimulate perception of the earth, and of the physical body, as a source of nourishment and support. Incarnation into the body then becomes more harmonious.

Within two years this client had defeated her paralysis – mainly by the use of Bach remedies to heal the emotional trauma of that Scorpio Moon and all her other Water planets. She had travelled to Australia, found a specialist who understood, and most importantly, named the condition, which was validated and could therefore be overcome. Cognitively it is extremely difficult to fight something which is not supposed to exist. She founded an association for fellow sufferers, and although there were few they were at least able to share information and hope of a cure. As she could not resolve the problem of heredity, she hoped that by tackling the cause of the disease within herself, she could prevent future generations from having to cope with such an intractable condition. As she said, although it was valuable for her own development it was 'oh so very wearying, so much, too much'.

The same feeling pertains to all karmic burdens and baggage, and it is the pressure of everything becoming 'too much' which pushes the soul into discarding or dealing with the underlying cause and present-life manifestation. As comedienne Ruby Wax so eloquently expressed it: 'It's not the grossness of the experience that drives people crazy, it's how long you let it ferment inside.'

STILLBIRTH AND SUICIDE

Questions which always seem to arise in reincarnation workshops are 'What happens to suicides?' and 'Can you explain stillbirth or cot death?'. There appear be a number of answers to both these questions and little in the way of astrological indications, although certain specific aspects such as Mars-Neptune, Saturn-personal planets, Saturn-Jupiter and some difficult Pluto aspects do seem to share a propensity to suicide.

It appears that for suicides the motive behind the act can be an important factor in determining the next-life conditions. If the incarnated soul feels on the deeper levels that it has worked on its difficulties as far as it can, and therefore decides to opt out as, for example, when a cancer patient makes the choice to 'die with dignity' to save other people the agony of watching a slow death – then a different kind of karma is generated from that of a soul who has 'escaped' from a situation it feels it cannot handle, avoiding a lesson which may well be repeated in the next life.

Similarly, a variety of factors operate for both stillbirth and cot death. It has been suggested that some suicides, or accident victims for whom death was sudden and unexpected, need to incarnate again for a short time in order to have time to adjust to the transition. In the case of some traumatic deaths a gentle intra-uterine experience may help the soul to prepare for another physical life at a later date. Infant mortality may also be linked to the incarnating soul changing its mind, particularly when conditions have altered within the family environment. Another explanation may be that the soul, having incarnated solely to bring its present-life parents a karmic lesson, or to fulfil their in-built expectation, may not have intended to incarnate for a long period.

Fig. 23 is the chart of a baby who was stillborn by Caesarean section, following a painful and difficult labour, at the appropriate time of 13.13 on Good Friday. The chart has seven planets in Earth, including Mars in Capricorn in the sixth house, which indicates karmic difficulties around being in a physical body, with Mars quintile Pluto which points to the possibility of the 'fate' of a traumatic and violent death, both

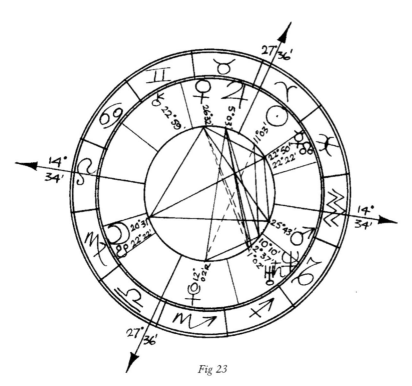

Fig 23

in the past and the present life (Pluto-Mars contacts often
signify an old, aggressive conflict, particularly on the psychological level). The chart for the commencement of labour has
the Capricorn Saturn-Uranus-Neptune conjunction right on
the Ascendant, indicating a deep ambivalence about incarnating into the physical body and, perhaps that self-sacrifice was
chosen in order that karmic lessons may be learnt by others.
It would appear from the chart that had the baby survived, she
could well have been brain-damaged or autistic: indeed the
hospital abandoned resuscitation for this reason.

 The child, who would have been much loved (tenth
house Venus and Jupiter), was clearly bringing a lesson to her
young parents as they faced the pain and loss of her death together (fourth house Pluto). Her mother's Saturn, opposing her
Moon, was conjunct the child's Sun, and her Pluto conjunct
the child's Moon and South Node, indicating an old debt and
mothering karma. The mother's Saturn opposition to the

Moon, which shows she lacks confidence and undervalues herself, indicated old emotional pain and isolation as well as her sense of worthlessness, and on an occasion prior to the baby's death she had said that she 'killed what she loved' when referring to her pets, although it would perhaps have been truer to say that what she loved, died. The child's North Node-Mercury was conjunct her parents' Chiron in Pisces, activating their spiritual pain and alienation and the deep wound in their contact with the cosmos. After their baby's death both were convinced that there was no god – a suspicion which both had voiced earlier. Her Chiron was also conjunct her father's Saturn conjunction to the Sun, opposing the Moon, which brought out his underlying emotional pain – but also his inner strength. The child's Saturn-Uranus-Neptune squared the father's Sun-Moon opposition, his Uranus was conjunct her Moon-South Node, his Pluto conjunct her Moon, and his South Node conjunct her Pluto: his lesson was to let go.

The pregnancy had been punctuated by trauma (reflecting the Mars quintile to Pluto). Very early on a beloved uncle had died; at four months the mother fell downstairs; at five months the car in which the mother was travelling was hit on the motorway by another car; at eight months the husband's car went up in flames while the mother watched helplessly and hysterically. Fortunately, it was stationary at the time and he was unhurt. They spent all their savings on another car which turned out to be worthless, and the shock induced labour. The baby's heart stopped when the hospital intervened in the birth and broke the membranes to speed up labour. The mother had intuitively felt that a Caesarean was needed, but did not have the confidence to say so. After the baby's death, she believed that this baby had just not been meant to be, and that it had happened for some unknown purpose, but she also knew that the baby would come back to them when ready to incarnate.

Fig. 24 is the chart of a child born to the same parents fourteen months later, again by Caesarean section in life-threatening circumstances indicated by the Scorpionic Pluto close to the Ascendant. Labour had been induced (often a feature of

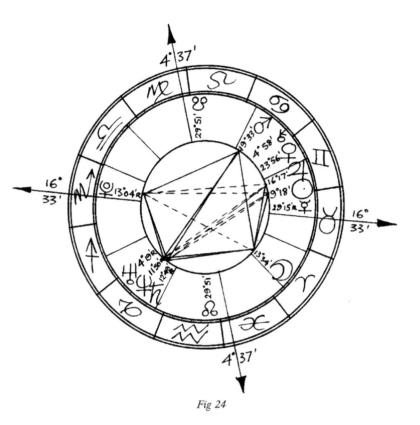

Fig 24

Plutonian births), but the cervix was not dilating and the hospital were again threatening to rupture the membranes in order to speed up the process. This time the mother had enough confidence in her own intuition to refuse: she demanded a Caesarean. Her fear was that the pattern would repeat itself and that she, through her body, would let the baby down at birth (Pluto in Virgo). Her Saturn-Moon opposition meant that she felt inadequate as a mother and she needed to find her own inner strength and resilience. This time the baby lived, but she was initially separated from her mother (Moon square Saturn) by the effects of the anaesthetic (Neptune). However, she was fed by her father (whose Sun in Aries is close to her Moon) immediately after birth (nurturing Mars in Cancer completing the T-square).

This chart has a better balance of elements, although it

is short on the Fire energy, reflecting the inertia of birth and the child does find it difficult to carry things through, quickly giving up in the face of challenge. It has Sun inconjunct Pluto as in the first chart, but this time incorporated into a Finger of Fate with Jupiter and the Moon, indicating the need to expand beyond the old parenting karma; another Finger of Fate incorporating the Uranus-Saturn-Neptune conjunction indicates the possibility of transformation. Pluto has returned to the same place; as has Neptune, but this time Pluto trines Mars reflecting the possibility of resolution of the issues of old trauma and violent death. (In a past life reading by Lila Beck this child was seen as an Egyptian Pharaoh and her younger sister as an opposing General – which explained the constant power battles they experienced in the present life. Both had come to an untimely end.) The Aries Sun of the first child is conjunct the Moon of the stillborn, reflecting the esoteric teaching according to which the Moon in the present life is the past-life Sun. The Chiron of the first child conjuncts the second child's Jupiter-Venus conjunction, and Venus in each chart both aspects the nodal axis of its own chart and squares the nodal axis of the other chart, indicating the possibility of resolution of the nodal conflict and of the Chiron wound through a loving experience which brings harmony to the incarnating soul. The North Node of the Moon conjuncts the mother's Sun, a growth aspect for them both and indicative of an old soulmate contact.

This child may well heal the mother's in-built expectation (Saturn opposed Moon) of pain and loss associated with mothering, and the mother could heal the child's Moon inconjunct Pluto difficulties around nurturing and creativity. Chiron is in the eighth house, indicating a life change following a significant death, and its placement in Cancer indicates an old suffering around nurturing which can now be transcended. This seems to be the same child incarnating again, this time with a chart which shows healing potential to overcome an old sense of helplessness and powerlessness (Saturn-Neptune opposed Mars, T-square Moon, eighth house Chiron, and the Moon-Pluto-Sun-Jupiter Finger of Fate). The chart also appears to be typical of one of the Age of Aquarius old-soul children who are incarnating to help the birth into the New Age (third house Aquarian North Node). Her chart has tremendous psychic and healing power from the Scorpionic Pluto on the Ascendant inconjunct the Moon, Mars opposition to Neptune, the eighth house Chiron, and a reservoir of old skills and transpersonal abilities in the second house Uranus, Saturn and Neptune.

Fig. 25 is the chart of an alcoholic who committed suicide in an emotional blackmail attempt which went wrong (Neptune inconjunct the Moon). Although not aware of the fact, he only had a few months to live as he had an undiagnosed kidney failure (Chiron conjunct the South Node in Pisces on the cusp of the sixth house and inconjunct Pluto). Fig. 26 is the chart for his death and transition to another life. The Ascendants are

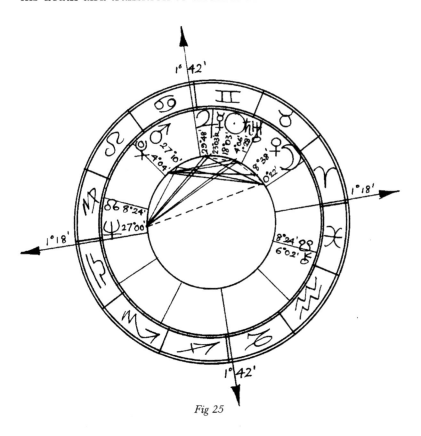

Fig 25

almost conjunct (there is some confusion about the exact time of death) and the natal Ascendant is being transited by Pluto-South Node-Mars-Jupiter-Uranus inconjunct Saturn, forming a Finger of Fate with his wife's Moon in Scorpio. Following his death his estranged wife was told by a medium that he would try to return to her. Some yeas later as Neptune transited her Sun-Mercury and opposed his natal Saturn-Uranus, she became aware that he was an earth-bound spirit and worked at releasing him. Three months later she miscarried a child on an anniversary of his death and, despite the fact that she was much relieved, she was aware of a deep sadness and of her body grieving for the child. Again, a medium told her that her husband was trying to return to her and would incarnate into her family if she was not willing to mother him.

Nine months later her nephew (Fig. 27) was born and she saw him when he was only a few minutes old: her hus-

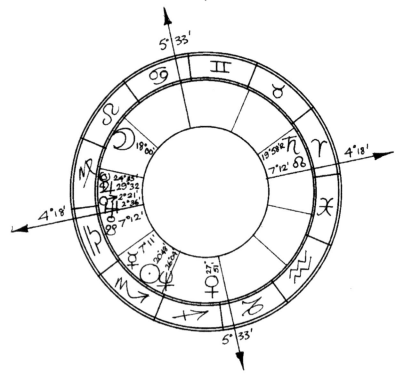

Fig 26

band looked at her out of his eyes. The child's chart has karmic inconjunct aspects requiring resolution, including a Mercury-Neptune-Mars Finger of Fate. Although not in the same sign, less than a minute separates the Moon in the first natal chart from the Sun in the chart of her nephew, who was a reluctant forceps delivery. Chiron in the first chart conjuncts Chiron in Pisces in the second, indicating a deep wound in the soul, while Venus in the first chart is conjunct the child's South Node-Jupiter, Jupiter conjuncts Moon-Venus and Uranus opposing Moon-Venus offers a transformation of the old emotional pattern. Neptune opposing the Sun and squaring the nodal axis and Saturn conjuncting Pluto-Mars suggests a transmutation of the self-destructive energies and a movement towards the spiritual insights made available by the child's Mercury conjunction to the Pisces North Node. In the synastry between the husband's death chart and the child's chart the

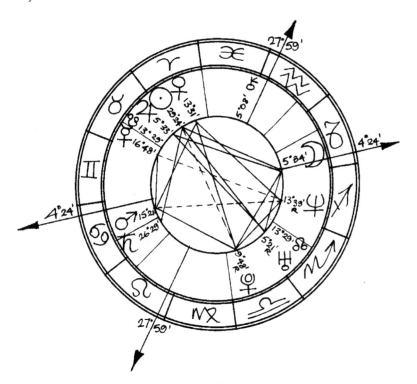

Fig 27

Sun and Mercury bracket the child's North Node and the Moon squares it; the child's Moon squares the nodal axis of the death chart; the South Node-Mars-Uranus-Ascendant conjunct Pluto and Saturn, the Lord of Karma, and the North Node is conjunct Venus.

There are replicate planetary interactions in the two natal charts and similar life patterns were experienced by the husband and the nephew. Both were the eldest child and both were supplanted by the birth of a sibling on whom the parents doted. As a teenager the husband was thrown out of his home on many occasions for arguing with his father; as a young child the nephew was threatened: 'We will send you to the naughty boy's home if you don't behave,' and his mother packed him a case when he was only four. When he was 21, (the age at which as a man he had gone away to sea on a journey that lasted six months), he 'disappeared' from University, undergoing a severe emotional breakdown. He was 'missing' for six months. His parents believed he must be dead. And yet he was still living at his old address – they did not go there to check. Both charts have the Moon-Pluto contact which indicates mothering karma; both man and child had powerfully instinctual mothers who held the power within the family. Both charts have Mars-Saturn aspects; both their lives were dominated by another person and each felt helpless and powerless. The man longed to go to sea from early childhood (twelfth house Neptune, Jupiter on the Midheaven and five ninth house planets) and he became a sailor, only returning home to die. The child was fascinated with the stars, and wanted to become an astronaut.

Both had the escapist Neptune-Mars contacts. In the man's case these became self- destructive when he died from a mixture of drink and drugs (a transit activated his Neptune sextile to Mars, square to the Sun-Mercury conjunction, trine to the Saturn-Uranus conjunction, and inconjunct to the Moon). The child incarnated with a Finger of Fate (Saturn-Mars inconjunct Neptune, inconjunct Mercury), indicating that he had to integrate and resolve the energies which had proved his 'downfall' in the last incarnation. When he had his breakdown he refused to be treated with drugs or electro-con-vulsive therapy, preferring to use natural approaches. When he recovered, he went to work as a porter in a hospital 'to be of service to others'. His dis-ease appeared to be at an end.

Conclusion

Moving Beyond Karma

With reincarnation man is a dignified immortal being, evolving towards a glorious end, without it, he is a tossing straw on the stream of chance circumstances, irresponsible for his character, his actions, his destiny.

Annie Besant, The Ancient Wisdom

Who Was I?

People often come to me thinking they were someone famous in the past. They want to know how to 'prove' it from the charts. I really don't think you can do this, although it is possible is to look at similar patterns as mapped by the two charts and within the lives. However, does it really matter who you were? After twenty five years, I don't believe it does. What I feel is important is that evolution and soul growth continue. An understanding of karma can contribute to that soul development, but there is a need to move on.

What Are We Here For?

According to the eleventh century nun Hildegard of Bingen, our task on earth is that defined by one of the most fiery of the Old Testament prophets, Ezekiel, who exhorted his followers to: 'Throw away from you all your collusions in which you have walked crookedly and make a new heart and spirit for yourselves'. Overcoming karmic patterns leads to the fulfilling of potential and to the expression of the highest octave of the chart, moving towards integration and wholeness of the physical, mental, emotional and spiritual states of Being. Within wholeness comes a shift of emphasis to a spiritual perspective, with reclamation of old knowledge and power.

The oldest question known to man must surely be: 'Why are we here?'. It provides the impetus and basis for all religions and all religions attempt to answer it in their own way. The concept of reincarnation, however, is not a religious answer; it is a philosophical, ethical and spiritual one. It teaches that each soul is the sculptor of its life, fashioned on the loom of experience by the power of action and thought, and therefore places the responsibility for the soul's conduct squarely on itself. We cannot blame external forces in the shape of 'fate' or 'nemesis', we can only look within to perceive the cause and manifested effect. When we come to realise that difficulties are the fibre from which inner strength is built, then we face up to problems and get on with the business of living. The doctrine of reincarnation can offer the opportunity for a soul to make recompense for past wrongs, not by undergoing punishment or taking on retaliatory handicaps or events but through service to others which will restore the balance and harmony lacking in the total experience. When life, and in particular the universal problem of suffering, is seen as having a definite purpose and, what is more important, a potential end, then the exercise of choice and free will becomes mandatory for spiritual growth and the birthchart is recognised as the map for the journey to perfection.

However, we do not have to wait until our North Node is in the twelfth house or our Sun is in Pisces to reach a point of release from our karma. We merely have to change our level of awareness and shift our mode of becoming into Being to know that we are cosmic, eternal and therefore already perfect, and free to create our own reality and our destiny. As Richard Bach points out in Illusions:

> You are led
> through your lifetime
> by the inner learning creature, the playful spiritual being
> that is your real self.
>
> Don't turn away
> from possible futures
> before you're certain you don't have
> anything to learn from them.

CONCLUSION

You're always free
to change your mind and
choose a different future, or
a different past.[1]

To the question: 'Why are we here?', we can reply: 'To learn and expand spiritual awareness through a life of harmony and love and to begin the next stage of the evolution of humankind into a state of higher consciousness.' Just as Freud rediscovered the existence of the Unconscious which had remained virtually unrecognised for centuries, so we are now learning that there is a higher consciousness linked to a divine spark buried deep within the soul: the Self. And, just as the unconscious is connected to the collective level, the Self unites with the whole of creation in cosmic selfhood. Attunement to the Self comes about through listening in the silence of meditation and spiritual discipline, which are tools for the Aquarian Age. The Self then becomes the guiding star for the soul's journey.

When the incarnated soul reaches the point of grace and enlightenment it moves beyond karma. The karmic journey is over. All possibilities are open. It could continue its sojourn on earth as a Master aiding others on their journey, but other planes of being await exploration:

Beyond the stars are Stars in which there is no combust or sinister aspect.
Stars moving in other heavens not the Seven Heavens known to all.
Stars immanent in the radiance of the Light of God,
neither joined to each other or separate.
Who so hath his future from these Stars, his soul drives off and consumes the unbeliever.[2]

NOTES

FOREWORD

1. *The Prophet* by Kahlil Gibran, William Heinemann, London, 1980 edition, p.73.
2. For further details, see Chapter 2, p.75 and Chapter 5, p.205.
3. Note that Louis XIV, the 'Sun King', died in 1714, not long before the next transit of Pluto through Sagittarius which was 1748 - 1762. He was the prime representative of the collective or archetypal Solar King with absolute rule. The next Pluto cycle was perhaps about individualising the notion of the Central Sun as personal Ego. It is this cycle which is now ending.

CHAPTER 1

1. Extract from *Echoes of the Orient,* quoted in J. Head and S. L. Cranston (eds.), *Reincarnation: An East–West Anthology,* The Julian Press Inc., New York, NY, 1961, p.2
2. Benjamin Walker, *Masks of the Soul: Facts behind Reincarnation,* The Aquarian Press, Wellingborough, Northants, 1981, p. 13.
3. ibid.,p.21
4. Liz Greene, *The Astrology of Fate,* George Allen & Unwin, London, 1984, p. 10.
5. ibid., p 10.
6. ibid., p.11, 6.
7. Pauline Stone, *The Astrology of Karma,* The Aquarian Press, Wellingborough, Northants, 1988, p.20.
8. Thorwald Dethlefsen, *The Challenge of Fate: Ancient Wisdom as the Path to Human Wholeness,* tr. C. McIntosh and E. M. Loewe, Coventure, London, 1984, p. 92.
9. Liz Greene, *The Astrology of Fate*, p. 8.
10. George Ritchie, *Return from Tomorrow,* Kingsway Publications, NY 1978, p.56.
11. Alan Oken, *Complete Astrologer,* Bantam Books, New York, NY, 1980, p.507.
12. Liz Greene *Saturn - A New Look at an Old Devil,* Arkana, London, 1990.
13. Gina Cerminera, Many Mansions, New American Library, New York, NY 1981, p. 98.
14. Origen, quoted in J. Head and S. L. Cranston (eds.), *Reincarnation: An East–West Anthology,* p. 36.
15. St Gregory, ibid., p. 36.
16. St. Augustine, ibid., p. 38.

17 Dr Ian Stevenson, *Twenty Cases Suggestive of Reincarnation,* University Press of Virginia, Charlottesville, VA, 1988.

18 Benjamin Walker, *Masks of the Soul,* p. 8.

19 William James, *Varieties of Religious Experience,* Harvard University Press, Cambridge, MA, 1985.

20 H. Carrington and S. J. Muldoon, *Projection of the Astral Body,* Psychic Book Club, Rider, London, p.2.

21 Drs Glenn Roberts and John Owen, 'The Near Death Experience'. *British Journal of Psychiatry,* London, 153, 1988, pp. 607–17.

22 ibid.

23 ibid.

24 ibid.

25 Robert Hand, 'The Emergence of an Astrological Discipline', *Astrological Journal,* May/June 1988, p. 117.

26 C.J. Jung, *The Visions Seminars,* Spring Publications, Dallas, TX, 1983.

27 Benjamin Walker, *Masks of the Soul,* p. 127.

28 Rupert Sheldrake, 'Morphic Resonance', *Caduceus,* 4.

29 Alan Jewsbury, 'A New Hypothesis to Explain Astrology', *Astrological Journal,* November/December 1988, p. 298.

30 Robert Hand, 'The Emergence of an Astrological Discipline'.

31 ibid.

32 Alan Jewsbury, 'A New Hypothesis to Explain Astrology'.

33 Tyrell, *The Personality of Man,* Penguin, London, 1947.

34 Joan Grant and Denys Kelsey, *Many Lifetimes,* Corgi, London, 1976.

35 E. H. Whinfield (ed.), *Teachings of Rumi: Mathnawi,* Octagon Press, London, 1979.

CHAPTER 2

1 Pauline Stone, *The Astrology of Karma,* The Aquarian Press, Wellingborough, Northants, 1988, p.20.

2 Mary Devlin, *Astrology and Past Lives,* Para Research Inc., Gloucester, MA, 1987.

3 Tracy Marks, *The Astrology of Self Discovery,* CRCS, Reno, NV, pp. 15ff.

4 M. Scott Peck, *The Road Less Travelled,* Rider, London, 1978, p. 119.

5 ibid., p. 116.

6 Paul Wright, *The Literary Zodiac,* Anodyne, Edinburgh, 1988, p. 20.

7 *Concise Oxford Dictionary.*

8 Liz Greene, *Star Signs for Lovers,* Arrow, London, 1980.

9 M. Scott Peck, *The Road Less Travelled,* p. 83.

10 *Concise Oxford Dictionary.*

11 M. Scott Peck, *The Road Less Travelled,* p. 131.

12   Jeff Mayo, *Teach Yourself Astrology,* Hodder & Stoughton, London, 1980.

13   Liz Greene, *Star Signs for Lovers.*

14   Debbie Boater, article in *Metamorphosis,* Autumn 1984.

15   Liz Greene, *Relating: Astrological Guide to Living with Others on a Small Planet,* Coventure, London, 1986.

16   Howard Sasportas, *The Twelve Houses,* The Aquarian Press, Wellingborough, Northants, 1985.

17   Liz Greene, *Relating.*

18   Quoted from Martin Luther King's famous speech, 'I Have a Dream', made at an anti-racist rally on 28 August 1968.

19   ibid.

20   ibid.

21   ibid.

22   M. Scott Peck, *The Road Less Travelled,* p. 302.

23   Christine Hartley, *A Case for Reincarnation,* Robert Hale, London, 1987, p. 62.

24   Alan Oken, *Soul Centered Astrology,* Bantam, New York, 1990.

25   Stephen Arroyo, *Astrology, Karma and Transformation,* CRCS, Vancouver, 1978 p.109.

26   Alan Epstein, *Understanding Aspects - The Inconjunct,* Trines, Reno, NV, 1997.

CHAPTER 3

1   Christine Hartley, *A Case for Reincarnation,* Robert Hale, London, 1987, p. 109.

2   Liz Greene, *Saturn: A New Look at an Old Devil,* Weiser, York Beach, ME, 1976, p.121.

3   Roberto Assagioli, *The Act of Will,* Penguin, London, 1974.

4   Anne Parker, *Astrology and Alcoholism: Genetic Key to the Horoscope,* Weiser, York Beach, ME, 1983, p. 34.

5   Stephen Arroyo, *Astrology, Karma and Transformation,* CRCS, Vancouver, 1978, p. 139.

6   ibid. p. 140.

7   Liz Greene, *Saturn,* Weiser, York Beach, ME, 1976.

8   Dr Susan Forward, *Men Who Hate Women,* p. 113.

9   Nor Hall, *The Moon and the Virgin,* The Women's Press, London, 1980.

10   ibid.

11   Dr Susan Forward, *Men Who Hate Women,* p. 111.

CHAPTER 4

1   Commentary extract from *Cities Fit to Live In,* Channel 4, 1988.
2   Robin Skynner and John Cleese, *Families and How to Survive Them,* Methuen, London, 1983.
3   Dr Susan Forward, *Men Who Hate Women and the Women Who Love Them,* Bantam Books, New York, NY, 1989, p. 43.
4   Chuck Spezzano, *The Enlightenment Book,* p. 49
5   ibid.
6   Jeff Green, *Pluto, the Evolutionary Journey of the Soul,* Llewellyn Publications, St Paul, MN, 1985, p. 215.
7   Howard Sasportas, *The Twelve Houses,* The Aquarian Press, Wellingborough, Northants, pp. 98ff.

CHAPTER 5

1   Elisabeth Kubler-Ross, *Death, the Final Stage of Growth,* Spectrum, New Jersey, 1975, p. 165.
2   Phyllis Krystal, *Cutting the Ties that Bind,* Element Books, Shaftesbury, Dorset, 1989, p. 9.
3   Alan Oken, *Complete Astrologer,* p. 499.
4   Debbie Boater, from the article in *Metamorphosis,* Autumn 1984.
5   Suzanne Lilley-Harvey, Thomas Merton: A Study of the Saturn–Uranus Dilemma', *Astrological Journal,* September / October 1987, p.21.
6   ibid.
7   ibid.
8   Mother Teresa, quoted in *Radio Times,* 1987.
9   Liz Greene, *Saturn,* Weiser, York Beach, ME, 1976, p. 4.
10 Anne Parker, *Alcoholism and Astrology,* Weiser, York Beach, ME, 1988, p. 136.
11 Jan Spiller and Karen McCoy, *Spiritual Astrology,* Simon and Schuster, NY 1988, p. 177.

CHAPTER 6

1   Melanie Reinhart, *Chiron and the Healing Journey,* Arkana, London 1989.
2   Howard Sasportas, *The Twelve Houses.*
3   Christine Hartley, *A Case for Reincarnation,* p. 121
4   Jonathan Cott, *The Search for Omm Sety,* Doubleday, New York, NY, 1987.
5   ibid.
6   Carl Jung, *The Collected Works, vol 4.*

CHAPTER 7

1 Talat Sait et al., Dost Yayinlan, *Celaleddin Rumi & the Whirling Dervishes.*
2 Extract from untitled American newspaper cutting in the author's collection, undated.
3 ibid.
4 Glen Williston and Judith Johnstone, *Discovering Your Past Lives,* The Aquarian Press, Wellingborough, Northants, 1988, p. 86.
5 Stephen Arroyo, *Astrology, Karma and Transformation,* CRCS, Vancouver, 1978, p. 79.
6 Stephen Arroyo, *Astrology, Psychology and the Four Elements,* CRCS, Reno, NV, 1975 p. 75.
7 ibid., p.120.

CONCLUSION

1 Richard Bach, *Illusions,* Pan, London, 1979, p. 51.
2 E. H. Whinfield (ed.), *Teachings of Rumi: Mathnawi,* Octagon Press, London, 1979.

GLOSSARY

Akashic Record   Esoteric record in which each individual soul's experience is chronicled, and which can be read by those trained to access it.

Angles   The Ascendant, Descendant, MC (Midheaven) and IC.

Ascendant   The degree of the zodiac rising over the eastern horizon at the moment of birth, forming the cusp of the first house. The opposite point, forming the cusp of the seventh house, is known as the Descendant.

Aspect   The distance between two planets measured around the zodiac, The major aspects are the conjunction (00^0) sextile (60^0), square (90^0), trine (120^0) quincunx (150^0) and opposition (180^0).

Being   A state in which the incarnating soul is totally attuned to the Self and simply *is*.

Cardinal   The initiating Cardinal signs are Aries, Cancer, Libra, Capricorn.

Cusps   The division points dividing the zodiac into houses.

Ecliptic   The circle *apparently* traversed by the Sun in a year.

Elements   The astrological elements are the active and intuitive Fire (Aries, Leo, Sagittarius), the communicative Air (Gemini, Libra, Aquarius), the practical Earth (Taurus, Virgo, Capricorn), and the emotional Water (Cancer, Scorpio, Pisces) energies.

Finger of Fate   An aspect pattern formed from two quincunxes radiating out from a planet to two other planets, themselves joined by a sextile.

Fixed   The constant Fixed signs are Taurus, Leo, Scorpio, Aquarius.

Free Will   The ability to choose one's actions and destiny.

Grand Cross   An aspect pattern formed by four squares and *two* oppositions linked together.

Grand Trine   An aspect pattern formed by three trines linked together.

House   The zodiac is divided into twelve houses each representing a sphere of experience.

Interaspect   A planet in one natal chart aspecting a planet in another natal chart.

Karma   The law of cause and effect, according to which for every action there is a reaction. Karma is the causal factor behind fate or destiny.

Kite   An aspect pattern formed from a Grand Trine with an opposition to a fourth planet which is sextile to two of the planets forming the Grand Trine.

MC (Midheaven) The highest degree reached by the ecliptic at a particular time and place, the tenth house cusp in the Placidus house system. The opposite point, the IC, forms the cusp of the fourth house.

Moon's Nodes   Points indicating the intersection of the Moon with the ecliptic of the earth as it passes from North to South. The nodal axis is an exact opposition aspect.

Mutable   The adaptable Mutable signs are Gemini, Virgo, Sagittarius, Pisces.

Natal chart   A map of the planets at the moment of birth.

Natal planet   The position of a planet at the moment of birth.

Negative signs   The Negative astrological signs (Taurus, Cancer, Virgo, Scorpio, Capricorn, Pisces) are self-repressive, passive and receptive.

Nodal return   The conjunction of the transiting Node to its natal placement. The Node takes eighteen and a half years to travel around the zodiac.

Personal planets   Sun, Moon, Mercury, Venus, Mars.

Placidus   System of house division.

Positive signs   The Positive astrological signs (Aries, Gemini, Leo, Libra, Sagittarius, Aquarius) are self-expressive, active and outgoing.

Psychic   Pertaining to the Psyche. Able to utilize extra-sensory perception and expanded states of consciousness to interact with other levels of being.

Orb   The number of degrees allowed for an aspect between planets.

Reincarnation   The successive taking on a physical incarnation, following a previous death.

Self   The eternal, divine, essence of Man.

Soul   The portion of the Self which takes on a physical body at incarnation.

Synastry   The interaction between two natal charts, depicting the relationship between two people.

Transit   When a planet in the heavens at a given moment crosses or aspects a planet on the natal chart.

T-square   Two planets forming an opposition with a third planet squaring them both.

CHART SOURCES

BAKER, DOUGLAS: Private source
CLEESE, JOHN: Frank Clifford *British Entertainers, The Astrological Profiles*
DEBUSSY, CLAUDE: Astrological Association
DUPRE, JACQUELINE: Her mother
DYLAN, BOB: Jeff Green
FELIX, JULIE: Herself
GARBO, GRETA: Alan Oken
GELDOF, BOB: Prediction
HALLIWELL, KENNETH: John Lahr
HARTLEY, CHRISTINE: Herself
HIGGS, DR MARIETTA: Stuart Bell
KENNEDY, JACQUELINE: Jeff Green
KENNEDY, JOHN F.: Alan Oken
KENNEDY, ROBERT: Jeff Green
KING, MARTIN LUTHER: Alan Oken
KUBLER-ROSS, ELISABETH: Herself
LENIN, VLADIMIR ILYICH: Astrological Association
MERTON, THOMAS: Suzanne Lilley-Harvey
MONROE, MARILYN: Alan Oken
MOZART, WOLFGANG AMADEUS: Jeff Green
OMM SETY: Jonathan Cott
ORTON, JOE: John Lahr
PATTON, General: Jeff Greene quoting Lois Rodden
WATERS, ROGER: Private source

HOW TO READ A BIRTHCHART

The chart is read from the Ascendant on the left hand side, in
an anti-clockwise direction, so that the first house falls **below**
the Ascendant. The other houses and signs follow in order
around the wheel, ending up back **above** the Ascendant, with
the twelfth house.

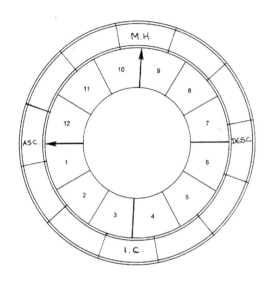

☉	Sun	♈	Aries	☌	Conjunction
☽	Moon	♉	Taurus	☍	Opposition
☿	Mercury	♊	Gemini	△	Trine
♀	Venus	♋	Cancer	□	Square
♂	Mars	♌	Leo	✳	Sextile
♃	Jupiter	♍	Virgo	⊼	Quincunx/
♄	Saturn	♎	Libra		Inconjunct
♅	Uranus	♏	Scorpio		
♆	Neptune	♐	Sagittarius		
♇	Pluto	♑	Capricorn		
⚷	Chiron	♒	Aquarius		
☊	North Node	♓	Pisces		
☋	South Node				

BIBLIOGRAPHY

ASTROLOGY

ARROYO, S., *Astrology, Karma and Transformation*, CRCS, Vancouver, Canada, 1978.

CUNNINGHAM, D., *Healing Pluto Problems*, Weiser, York Beach, ME, 1986.

DEVLIN, M., *Astrology and Past Lives*, Para Research Inc., Gloucester, MA, 1987.

EPSTEIN A., *Understanding Aspects - The Inconjunct*, Trines, Reno, NV, 1997

GAMMON, M., (ed.), *Astrology and The Edgar Cayce Readings*, ARE Press, Virginia Beach, VA, 1973.

GREEN, J., *Pluto, the Evolutionary Journey of the Soul*, Llewellyn Publications, St Paul, MN, 1985.

GREENE, L., *Astrology of Fate*, George Allen & Unwin, London, 1984.

GREENE, L., *Saturn: A New Look at an Old Devil*, Arkana, London, 1990.

HALL, J. *The Hades Moon: Saturn in Aspect to Pluto*, Samual Weiser, Maine 1998.

HALL, J. *Karmic Astrology* Godsfield Press, London, 2000.

HALL, J. *The Zodiac Pack*, Findhorn Press, Scotland, 1998.

HALL, J. *The Illustrated Guide to Astrology*, Godsfield Press, UK 1999.

MARKS, T., *The Astrology of Self Discovery*, CRCS, Reno, NV, 1985.

OKEN, A., *Alan Oken's Complete Astrology*, Bantam, NY 1980

OKEN, A., *Soul Centered Astrology*, Bantam, NY, 1990

REINHART, M., *Chiron and the Healing Journey*, Arkana, London, 1989.

SASPORTAS, H., *The Twelve Houses*, The Aquarian Press, Wellingborough, Northants, 1985.

STONE, P., *The Astrology of Karma*, The Aquarian Press, Wellingborough, Northants, 1988.

REINCARNATION, ETC

CARRINGTON, H., and MULDOON, S. J., *The Projection of the Astral Body*, Rider, London, 1929.

CERMINERA, G., *Many Mansions*, New American Library, New York, NY, 1988.

CERMINERA, G., *Many Lives, Many Loves*, De Vorss, Marina del Rey, CA, 1981.

CHALLONER, H. K., *The Wheel of Rebirth*, Theosophical Publications House, Wheaton, IL, 1976.

CROOKHALL, R., *The Study and Practice of Astral Projection*, Citadel Books, Secausus, NJ, 1987.

DEVLIN, B. L. *I am Mary Shelley*, Condor, Souvenir Press, London.

EBON, M., *Reincarnation in the Twentieth Century*, Signet, New American Library.

FISHER, J., *The Case for Reincarnation*, Grafton Books, London, 1986.

GLASKIN, G. M., *Windows of the Mind*, Prism Press, Bridport, Dorset, 1989.

GRANT, J., *Eyes of Horus*, Arid OH, Columbus, OH, 1988.

GRANT, J., *Far Memory*, Corgi, London, 1975.

GRANT, J., *Lord of the Horizon*, Ariel OH, Columbus, OH, 1988.

GRANT, J., and ICELSEY, D., *Many Lifetimes*, Corgi, London, 1976.

GREEN, C., *Lucid Dreams*, Institute of Psychophysical Research, London, 1968.

GREEN, C., *Out of the Body Experiences*, Institute of Psychophysical Research, London, 1968.

GREEN, C., and MCCREERY, C., *Apparitions*, Institute of Psychophysical Research, London, 1977.

GREY, M., *Return from Death, an Exploration of the Near Death Experience*, Penguin Books, Harmondsworth, 1985.

GUIRDHAM, A., *A Foot in Both Worlds*, Neville Spearman, Saffron Walden, Essex, 1990.

GUIRDHAM, A., *We are One Another*, Newcastle Publications, North Hollywood, CA, 1985.

GUIRDHAM, A., *The Cathars and Reincarnation: The Record of a Past Life in Thirteenth-Century France*, Neville Spearman, Saffron Walden, Essex, 1990.

HAICH, L., *Initiations*, tr. J. P. Robertson, Unwin Paperbacks, London, 1979.

HALL, J., *Deja Who? A Fresh Look at Past Lives*, Findhorn Press, Scotland, 1998.

HALL, J., *Hands Across Time: the Soulmate Enigma*, Findhorn Press, Scotland, 1998.

HALL, J., *Principles of Past Life Therapy*, Thorsons, London, 1998.

HALL, J., *Principles of Reincarnation*, Thorsons, London, 2000.

HALL, J., *Principles of Psychic Protection*. Thorsons, London, 1999.

HALL, J., *The Art of Psychic Protection* Findhorn Press, Scotland, 1996.

HARTLEY, C., *A Case for Reincarnation*, Robert Hale, London, 1987.

HEAD, J. and CRANSTON S. L., (eds.), *Reincarnation: An East–West Anthology*, The Julian Press Inc., New York, NY, 1961.

IVERSON, J., *More Lives Than One*, Pan, London, 1977.

LANGLEY, N., *Edgar Cayce on Reincarnation*, Warner Books, New York, NY, 1967.

LUNDALL, C., *A Collection of Near Death Research Readings*, Nelson-Hall, Chicago, IL, 1982.

MONROE, R., *Journeys out of the Body*, Doubleday, New York, NY, 1977.

MOODY, R., *Life After Life*, Bantam Books, New York, NY, 1983.

RICHARDSON, A., *Dancers to the Gods: The Magical Records of James Seymour and Christine Hartley*, The Aquarian Press, Wellingborough, Northants, 1985.

RICHARDSON, A., *Gate of the Moon: Mythical and Magical Doorways*, The Aquarian Press, Wellingborough, Northants, 1984.

ROGO, S. D., *Life after Death: A Case for the Survival of Bodily Death*, The Aquarian Press, Wellingborough, Northants, 1986.

RUSSELL, B, *Design for Destiny*, Neville Spearman, Saffron Walden, Essex 1973.

RYALL, E., *Second Time Around*, Macdonald Optima, London, 1989.

SHELDRAKE, R., *A New Science of Life*, Paladin Books; London, 1987.

SHELDRAKE, R., *The Presence of the Past*, William Collins, London, 1988.

SPEZZANO, C., *The Enlightenment Pack*, Rider, London, 1996.

STEMMAN, R., Reincarnation: Amazing True Cases from Around the World Piatkus London 1997

STEVENSON, I., *Where Reincarnation and Biology Intersect*, Praeger, Westport CT 1997.

STEVENSON, I., *Twenty Cases Suggestive of Reincarnation*, University Press of Virgina, Charlottesville, VA, 1988.

STEWART, A., *Died 1513, Born 1929*, Macmillan, London, 1978.

TOYNBEE, A., *Life after Death*, Weidenfeld & Nicolson, London, 1976.

UNDERWOOD, P. and WILDER, L., *Lives to Remember*, Robert Hale, London, 1975.

WALKER-MCCLAIN, F., *Past Life Regression*, Llewellyn Publications, St Paul, MN, 1986.

WALKER, J., *Masks of the Soul*, The Aquarian Press, Wellingborough, Northants, 1981.

WAMBACH, H., *Reliving Past Lives*, Century Hutchinson, London, 1979.

WAMBACH, H., *Life Before Life*, Bantam Books, New York, NY, 1979.

WATSON, L., *The Romeo Error*, Coronet, London, 1979.

WILLISTON, G., and JOHNSTONE, J., *Discovering your Past Lives*, The Aquarian Press, Wellingborough, Northants, 1988.

WILSON, C., *C. C. Jung, Lord of the Underworld*, The Aquariarin Press, Wellingborough, Northants, 1988.

WILSON, I., *All in the Mind*, Doubleday, New York, NY, 1978.

WOOLGER, R. J., *Other Lives, Other Selves*, Crucible, Chatham, 1990.

COPYRIGHT PERMISSIONS

by Pauline Stone; *The Twelve Houses* by Howard Sasportas; and *Discovering Your Past Lives* by Glen Williston and Judith Johnstone.

The late Maurice Barbanell, for permission to quote from Psychic Press and Psychic Book Club books.

The Society of Authors, as the literary representative of the Estate of John Masefield, for 'A Creed'.

The extract from 'Healing', by D. H. Lawrence, is included by kind permission of Laurence Pollinger Limited and the Estate of Mrs Frieda Lawrence Rowagh.

The extract taken from *The Astrology of Fate* by Liz Greene, reproduced by kind permission of Unwin Hyman, © Liz Greene, 1984.

Samuel Weiser, Inc., for *Saturn: A New Look at an Old Devil* by Liz Greene, © 1976 Liz Greene (York Beach, ME, Samuel Weiser, Inc., 1976). Used by permission. Published in the UK by Arkana. Also for *Astrology and Alcoholism: Genetic Key to the Horoscope* by Anne B. Parker, © 1981 Anne E, Parker (York Beach, ME, Samuel Weiser, inc., 1981). Used by permission. See Chapter Notes for pages details of each work.

NOTE: Every effort has been made to trace the copyright holders of works quoted from in this book, but in some cases this has not proved possible. The author and publishers therefore wish to thank the authors or copyright holders of any material which is included without acknowledgement above.

ASTROLOGICAL SCHOOLS AND ORGANISATIONS

This is by no means a definitive list, and apologies to any organisation that feels they have been missed out. It is however a good starting point for anyone thinking of studying astrology.

The Astrological Association
Lee Valley Technopark, Tottenham Hale, London N17 9LN.
Tel: 0208 880 4848, Fax: 0208 880 4849,
email: astrological.association@zetnet.co.uk.
website: www.astrologer.com/aanet
The AA publishes a bi-monthly Journal and runs an annual conference which is attended by astrologers from all over the world. Its main objectives are to facilitate the exchange of information within the astrological community, and promote the good name of astrology in general.

The Astrological Lodge of London
50, Gloucester Place, London W1H 4EA
The Astrological Lodge holds regular classes in London. It supports all branches of astrology, whilst encouraging the study and understanding of the philosophical, historical and symbolic aspects of astrology. Its magazine, The Astrological Quarterly, is free to members.

British Association for Vedic Astrology
19, Jenner Way, Romsey, Hants. SO51 8PD
Tel: 01794 524178
email: bava@btinternet.com
website: www.bava.org
BAVA runs regular classes in London, and an annual conference which attracts speakers from all over the world.

British Astrological and Psychic Society
Robert Denholm House, Bletchingly Road, Nutfield Surrey, RH1 4HW
Tel: 0906 4700827
email: baps@tlpplc.com
website: www.bapsoc.co.uk
BAPS runs certificate courses in astrology, tarot and palmistry. It also provides a register of members, with details of local courses and discussion nights.

The Centre for Psychological Astrology (CPA)
Box 1815, London WC1N 3XX
Tel: 0208 749 2330
email cpalondon@aol.com website: www.astrologer.com

Director: Liz Greene PhD, DFAstrolS, Dip Analyt Psych. The CPA is the outstanding centre in the world for the study of astrology in relationship to depth psychology. It runs regular courses and seminars in London and occasional additional seminars in Zurich. The CPA 3-year Diploma seminar programme, based at Regent's College in London, is also open to members of the public. High quality books presenting seminar material by CPA tutors are available from the CPA Press via Midheaven Books (tel 0207-607-4133) where Apollon, the exciting new quality Journal of Psychological Astrology, can also be ordered.

The Company of Astrologers
PO Box 3001, London, N1 1LY
Tel: 01227 362427
email: admin@coa.org.uk
website:: www/hubcom.com/coa
The Company is the home of divinatory astrology. It runs certificate courses as well as seminars and an annual conference.

The English Huber School of Astrological Counselling
PO Box 118, Knutsford, Cheshire, WA16 8TG
Tel/Fax: 01565 651131
email: huberschool@btinternet.com
website: www.ncsa.es/eschuber.sch
The English Huber School provides correspondence courses and workshops for all levels of astrology.

The Faculty of Astrological Studies
BM7470, London WC1N 3XX
Tel: 07000 790143
Fax: 01689 603537
email: info@astrology.org.uk
website: www.astrology.org.uk
The Faculty provides tuition at all levels of astrology, through home study courses, evening classes in London, seminar tapes and annual summer schools in Oxford.

The Mayo School
Alvana Gardens, Tregavethan, Truro, Cornwall, TR4 9EN
Tel: 01872 560048
email: jackie.h@virgin.net
website: www.astrology-world.com/mayo
Founded by Jeff Mayo, the school offers correspondence courses at certificate and diploma level and issues a list of their qualified consultants who have gained the diploma.

INDEX